PROTESTANT CHURCH MUSIC
IN AMERICA

A Short Survey of Men and Movements
from 1564 to the Present

PROTESTANT CHURCH MUSIC
IN AMERICA

A Short Survey of Men and Movements
from 1564 to the Present

BY ROBERT STEVENSON

W · W · NORTON & COMPANY · INC · NEW YORK

OH! king of Heaven!
Most perfect harmony is giv'n:
Whilst happy saints in concert join
To make the music more divine,
And with immortal voices sing
Hosannahs to their glorious King.

Hail heav'n born music! by thy pow'r we raise
Th' uplifted soul to acts of highest praise:
Oh! I would die with music melting round,
And float to bliss upon a sea of sound!

Francis Hopkinson, *Ode on Music* (1754) and
Description of a Church (1760/1762)

CONTENTS

PREFACE   xi

1. EARLY CONTACTS WITH THE ABORIGINES   3

Huguenots in Florida, 1564 — Drake's men in California, 1579 —
Puritans and "Praying Indians" in New England

2. NEW ENGLAND PURITANISM, 1620–1720   13

Ainsworth Psalter — Bay Psalm Book, 1640 — Revisions of 1651
and later — Samuel Sewall's precentorship — Changing repertory
of tunes at the turn of the century

3. "REGULAR SINGING," 1720–1775   21

Reaction against improvised embellishment of psalm tunes — Early
musical reformers: John Tufts, Thomas Walter, Cotton Mather,
Thomas Symmes — Rise of singing schools in New England, Pennsylvania, and Virginia

4. PENNSYLVANIA GERMANS   32

Johannes Kelpius (1673–1708) and "The Lamenting Voice of the
Hidden Love" — Johann Conrad Beissel (1690–1768) and the
Ephrata experiment — Moravian musical mentors: Jeremias
Dencke (1725–1795), John Antes (1741–1811), Johann Friedrich
Peter (1746–1813), and others

5. NATIVE-BORN COMPOSERS IN THE MIDDLE
   ATLANTIC COLONIES   46

Francis Hopkinson (1737–1791), signer of the Declaration of Independence — Availability of organs for accompaniment and use
of figured bass — James Lyon (1735–1794), compiler of *Urania*

6. THE SOUTH BEFORE 1800   53

Musical life in Virginia, 1710–1774 — Composers in South Carolina: C. T. Pachelbell (1690–1750), Peter Valton (*ca.* 1740–
1784), J. H. Stevens (1750–1828)

7. SINGING-SCHOOL MASTERS IN THE
    NEW REPUBLIC   59

British precedents — Musical idiom in early American tunebooks
— William Billings (1746–1800) — Lewis Edson (1748–1820) and
Daniel Read (1757–1836), fuging-tune composers — The New
England anthem

8. THE HALF-CENTURY PRECEDING THE
    CIVIL WAR   74

Changes wrought by immigrant "scientific" composers — Lowell
Mason (1792–1872) and his circle — "Set pieces" — Adaptations
from Roman Catholic composers — Shape notes and other schemes
for simplifying music notation — Fasola folk in the West and
South: Elkanah Kelsay Dare (1782–1826), Lucius Chapin (1760–
1842), Ananias Davisson (1780–1857), James P. Carrell (1787–
1854), William Walker (1809–1875), William Hauser (1812–
1880)

9. NEGRO SPIRITUALS: ORIGINS AND
    PRESENT-DAY SIGNIFICANCE   92

Samuel Davies in Virginia, 1755–1758, and musical propaganda
among the Negroes in South Carolina, 1745 — Reactions of Russian and English visitors to antebellum Negro religious singing —
Slave Songs, 1867 — Periodical literature on Negro spirituals published in the same year — The "shout" — *Jubilee Songs,* 1872 —
Cabin and Plantation Songs, 1875, and other pioneer collections
— Interrelationship of white and Negro spirituals — Spirituals as
documents of social protest — Present-day repertory

10. DIVERGING CURRENTS, 1850–PRESENT   106

"Upper-class" Eastern seacoast music: Henry Wilson (1828–1878)
and S. Parkman Tuckerman (1819–1890) — Rise of gospel hymnody: William B. Bradbury, Ira D. Sankey, Philip P. Bliss,
Charles H. Gabriel — Heyday of the mixed quartet — Dudley
Buck (1839–1909) — John Knowles Paine (1839–1906) — Horatio W. Parker (1863–1919) — Twentieth-century composers of
"elevated" church music: D. S. Smith, Roger Sessions, Randall
Thompson, Leo Sowerby, and their contemporaries — The younger
generation of scholars and composers

SELECTIVE BIBLIOGRAPHY   133

INDEX   152

PLATES

(*between pages 78 and 79*)

1. Two pages from John Tufts, *An Introduction To the Singing of Psalm-Tunes* (1738).

2. Page from Conrad Beissel, *Das Gesäng der einsamen Turteltaube* (Library of Congress MS).

3–6. Two pieces from *Frances Hopkinson His Book,* and the same pieces as printed in James Lyon, *Urania* (1761).

7. Frontispiece from William Billings, *The New-England Psalm-Singer* (1770).

8. JUDEA, from Billings, *The Singing Master's Assistant* (1778).

9–10. Two letters to Andrew Law, from Elkanah Kelsay Dare (1811) and Lucius Chapin (1812).

11. Page from shape-note edition of Lowell Mason, *The Sacred Harp* (1835).

12. ANTIOCH, from Mason, *Occasional Psalm and Hymn Tunes* (1836).

13. Page from *Ka Lira Hawaii* (1844).

14. Page from autograph of Horatio Parker, *Hora Novissima* (1892).

15. Page from autograph of George W. Chadwick, *Noël* (1909).

PREFACE

WITH THE KIND PERMISSION of G. Schirmer, Inc., the section "Diverging Currents" at the close of the present conspectus incorporates several paragraphs from my essay "Church Music: A Century of Contrasts," published in *One Hundred Years of Music in America*, 1961. My hearty thanks are due not only to Paul Henry Lang, who kindly encouraged the writing of that essay, but also to Nathan Broder, who offered many valuable suggestions for its improvement and who on behalf of W. W. Norton & Company commissioned the American chapter in Friedrich Blume's *History of Protestant Church Music* out of which the present study grew.

Since my purpose in publishing the present résumé is to provide a compressed text for use in seminaries, choir schools, and colleges, I have had to omit much important data and have been obliged to consign many men and movements to a mere passing mention. As for musical examples, only such short vocal works as fall within the scope of a modest seminary choir (and those chosen mostly from the earlier periods) have been inserted.

Had space allowed, I should keenly have enjoyed pursuing such fascinating precursors as:

(1) Thomas Walter, who salved Puritan conscience by ingeniously justifying three-part congregational singing of the Davidic psalms on Scriptural grounds;

(2) Samuel Sewall, who in his Diary (1694–1718) frequently mentioned leading the Old South Church at Boston in such tunes as *Vater unser in Himmelreich* and Orlando Gibbons's WESTMINSTER (printed at Boston in three-part harmonization, 1721, 1723, 1726);

(3) Josiah Franklin, father of Benjamin, and so able a musician

xi

that Samuel Sewall suggested him for the Old South Church precentorship in 1718;

(4) Giovanni Palma, whose concert in Philadelphia George Washington attended on March 17, 1757, and who contributed a two-part setting of the popular hymn beginning "While shepherds watch'd their flocks by night" to James Lyon's *Urania,* published at Philadelphia only four years later;

(5) Francis Hopkinson, whose setting of the Twenty-third Psalm is also in *Urania;*

(6) Philip Fithian, who met Lyon, "that great master of music," on April 22, 1774;

(7) Samuel Davies, who began teaching the Negroes to sing Watts's hymns as early as 1755;

(8) or the white missionary in Charleston, S. C. who so successfully had the Negroes learning to "sing psalms" there in 1745 that he was briefly imprisoned for turning their assemblies into a "nuisance to the neighborhood."

All these intriguing facets of American musical history, and many others similarly zestful, gain only passing allusion in the pages that follow—but will hopefully enjoy the attention that they merit in a full-length history of musical America to be published shortly.

My indebtednesses for helpful advice during the writing of this preliminary text cannot be discharged by any mere passing nod in a prefatory note. But not to mention Irving and Violet Lowens would be to omit two investigators who have changed the whole course of American musicology in our time. When I think of the many others whose researches have aided and inspired me, I find myself repeating the living authors listed in the bibliography at the close of this book.

To keep it within manageable limits, this bibliography includes only such materials as are listed under ML in the Library of Congress system; or books outside the field of music that have nonetheless offered useful documentation. Since the running text has had to be so curtailed, some readers may question the abundant bibliographic detail added in the footnotes. By way of explanation: the students whom I have guided in this field, first at the Westminster Choir College (1946–1949) and later at UCLA (since 1949), have usually lacked the expertise needed in tracking down primary sources. In a stream still muddied with the mere opinions of such nineteenth-century partisans as Hood, Gould, and Ritter, only original documents can at this late date clear up the waters of historical research.

To the primary sources, I therefore constantly invite the student's attention in the numerous footnotes.

In several previously published essays (see the bibliography) and in the compilation published by Duke University Press in 1953, *Patterns of Protestant Church Music,* I dealt at length with the historic texts sung by American choirs and congregations and with the doctrinal problems which the texts raise. To redress the balance, the music itself—rather than the words sung—is emphasized throughout the present synopsis.

Does the music, as such, merit the attention now reserved for European art? Thanks to Britton, Lowens, Hamm, and others, the small gems mined by New Englanders such as Read, who stayed at home, or Lucius Chapin, who traveled, no longer need apology. Negro spirituals obviously enjoy the cachet of approval by critic and public alike. The role that distinguished research and performance have played in fomenting interest in another phase of the American heritage—the Moravian—and towards establishing it as a pre-eminent body of art music, is known to all. With these successes in mind, perhaps it is not too much to hope that even such major musical efforts of the now unfashionable late Romantic period as Paine's and Parker's oratorios may soon enjoy the accolades that only worthy performances can bring. In a country so rich as the United States, do not our own late nineteenth-century forebears deserve, at least occasionally, the kind of attentive and costly performance without which even a Brahms *German Requiem* and an Elgar *Dream of Gerontius* lose their impact?

PROTESTANT CHURCH MUSIC
IN AMERICA

A Short Survey of Men and Movements
from 1564 to the Present

∽ 1 ∽

EARLY CONTACTS WITH
THE ABORIGINES

ALTHOUGH Jamestown was not founded until 1607, Plymouth until 1620, and Massachusetts Bay until 1630, these seventeenth-century English colonies by no means initiated Protestant forays into North America. As early as the spring of 1564 three shiploads of Huguenots under the command of René de Laudonnière settled ten miles down St. Johns River from what is now Jacksonville, Florida. Their principal recreation consisted in singing Marot psalms. The sturdy Calvinist tunes to which these were sung caught the immediate fancy of the surrounding Florida Indians, who came from far and near to enjoy the Huguenots' music. Before long the natives were singing the same tunes, learned by rote. After the Spaniards massacred the encroaching French colonists, the Indians for many years continued to sing snatches of these vigorous Huguenot tunes as "codewords" to determine whether any stragglers along the seacoast were friendly French or sullen Spanish.

Nicolas Le Challeux's *Brief Discovrs et histoire d'vn voyage de quelques François en la Floride,* published at Geneva in 1579 as an appendix to Girolamo Benzoni's *Histoire novvelle dv Novveav monde,* specifies the very tunes that were used as signals—those for Psalms 128 and 130. He writes that the Florida Indians "yet retain such happy memories that when someone lands on their shore, the most endearing greeting that they know how to offer is *Du fons de ma pensée* [Ps. 130] or *Bienheureux est quiconque* [Ps. 128], which they say as if to ask the watchword, are you French or not?" Le Challeux continues that the Indians do so because "the French while there taught them how to pray and how to sing certain psalms, which they heard sung so frequently that they still retain two or three words of those psalms." [1]

<hr>

[1] Printed by Eustace Vignon; p. 96: "Et de fait ils en ont encore si bonne souuenance, que quand quelqu'vn arriue à leur bord, la plus belle caresse qu'ils luy

Both Psalms 128 and 130 had been published *a 4* in Louis Bourgeois's *Pseavlmes cinqvante, de David* (Lyons, 1547), with the congregational melody confided to the tenor.[2] A comparison of the
Huguenot tune for Psalm 128, as taught the Florida Indians in 1564
and 1565, with the tune as it was published in a pioneer Germantown
psalm book of 1753 shows how remarkably faithful to their primitive

Example 1a

Octante trois pseavmes de David (Geneva: Jean Crespin, 1554)

Example 1b   *Der CXXVIII. 128. Psalm*

*Neu-vermehrt und vollsta^endiges Gesang-Buch Worinnen sowohl die Psal-
men Davids* (Germantown: Christopher Saur, 1753), p. 186

tunes the Calvinists in America remained after two centuries (see
Example 1). The Bourgeois version (this became definitive throughout the French-speaking Calvinist world with its republication at

---

sauent faire, c'est de luy dire *Du fons de ma pensee,* ou *Bien-heureux est quiconques
sert à Dieu volontiers.* C'est comme luy demander le mot du guet, pour sauoir s'il
est François ou non: à cause que les François estans en ce pays la leur apprenoyent
à prier Dieu, & à chanter des Pseaumes: ou bien ils ont retenu les deux ou trois mots
de ces Pseaumes la, pour les auoir ouy souuent chanter à nos gens."

[2] Pierre Pidoux, *Le Psautier huguenot du XVIe siècle: Mélodies et documents*
(Basle: Bärenreiter, 1962), I, 116, 119; II, 36. Still earlier, the tune of Psalm 128
had been published in *La Forme des prieres et chantz ecclesiastiqves* (Strassburg:
Johann Knobloch, 1545 [only known copy destroyed in 1870: see Pidoux, II, 29])
and of Psalm 130 in *Avlcvns pseaulmes et cantiques mys en chant* (Strassburg:
[Knobloch], 1539). The first polyphonic version of Psalm 128 to be published in
America came out with Goudimel's harmonization (1565), adapted, in *A Collection
of the Psalm and Hymn Tunes, Used by the Reformed Protestant Dutch Church of
the City of New-York, agreeable to their Psalm Book, published in English. In Four
Parts, Viz. Tenor, Bass, Treble, and Counter* (New York: Hodge and Shober, 1774).
See Carleton Sprague Smith, "The 1774 Psalm Book of the Reformed Protestant
Dutch Church in New York City," in *The Musical Quarterly,* XXXIV/1 (Jan., 1948),
93, n. 21.

Geneva in *Pseaumes octante trois de Dauid,* 1551, and *Octante trois pseavmes,* 1554) differs from that printed in 1753, 1763, and 1772 by Christopher Saur [3] for the Pennsylvania Reformed Church in only such small details as the addition of leading-tone accidentals and some time adjustments at phrase endings.

Saur's 1753 psalm book heads the long list of Calvinist musical publications in America with German text. The first American psalter with English text to include this same *Bienheureux est quiconques* tune saw light at New York only fourteen years later in a 479-page collection sponsored by the Reformed Dutch Church. Francis Hopkinson (1737–1791), the famous signer of the Declaration of Independence, was, however, forced to fit a different psalm text to the old tune. Finding that the English iambic Psalm 128 in the Tate and Brady New Version (1696) did not match the trochaic Geneva tune, he wedded the tune to verse of similar sentiment (Psalm 112) in 7.6.7.6. D. meter (see Example 2). As a result the historic tune sur-

Example 2

The Psalms of David (New York: James Parker, 1767), pp. 355–356

* Half this time-value in the first strophe, corrected in the second and third strophes. The wealth of the Dutch congregation enabled Parker to print the melody afresh for every strophe.

vives almost unscathed in *The Psalms of David . . . Translated from the Dutch For the Use of the Reformed Protestant Dutch Church of the City of New-York* (New York: James Parker, 1767).[4] Hopkinson's tact in finding alternate psalms to mate with traditional tunes— which might otherwise have died spinsters' deaths—won such approval that he could write Benjamin Franklin a letter on December 13, 1765, rejoicing that: "I have finished the Translation of the Psalms of David,

[3] Reprinted from a Marburg Reformed book of identical title, the Saur publication contains 123 tunes for the 150 psalms, as translated by Ambrosius Lobwasser (1515–1585). See National Society of the Colonial Dames of America: Pennsylvania, *Church Music and Musical Life in Pennsylvania in the Eighteenth Century* (Philadelphia [Lancaster: Wickersham Printing Co.], 1947), III, ii, 291–294.

[4] See Virginia L. Redway, "James Parker and the 'Dutch Church,'" in *The Musical Quarterly,* XXIV/4 (Oct., 1938), opposite p. 489, for facsimile of pp. 66–67 of the 1767 psalter. At p. 481 of her article she cites "three great bibliographers, Charles Hildeburn, Charles Evans, and Frank Metcalf" in support of this psalter's claim to be "the first book of music printed from type in America."

to the great Satisfaction of the Dutch Congregation at New York & they have paid me £145 their Currency." [5]

The longevity of the *Bienheureux est quiconques* tune—first brought to North America in 1564—can be matched by the success of that other tune taught the Florida tribesmen by pioneer Huguenots, *Du fons de ma pensée*. Taken over into Henry Ainsworth's *The Book of Psalmes: Englished both in Prose and Metre* (Amsterdam: Giles Thorp, 1612) as the proper tune for no less than nine different Psalms (7, 10, 14, 16, 74, 83, 90, 116, 143),[6] the Ainsworth [7] version of the *Du fons* tune differs from its French prototype in only a single insignificant trait. Where Ainsworth (Example 3) repeats a note before the final of a phrase, the French version combines the repeated notes.

Example 3

The Book of Psalmes (Amsterdam: Giles Thorp, 1612), p. 16

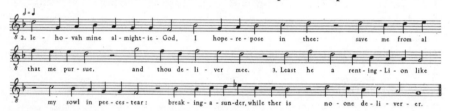

The psalter of Ainsworth,[8] in use at Plymouth until 1692,[9] guarantees the currency of the *Du fons de ma pensée* tune among the Pilgrims. This same tune had also been printed in at least fifteen Sternhold and Hopkins psalters before 1600,[10] and was again to be re-

---

[5] *Ibid.*, p. 495; Smith, p. 88; George E. Hastings, *The Life and Works of Francis Hopkinson* (Chicago: University of Chicago Press, 1926), p. 75.

[6] Waldo S. Pratt, *The Music of the Pilgrims: A Description of the Psalm-book brought to Plymouth in 1620* (Boston: Oliver Ditson Co., 1921), p. 31.

[7] Henry W. Longfellow refers to this psalter in the familiar quatrain (lines 47–50) from part 3 in *The Courtship of Miles Standish* (published in 1858).

[8] For a useful bibliography, see Samuel A. Ives, "Henry Ainsworth, a Founding Father of Congregationalism," in *Transactions of the Wisconsin Academy of Sciences, Arts and Letters* (Madison: 1957 [1958]), XLVI, 197–199. Ainsworth's last days were devoted to an iambic pentameter rhyming couplet paraphrase of the Song of Songs (printed at Amsterdam in 1623, the year after his death). The anonymous editor claimed that "he hath (like the Swan, as some report at his death) sung sweetliest in this." In his *Annotations Upon the second book of Moses* (Amsterdam: n. p., 1617, fol. K4v.; also London: John Bellamie, 1627, p. 53), Ainsworth's versification of Exodus 15 is preceded by the suggested tune above the verse ("This may be sung also as the 113. Psalme").

[9] Thomas Symmes, *Utile dulci. or, A Joco-Serious Dialogue, Concerning Regular Singing* (Boston: B. Green, for Samuel Gerrish, 1723), pp. 14–15.

[10] Maurice Frost, *English & Scottish Psalm & Hymn Tunes, c. 1543–1677* (London: Oxford University Press, 1953), p. 181. The Marian exiles adopted the tune in

peated as the proper tune for Psalm 130 in Thomas Ravenscroft's *The Whole Booke of Psalmes . . . Composed into 4 parts* (London: Stationers' Company, 1621).[11] Because of the early vogue of the Ravenscroft psalter among Massachusetts Bay colonists, his version (Example 4) certifies that the psalm-singing Bostonians knew the

Example 4
The Whole Booke of Psalmes (London: Stationers' Company, 1621), pp. 228–231

Lord to thee I make my mone when dan-gers mee op-presse: I call, I

sigh, plaine and grone, trust - ing to finde re lease. Heare now O Lord my re - quest,

for it is full due time: And let thine eares aye be prest vn - to this pray - er of mine.

• 9. French Tune. Tenor, or Faburden. Ravenscroft adjusts printed text to all three added parts.

Du fons de ma pensée tune with a much richer overlay of accidentals than did the Knickerbockers for whom Francis Hopkinson compiled *The Psalms of David* in 1767.

Psalmes of David in Englishe Metre by Thomas Sternehold and others and *Fovr Score and Seven Psalmes of David in English mitre by Thomas sternehold,* both printed at Geneva (in 1558 and 1561; see Frost, pp. 4 and 8). Ravenscroft calls it the "9. French tune," assigns it to the tenor voice (only very exceptionally, as in Psalm 25, does Ravenscroft put the "tune" in the cantus), and calls the tune a "Faburden." He calls the French tunes for Psalms 50, 111, 125, and 130 "Faburdens" along with a few other foreign tunes. He calls other tenors "Playnsongs." In "The Ravenscroft Psalter (1621): The Tunes, with a background on Thomas Ravenscroft and Psalm Singing in his Time," University of Southern California D. M. A. dissertation, 1959, pp. 356–361, William Paul Stroud learnedly discusses *9. French Tune.* To appreciate Ravenscroft's artistry, his harmonization need only be compared with that of so peerless a master as Orlandus Lassus (printed in O. Douen, *Clément Marot et le psautier huguenot,* II [Paris: Imprimerie Nationale, 1879], pp. 215–217; discussion, p. 56).

[11] Just as Ainsworth's 1612 psalter (later editions, 1617, 1626, 1639, 1644, 1690; see Pratt, p. 8) provided the Plymouth and Salem congregations with their tunes, so Ravenscroft bequeathed to the Puritans of Massachusetts Bay the tunes first sung at

The text in Ravenscroft's *Whole Booke* conforms with that sung after 1640 by Anglicans throughout the American colonies—the so-called "Old Version," [12] i.e., Sternhold and Hopkins version. This was sung in California as early as 1579. Sir Francis Drake's chaplain, Francis Fletcher, recounts the enthusiasm of the California Indians for the psalm-singing of Drake's men on June 26, 1579:

Our generall with his company in the presence of those strangers fell to prayers. . . . In the time of which prayers, singing of psalms, and reading of certain chapters in the Bible, they sate very attentively; and observing the end of every pause, with one voyce still cryed, oh, greatly rejoycing in our exercises. Yea, they took such pleasure in our singing of psalmes, that whensoever they resorted to us, their first request was commonly this, *Gnaah,* by which they intreated that we should sing.[13]

" 'Gnaah' was an imitative word, representing the nasal tone in which, we have been told, the Puritans sang" [14]—or at least so thought Otto Kinkeldey, the dean of American musicologists. However, Percy Scholes countered by observing that "such tone was evidently not a Puritan characteristic since Drake and his men were certainly not, as a body, Puritans." [15]

On whichever side justice may lie, the Puritans can at least take credit for the first Protestant metrical psalter in an Indian tongue. That same fondness for Calvinist psalm tunes which left *Du fons de ma pensée* and *Bienheureux est quiconques* so deeply etched in the memories of the Florida Indians with whom Laudonnière's Huguenot troupe came into contact in 1564, had a similar effect in the Massachusetts Bay colony. The pioneer minister at Cambridge records this

Boston and Cambridge. Gov. John Endecott (*ca.* 1589–1665) owned a copy—still extant. It was to Ravenscroft that compilers of the so-called "Bay Psalm Book" (*The Whole Booke of Psalmes Faithfully Translated into English Metre* [Cambridge: Stephen Day, 1640]) turned for the tunes to which the psalms printed in 1640 "may be sung" (see Irving Lowens, "The Bay Psalm Book in 17th-Century New England," in *Journal of the American Musicological Society,* VIII/1 [Spring, 1955], 23 [n. 5], 24; or, *Music and Musicians in Early America* [New York: W. W. Norton, 1964], pp. 27, 29).

[12] Before 1640 the Massachusetts Puritans sang the rugged Sternhold and Hopkins metrical psalms, just as did Laudians—but only for lack of a more literal version. See Wilberforce Eames, ed., *The Bay Psalm Book* (New York: Dodd, Mead & Co., 1903), p. [v].

[13] Francis Fletcher, *The World Encompassed by Sir Francis Drake* (London: Nicholas Bourne, 1652), p. 72.

[14] Percy Scholes, *The Puritans and Music in England and New England* (London: Oxford University Press, 1934), p. 257.

[15] Cyclone Covey, "Puritanism and Music in Colonial America," in *William and Mary Quarterly,* 3rd ser., VIII/3 (July, 1951), 378–388; also: IX/1 (Jan., 1952), 129–133, criticizes Scholes's techniques of special pleading.

fondness in a tract published in 1648.[16] Psalm-singing was therefore one of the first habits that the Massachusetts natives picked up from the English.

The Narragansetts of Rhode Island even preserved a tradition (first put in print in 1845) that before the Pilgrims landed they had already heard Calvinist canticles. In *Indian Melodies* composed by Thomas Commuck, "a Narragansett Indian," and harmonized by the famous Thomas Hastings (New York: G. Lane & C. B. Tippett, 1845), Commuck inserts one OLD INDIAN HYMN at page 63 with the following footnote:

The Narragansett Indians have a tradition, that the following tune was heard in the air by them, and other tribes bordering on the Atlantic coast, many years before the arrival of the whites in America; and that on their first visiting a church in Plymouth Colony, after the settlement of that place by the whites, the same tune was sung while performing divine service, and the Indians knew it as well as the whites. The tune is therefore preserved among them to this day, and is sung to the words here set.

Long before Commuck, this tune had obviously blossomed with the kind of thick passing-note foliage recommended by the author of *A New and Easie Method . . . applied to the promoting of Psalmody* (London: William Rogers, 1686, p. 101). Whether or not it was taught the seventeenth-century Narragansetts in anything like the form notated by Commuck, the 1845 version deserves insertion here (Example 5). (The rest of Commuck's collection consists of "original tunes" by a "*son of the forest*," as he calls himself, and shows Hastings's heavy correcting hand. But such "correction" was of course to be the fate of most "Indian" airs published on both sides of the Atlantic before 1900.[17])

Example 5   *Old Indian Hymn.* C.M. (Double)

Thomas Commuck, *Indian Melodies* (New York: G. Lane and C. B. Tippett, 1845), p. 63

[16] Thomas Shepard, *The Clear Sun-shine of the Gospel breaking forth upon the Indians in New-England* (London: R. Cotes, 1648), p. 33.

[17] For a discussion of *The Cherokee Singing Book* (Boston, 1846), edited by Dr. Samuel A. Worcester and the Indian Elias Boudinot, and of other Indian-language hymnals, see J. Vincent Higginson, *Hymnody in the American Indian Missions* (New York: Hymn Society of America, 1954), pp. 17–18, 32–33, and *passim*.

Missionary work amongst the Indians was "a principal end of our coming hither," vouched John Endecott (*ca.* 1589–1665, first Massachusetts Bay governor) in his letter of August 27, 1651, to the president of the "Corporation established in Parliament for Promoting the Gospel among the Heathen in *New-England*." Earlier in the month he had visited a settlement of "praying Indians" thirty-eight miles away. John Eliot (1604–1690), their evangelizer, had already finished metrical translations of several psalms into their language (later he undertook the complete Psalter) and of the first books of both Old and New Testaments (the whole Bible was printed in their tongue at Cambridge in 1663). When Endecott arrived, one Indian began expounding two kingdom-of-heaven similitudes (Matt. 13:44–46). This lasted half an hour. About one hundred of his tribesmen and women listened attentively. Next, Eliot discoursed for three-quarters of an hour in the Massachusetts Bay language.

After all there was a *Psalme* sung in the *Indian* tongue, and *Indian* meeter, but to an *English tune,* read by one of themselves, that the rest might follow, and he read it very distinctly without missing a word as we could judge, and the rest sang chearefully, and prettie tuneablie.[18]

Such concrete evidence [19] strongly suggests that the missionaries in Massachusetts found "Calvinist" music no less popular with the Indians there than Motolinía and Sahagún in Mexico, Gerónimo de Oré in Peru, and Nóbrega in Brazil had been finding "Catholic" music to be with the indigenes farther south. For an outline of such a tune as Endecott would have heard the Natick Indians singing "chearefully, and prettie tuneablie" in early August of 1651, Psalm 1 is shown in Example 6, the English text being the Sternhold and Hopkins translation (with the tune to which the arriving Puritans sang it), and the Indian text being Eliot's *Wame Ketoohomae uketoohomaongash David* metrical version in *Up-Bookum Psalmes*.

In the firm conviction that nothing was so good for the Indians to learn as Calvinist psalm tunes, Dutch as well as English missionaries made it their first business to teach their converts psalms "upon our Notes." So much is certified in a lengthy letter written from Albany in 1694 by a pioneer Dutch missionary who signs himself

18 John Endecott, Letter in *Strength ovt of Weaknesse* (London: M. Simmons, 1652), p. 34.
19 Henry W. Foote, *Three Centuries of American Hymnody* (Cambridge: Harvard University Press, 1940), p. 56, provides later testimonials to the musicality of the Massachusetts Indians.

Example 6

The Whole Booke of Psalmes (Cambridge [England]: Cantrell Legge, 1623, p. 2, and

Wame Ketoohomae uketoohomaongash David (Cambridge [Massachusetts]: Samuel Green, 1685), Psalm 1

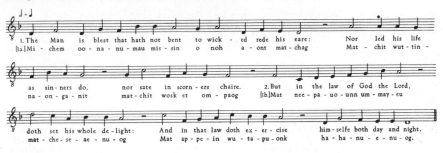

• ♩ in 1623.

"Godefridus Dellius" (published the same year in Matthew Mayhew's *A Brief Narrative of The Success which the Gospel hath had, among the Indians* [Boston: Bartholomew Green], p. 55). Although wars with the Indians blighted missionary labors toward the close of the century, especially when Christianized Indians in New England were expected to side with the colonists, still Cotton Mather could boast in 1705 (*A Letter; About the Present State of Christianity, among the Christianized Indians of New-England* [Boston: Timothy Green], p. 9) of their "Excellent Singing of Psalms, with most ravishing Melody." In 1721 he harped again on the same theme in his *India Christiana* (Boston: B. Green) when he called the Indians converted by Eliot *"Notable Singers"* of the metrical psalms in their own language (p. 32) and claimed that among the approximately thirty-eight New England congregations ministered to by some twenty-five Indian "teachers" in his own day, psalm-singing was frequently better than in "our English Assemblies" (p. 38).

2

NEW ENGLAND PURITANISM,
1620-1720

THE nonseparatist Puritans who began settling in and around Boston a decade after Plymouth was founded by the Pilgrim Forefathers (the Pilgrims were Separatists from the Church of England) took second place to no other colonists "in wealth, station, education or capacity." Nonetheless, they rejected the tunes in the Pilgrim psalter, preferring Ravenscroft's plainness to "the difficulty of *Ainsworths* tunes." [20] This difficulty had not so much to do with range as with length.[21] Moreover, Ainsworth used too many meters. The compilers of the so-called Bay Psalm Book, after laboring a quadrennium, produced a psalter in 1640 that incorporates only six kinds of meter. Ainsworth resorted to no less than fifteen.

Of course, Ainsworth himself professed to have chosen the "easiest tunes of the French and Dutch psalmes." [22] Daily converse with the Dutch doubtless taught the Pilgrims the fifteen tunes that had never before appeared in any English psalter.[23] If he took only the "easiest," then such a tune as that for Psalm 95 (Example 7) accounts for opposition to Ainsworth's novelties among the Massachusetts Bay Puritans who had never lived on the Continent.

Praising the vocal skill of the Pilgrims before their leaving Leyden, one trustworthy witness reports:

Wee refreshed our selves after our teares, with singing of Psalmes, making joyfull melody in our hearts, as well as with the voice, *there being many of*

[20] *The Whole Booke of Psalmes* (Cambridge: [Stephen Day], 1640), fol.**2.
[21] The tunes for Psalms 20, 67, 84, 113, 136; 37, 49, 119, 139; 49, 78, 80, 91, 94 call for 80 or more notes. See Pratt, pp. 60, 66, 59; Frost, pp. 158, 404, 401 (nos. 125, 331, 328). The Psalm 113 tune (also in Sternhold and Hopkins) begins with a repeated strain. However, as a rule Ainsworth's lengthy tunes eschew repeated strains.
[22] *The Book of Psalmes* (Amsterdam: Giles Thorp, 1612), preface. Since no tunes are "set of God," Ainsworth allows "ech people to use the most grave, decent, and comfortable manner of singing that they know."
[23] Frost, p. 394.

the Congregation very expert in Musick; and indeed it was the sweetest melody that ever mine eares heard.[24]

And many "very expert in Musick" would indeed have been required if the whole Pilgrim band grasped the rhythm of such a syncopated passage as measures 8–9,[25] or cleanly negotiated the skips that outline a downward minor seventh in measure 6.[26]

Example 7   *Psalm XCV*

The Book of Psalmes (Amsterdam: Giles Thorp, 1612), pp. 119 [music], 247 [text]

When in 1640 the Massachusetts Bay Puritans rejected the excessively long tunes, the multiplicity of metrical patterns, the extensive borrowing from Continental sources,[27] and the jaunty rhythms to which Ainsworth's 1612 psalter committed the Plymouth and Salem congregations, they merely conformed with a trend that before 1700 reduced the number of tunes "in general use" throughout the English-speaking world to scarcely more than a dozen.[28] Salem congregation itself dropped Ainsworth—after a church-meeting vote taken on May 4, 1667—for almost identical reasons. The first was "the difficulty of the tunes, and that we could not sing them so well as

---

[24] Edward Winslow, *Hypocrisie Vnmasked* (London: Richard Cotes for John Bellamy, 1646), pp. 90-91. Italics added.

[25] Of the three other irregularly accented Ainsworth tunes printed by Pratt, pp. 33, 37, 53, two derive from William Daman's *The Psalmes of David . . . with Notes of foure parts set vnto them* (1579) and *The former Booke* (1591). Cf. Frost, pp. 394, 21–22.

[26] This melody reappears as first or second tune for eight other psalms in Ainsworth —45, 53, 58, 72, 96, 103, 111, 147.

[27] Frost, p. 394, acknowledged having failed to find sources for four Ainsworth tunes (including Psalm 45).

[28] William Barton, *The Book of Psalms in Metre* (London: Thomas Snowden, 1692), typically prints but ten "general tunes." The one well-known psalm tune which he admits to having excluded is the "104th, which is counted too crabbed." According to Charles Burney, *A General History of Music* (London: Payne and Son, etc., 1789), III, 59, note e, the only two new tunes widely adopted in the century previous "are perhaps those of the 104th Psalm, and the Easter Hymn." The old 104th tune was "based upon the plainsong melody for *Iam Christus astra ascenderat*" (Frost, p. 152, quoting G. R. Woodward).

formerly." [29] The same story repeated itself at Plymouth. On May 17, 1685,

the Elders stayed the chh after the publick worship was ended & moved to sing Psal: 130: in another Translation, because in M[r] Ainsworths Translation which wee sang, the tune was soe difficult few could follow it, the chh readily consented thereunto.[30]

Seven years later, the knell sounded once again. John Cotton, Plymouth pastor from 1669 to 1697, was the son of that erudite patriarch of Boston, John Cotton (1584–1652),[31] who had published the Magna Charta of Puritan music in New England, *Singing of Psalmes A Gospel-Ordinance* (1647). John Cotton the younger, having grown up singing his father's Bay Psalm Book, naturally favored it. This preference can be condoned the more easily when one recalls that not only Psalm 23 but others in the Bay collection had been translated by his own father. On June 19, 1692 (*Plymouth Church Records,* I, 277), "after the Evening worship, the Pastour stayed the church, & propounded. . . . That seeing many of the Psalmes in M[r] Ainsworths Translation which wee now sung had such difficult tunes as none in the church could sett," they therefore find a way to bring in another version, with easier tunes. The following August 7, "at the conclusion of the sacrament, the Pastor called upon the church to expresse their Judgments as to the Proposall made about the Psalmes June, 19: & put to vote, whether they did consent, that when the Tunes were difficult in our Translation, wee should sing the Psalmes now in use in the neighbour-churches in the Bay." After "two bretheren vocally exprest their approbation . . . by a silentiall vote the whole church consented it should be soe, not one opposing" (*Records,* I, 278).

The contents of the so-called Bay Psalm Book did not change so utterly in fifty-odd [32] re-editions as those of another famous American

[29] George Hood, *A History of Music in New England* (Boston: Wilkins, Carter & Co., 1846), p. 53.

[30] *Plymouth Church Records 1620–1859,* Part I (*Publications of The Colonial Society of Massachusetts,* Vol. XXII [Boston: John Wilson and Son, 1920]), p. 160. This splendid hypolydian tune, surcharged with energetic syncopations, serves also for Psalms 13 and 88. See Pratt, p. 33; Frost lists it as one of the four Melchizedek tunes in Ainsworth (pp. 394–395).

[31] Cotton senior advocated congregational singing not only of the Davidic psalms but also of other scripture portions. Commending Ainsworth's swan song (see note 8 above), he wrote: "It were to be wished, that this Booke [Song of Songs] were turned into verse or meeter in each language, that we might sing the Canticles as the Hebrewes did" (*A Briefe Exposition Of the Whole Book of Canticles* [London: J. Young for Charles Green, 1648], p. 6).

[32] Eames, ed., *The Bay Psalm Book,* p. [ix].

bibliographical deceiver—the Little and Smith *Easy Instructor*—in thirty-four re-editions; [33] but the psalm book adopted at Salem in 1667 and at Plymouth in 1692 does differ from the 1640 edition. Because only the first edition can presently fetch $151,000 a copy in open market,[34] specialists in Americana often disregard the 1651 revision, published after "a little more of Art was employ'd upon" the psalms by Henry Dunster,[35] the president of Harvard who resigned in 1654 because he could no longer accept infant baptism as scriptural. Just as the New England translations cannot be judged without comparing the original editions (facsimiles of the 1640 imprint are conveniently accessible [36]) so also the variety of the tunes cannot be known without consulting original imprints. To show what melodies were recommended by the 1640 compilers [37] Irving Lowens has listed all forty-eight of the Ravenscroft psalm tunes that are mentioned in "An Admonition to the Reader" at fol Ll3v. of the first edition.[38] However, Ravenscroft (a copy of whose 1621 *Whole Booke* John Endecott brought over) and Richard Allison (a copy of whose 1599 *Psalmes of Dauid* William Brewster owned in 1643) had by 1698 fallen so much behind the times that all thirteen psalm-tunes in the 1698 Bay Psalm Book are copied from either the seventh (1674) or eighth

[33] Irving Lowens and Allen P. Britton, *"The Easy Instructor* (1798–1831): A History and Bibliography of the First Shape-Note Tune-Book," in *Journal of Research in Music Education,* I/1 (Spring, 1953), 31–55; or, Lowens, *Music and Musicians,* pp. 115–137, 292–310.

[34] Zoltán Haraszti, *The Enigma of the Bay Psalm Book* (Chicago: University of Chicago Press, 1956), p. v: "the highest price ever paid for a volume at a public sale."

[35] According to Cotton Mather, *Magnalia Christi Americana* (London: Thomas Parkhurst, 1702), p. 100, Richard Lyon aided Dunster. Hood, pp. 27–29, prints the Dunster-Lyon "improvements" of Pss. 1, 23, and 137. Neither of the previous editions had included versifications of Ex. 15:1–21; Deut. 32:1–43; Jud. 5:1–31; I Sam. 2:1–10; II Sam. 1:19–27; Song of Songs 1–8; Isa. 5:1–7; 12:1–6; 25:1–9; 26:1–21; 38:10–20; Lam. 3, 5; Jonah 2:2–9; Hab. 3:2–18; Luke 1:46–55, 68–79; 2:14; 29–32; Rev. 4:8, 11; 5:9–10, 12, 13; 7:10, 12; 15:3. In the twenty-sixth edition (Boston: J. Draper, for J. Blanchard, 1744), the Psalms of David end at p. 287, the other metrical scripture passages occupying pp. 288–346. The New England Puritans cannot be justly be accused of bias against singing when they insisted on so much scripture besides "David." Cf. note 31 for John Cotton's eagerness that the Song of Songs be turned into a singable version. Cotton, not Richard Mather, penned the memorable preface to the 1640 edition; he also versified Psalm 23. See Haraszti, pp. 19–27, 45–47; for comment on the tact shown in the Dunster-Lyon "refinements," pp. 59–60; for identification of the elusive Richard Lyon (who wrote the 1651 alternate Ps. 112), pp. 98–106.

[36] N. B. Shurtleff, ed., *A Literal Reprint of the Bay Psalm Book* (Cambridge: Riverside Press, 1862); Wilberforce Eames, ed., *The Bay Psalm Book* (see note 12); Zoltán Haraszti, ed., *The Bay Psalm Book* (Chicago: University of Chicago Press, 1956).

[37] Haraszti, *The Enigma of the Bay Psalm Book,* pp. 12–18, 31–60, explodes the myth that a triumvirate consisting of John Eliot, Thomas Welde, and Richard Mather acted as sole compilers.

[38] Lowens, "The Bay Psalm Book in 17th-Century New England," p. 25, n. 10.

(1679) editions of John Playford's *Brief Introduction to the Skill of Musick.*[39]

Samuel Sewall (1652–1730), whose diary gives the fullest picture of everyday New England life in his period, owned the 1679 edition of Playford.[40] A key figure in Boston cultural life throughout his long life, his services to music included 24 years (1694–1718) as precentor (director of congregational singing [41]) in the Old South Church. Long before he succeeded Captain Jacob Eliot (1632–1693) in this coveted office, he began recording his musical experiences. Three typical entries during 1687–1688 will illustrate: [42]

August 25, 1687: Benjamin Eliot [43] [youngest son of the "Apostle to the Indians" and co-translator of the Bay Psalm Book, John Eliot [44]] would

[39] *Ibid.,* p. 28. For sources of the tunes that were to be requisitioned in the 1698 Boston imprint, Playford had abundant variety from which to choose. See Frost (n. 10 above), who lists sources for CAMBRIDGE, HACKNEY, LITCHFIELD, MARTYRS, OXFORD, ST. DAVID'S, WINDSOR, and YORK at the following numbers: 45, 333a, 25, 209, 121, 235, 129, and 205. Henry W. Foote, who listed HACKNEY and the 115TH PSALM as the two tunes in the 1698 imprint that were dropped from subsequent musical supplements (*Three Centuries of American Hymnody,* p. 54), seems to have overlooked the alternate title for HACKNEY. This common meter tune appears in Thomas Walter's *The Grounds and Rules of Musick Explained* (Boston: J. Franklin, for S. Gerrish, 1721; and for forty years thereafter in re-editions) with the title of ST. MARY'S (cf. Boston edition: Benjamin Mecom, for Thomas Johnston, [1760]; facsimile in Louis C. Elson, *The History of American Music* [New York: Macmillan, 1925], p. 2). John Tufts (1698–1750) includes HACKNEY in *An Introduction To the Singing of Psalm-Tunes* as late as the eleventh edition (Boston: Samuel Gerrish, 1744 [fol. A2]). Cf. Symmes (n. 9 above), pp. 25, 37.

[40] Haraszti, *The Enigma,* p. 130, note 20: "He also had a copy of the 1698 edition of Playford's psalm book, 'with all the Ancient and Proper Tunes . . . Composed in Three Parts, Cantus, Medius, and Bassus' (both volumes are in the Prince Library [Boston Public Library])." Lowens's identification of the 1674=1679 Playford as the source of the 1698 first New England music imprint makes it easier to believe in Sewall's intervention. For a convenient summary of Sewall's musical entries, see Scholes, pp. 41–46, 49–50, 66–68, 262–264.

[41] Scholes sees the English parish clerk as the homeland predecessor of the New England precentor, pp. 261–262. Allen P. Britton, "Theoretical Introductions in American Tune-Books to 1800," University of Michigan Ph.D. dissertation, 1949, p. 83, distinguishes between the clerk who read the psalm line by line and the precentor who "set the tune."

[42] Samuel Sewall, *Diary 1674–1729,* in *Collections of the Massachusetts Historical Society,* Vols. V–VII, Fifth Series (Boston [Cambridge]: John Wilson & Son, 1878–1882), I [1674–1700], 187, 232, 233.

[43] Benjamin Eliot, who obtained his A.B. in 1665, attended Harvard at an epoch when "*Singing by Note* . . . was study'd, known and approv'd of in our *College.* . . . And besides, . . . the *Notes* of the Tunes were plac'd in our *New England Psalm Books* from the *Beginning,* with general *Directions* for Singing by *Note*" (Symmes, *Utile dulci,* p. 14; cf. quotation from *The Reasonableness,* below at p. 24).

[44] Haraszti's contention that Eliot's part in the Bay Psalm translations may be less than was once supposed (*The Enigma,* p. 16) finds some support in the *Wame Ketoohomae Uketoohomaongash David* version of Psalm 2 (this is unquestionably Eliot's). No other Bay translator dared anticipate Isaac Watts in the matter of modernizing David's psalms to include Jesus' name. Eliot's Indian version includes the name *Jesus* in verse 7, *Christ* in verse 12.

sing with me, which did; he read three or more staves of the Seventy first Psalm, 9 verses, his Father and Jnº Eliot singing with us; Mr. Benjamin would in some notes be very extravagant. Would have sung again before I came away.

October 17, 1688: The 132. Psal. sung from the 13ᵗʰ v. to the end. . . . Mr. [John] Eliot ordain'd [Nehemiah Walker]. . . . After Dinner sung Zech'ˢ Song from 76ᵗʰ v. to the end, and the Song of Simeon [*Benedictus* and *Nunc dimittis*].

October 23, 1688. Heard Mr. Bayly preach from Numb. 33. 8,9. Sung the prayer of Jonah.

Numerous similar diary entries attest the genuine popularity of public as well as private singing throughout the last decade of Captain Jacob Eliot's precentorship. As if the 150 psalms were not enough matter for singing, the other Old and New Testament passages versified in 1651 were also in constant demand.[45] Such "very extravagant notes" as Benjamin Eliot introduced—though later in New England history regarded as abusive—gave fancy its needed room to roam in the heyday of psalm singing.

Captain Eliot fell "sick from Muddy-River" and died, aged sixty-one, on August 16, 1693; whereupon Sewall wrote: "We shall hardly get another such sweet Singer as we have lost—he was one of the most Serviceable Men in Boston." [46] A quarter-century later when Sewall himself resigned the precentorship, aged sixty-six, he had to admit that his own "enfeebled" [47]voice had long lost the luster endearing the Captain's to everyone in Boston. At least Sewall had the wit, however, to retire betimes—not yielding to the Reverend Thomas Prince's blandishments that he continue until seventy-two.[48]

Pitching the tune properly and keeping the congregation on the same tune throughout an entire psalm proved Sewall's knottiest problems. As early as October 25, 1691, at an evening exercise he was not sure he "had [LITCHFIELD] tune till 2ᵈ line" although he "meant

---

[45] Cf. H. W. Foote, p. 51, who doubts that these "were much used in public worship."   -

[46] *Diary,* I, 382.

[47] *Diary,* III [1714–1729], 171. Symmes, *Utile dulci,* p. ii, names Thomas Foxcroft —preacher on the Sunday morning when Sewall decided that he must quit the precentorship—as one of the principal proponents of "Regular Singing" in Boston. Walter, *The Grounds and Rules,* lists Foxcroft at p. iii. Judge Sewall probably felt his discomfiture the more keenly in Foxcroft's presence.

[48] With considerable tact Prince (1687–1758), who had succeeded to the ministry of Old South only the year before (and who was to hold the post until death), urged Sewall to remain precentor "six years longer." Prince takes palmary honors as New England historian, assembler of antiquities, and hymnbook editor (Foote, pp. 157–159).

it." [49] On December 28, 1705, he again made the mistake of going "into a Key much too high" and of wandering from WINDSOR into HIGH DUTCH.[50] He thereupon wrote: "The Lord humble me and Instruct me." His final humbling came in the three weeks February 2–23, 1718. On the first Sunday he could not restrain the "Gallery" from shifting into ST. DAVID'S although he had started with YORK. The same happened on the last Sunday of the month.[51] Certain now that "this is the 2ᵈ Sign," he interpreted these contretemps as "an intimation and call for me to resign the Praecentor's Place to a better Voice."

The singer in the Gallery whom he selected as his best qualified successor was none other than the tallow-chandler Josiah Franklin, whose then sixteen-year-old son Benjamin was one day to write a string quartet and to render enough other musical services to merit an entry in *Grove's Dictionary*. Baptized in Old South Church, Benjamin thus enjoyed the twin advantages of Sewall's early influence, and of his father's. Nor did he forget his father when years later he reminisced in *The European Magazine and London Review*, XXIII (January, 1793), p. 20:

[My father's] voice was sonorous and agreeable; so that when he sung a psalm or hymn, with the accompaniment of his violin, with which he sometimes amused himself in an evening, after the labours of the day were finished, it was truly delightful to hear him.

The tunes mentioned in Sewall's diary tend to be those that gave the Judge trouble on one occasion or another. However, the sheer number mentioned by name gives some clue to their variety: [52] HIGH DUTCH (= 85TH PSALM in Tufts and Walter),[53] LITCHFIELD, LOW DUTCH (= CANTERBURY in Playford, Tufts, Walter),[54] MARTYRS,

[49] *Diary*, I, 351 (LITCHFIELD is Frost's no. 25).

[50] *Diary*, II [1699–1714], 151 (WINDSOR is Frost's no. 129, HIGH DUTCH his no. 180 [cf. n. 54 below]).

[51] *Diary*, III, 164; 171 (YORK is Frost's no. 205, ST. DAVID'S his nos. 234 and 235).

[52] Cf. Britton, pp. 83–84.

[53] Tufts, *An Introduction*, 5th and 11th [1726 and 1744] eds., p. 10 in musical supplement; Walter, 1721 ed., p. 37; 1760 [Mecom], p. 12 of supplement. Frost, no. 180; Pidoux, I, 113.

[54] Baptized LOW DUTCH in Ravenscroft (Frost, pp. 37, 71), it retained this name in Massachusetts as late as 1698, when it was printed in *The Psalms Hymns and Spiritual Songs* (= Bay Psalm Book), *The Ninth Edition* (Boston: B. Green and J. Allen) as the proper tune for Psalm 23. In 1671 and 1677 Playford renamed it CANTERBURY. See Frost, 19a, 19b. Sewall heard Thomas Walter, Dr. Cotton Mather's musical nephew (1696–1725), who published *The Grounds*, 1721 (see note 39), "set Low Dutch very well" in the presence of Governor Dudley, Friday October 24, 1718 (*Diary*, III, 201).

OXFORD, PSALM 72, PSALM 119, ST. DAVID'S, WESTMINSTER, WINDSOR, and YORK. HIGH DUTCH, thus newly baptized in Ravenscroft's *Whole Booke* of 1621 (pp. 196, 226), proves none other than the ancient Lutheran chorale *Vater unser im Himmelreich,* printed by Valentin Schumann in 1539, adapted to Marot's *Enfans qui le Seigneur servez* [Ps. 113] in *Pseavmes de David, mis en rime* (Strassburg: Wolfgang Köpfel, 1553), and the subject of at least seven of Bach's chorale preludes (*BWV* 636, 682, 683, 737, 760, 761, 762). It was into this 8.8.8.8.8.8 *Vater unser* tune (Ravenscroft, pp. 116, 152, 190 = Playford, *An Introduction,* 8th ed., p. 72) that Sewall inadvertently fell at the close of the Friday service on December 28, 1705, when he intended the common meter WINDSOR instead. Twice printed so early as 1591 nameless, WINDSOR awaited christening in Ravenscroft's classic 1621 *Whole Booke.*[55] WESTMINSTER—one of the sixteen tunes composed by Orlando Gibbons for George Wither's *The Hymnes and Songs of the Chvrch* (1623)—reappears identically in three collections: Playford's *Whole Book of Psalms* (1677), Tufts's *Introduction,* 5th ed. (1726), and Walter's *Grounds* (1721, 1723).[56] It remains still current today in *Hymns Ancient & Modern Revised* (1950, nos. 336, 511), *The Oxford Hymn Book* (1908, no. 4), and *The Hymnal 1940* (no. 573).

LITCHFIELD (Playford, *Brief Introduction,* 8th ed., p. 71), the tune that confused Sewall on October 25, 1691, joins HIGH DUTCH and WINDSOR in being another minor melody.[57] Evidence both external and internal confirms its more recent origin. When first printed (*Brief Introduction,* 1658), it was categorized by Playford as a "New Tune." [58] Liberal use of large leaps distinguishes not only LITCHFIELD but also ST. DAVID'S and YORK, the tunes that by twice painfully unhorsing Sewall in February of 1718 made him resign the precentorship after twenty-four years in the office. ST. DAVID'S, listed in Ravenscroft's

[55] Frost, pp. 161, 23–24 [1591 (B)]. Daman's four-part harmonizations of "all the tunes of Dauids Psalmes, as they are ordinarily soung in the Church" entrust the congregational tune to the tenor in *The former Booke,* to the cantus in *The second Booke.* In Scotland, where this same sturdy stepwise tune circulated widely, it was renamed DUNDIE from 1615 onwards (Frost, pp. 163, 36 [1615b]).

[56] Frost, no. 362c; Irving Lowens, "John Tufts' *Introduction to the Singing of Psalm-Tunes* (1721–1744)," in *Journal of Research in Music Education,* II/2 (Fall 1954), 98, col. 1.

[57] OXFORD and MARTYRS, both Scots tunes (Frost, nos. 121 and 209 [published 1564 and 1615]), inhabit minor—as do also Psalms 72 and 119 (Frost, nos. 233 and 132 [Tufts, 1726 ed., p. 11]). Two-fifths of all sacred music published in New England before 1800 are in minor. As late as 1794, William Billings avowed that "lovers of Music" in the main still preferred minor (*The Continental Harmony,* p. xxiii). See Britton, p. 234, for an illuminating discussion.

[58] Frost, p. 76.

1621 *Whole Booke* as a "Welch Tune," begins with fifths in every line but one; for every scale step there are 1.6 skips in this vigorous tune. YORK (first printed in the Scots *CL. Psalmes of David* [Edinburgh: Andro Hart, 1615]) receives as its more appropriate name in all Scottish tune books THE STILT.[59] The thirteen skips in this splendid major triadic tune (Ravenscroft changed its name from THE STILT to YORK) contrast with only eight scale steps.

Such numerous wide skips outlining chords leave open arteries for the many "extravagant notes" with which enthusiastic improvisers such as Benjamin Eliot liked to embolize their psalmody. True, the chords are only implied when the whole congregation stays together on the tune. But with individual singers lagging or running ahead, the harmony becomes explicit. When this happened, Puritans who had so long denied themselves the delights of harmony (because of Calvin's interdict) could at last enjoy the forbidden fruit of common chords with clear conscience.

[59] *Ibid.*, pp. 36, 256 (no. 205). Foote, p. 43, recalls the singing of this tune at the Harvard Tercentenary: "the old tune had a simple dignity and austere beauty all [its] own." For Benjamin Franklin's comment on Scots tunes such as THE STILT, see Gilbert Chase, *America's Music* (New York: McGraw-Hill, 1955), p. 93.

~~~ 3 ~~~

"REGULAR SINGING," 1720-1775

LIKE many later musical innovations in America, the "Regular Singing" movement of the 1720's kept pace with developments in the motherland. The Congregationalists in Boston took their cue from the Independents in London who in the previous decade had decided to promote the "delightful Exercise of Psalmody" by singing "according to the Rules of the *Gamut:* Without the Knowledge of which, it is impossible regularly to perform any Musick." The former custom of singing by ear must cease, the Independents at London were beginning to agree; and since "without the Knowledge of the *Gamut* Rules" no one can "judge, whether he sings true or false," every one in the congregation should know how to read music in G- and F-clefs.

To hurry the reform, a singing master signing himself "W.L." prepared a tune book (with a prefatory manual of psalmody) for the London congregation.[60] Among his precepts were many that were to be endlessly re-echoed in New England. Although the French use *ut* and *re* in their solfaing, "our English Masters have thought these four [mi fa sol la] sufficient," he wrote, stressing that of the four syllables the most important is *mi,* because it alone signals the keynote—a step above in major ("sharp") keys, a step below in minor ("flat") keys.

These and similar rules in the musical manual published in 1719 for the London Independents who "support and encourage the Friday lecture in Eastcheap" heralded a new epoch on both sides of the

---

[60] "An Introduction to Psalmody, in a New Method," by W. L. (initials not expanded) in *A Collection of Tunes, Suited To the various Metres in Mr. Watts's Imitation of the Psalms of David* (London: W. Pearson, for John Clark, 1719). All quotations are from the question-and-answer section (17 pages). The idea of printing an introduction explaining the gamut = staff, cliffs = clefs, notes, keys, time, and whatever else the psalm-singer needed to know, was no invention of W. L. Already in 1708 the famous sixth edition of *A Supplement to the New Version of Psalms* with thirty *"New Tunes"* (including William Croft's ST. ANNE and HANOVER) "composed by several of the Best Masters" had set the fashion with such an introduction. Nearly all eighteenth- and early nineteenth-century tune-collections printed in America were to include such a "rudiments of music" introduction.

Atlantic. As early as 1721, the twin tendencies to treat the psalm tunes as mere melody-types that—like a *maqam* [61]—could be embellished at will, and to transform the psalmody into "song tunes" [62] of ever more rustic flavor, had so aroused two Harvard graduates in touch with London co-religionists that they published almost simultaneously the first two music tutors printed in English America. Aiding John Tufts and Thomas Walter in the campaign for musical literacy there simultaneously sprang up a battalion of pamphleteers [63] whose trenchant prose still continues to be widely quoted in histories of American music. The profoundest of these was Cotton Mather; the saltiest, Thomas Symmes. Both shared the new-found zeal for "regular singing"—that is, by note, and according to musical rules.

Cotton Mather (1663–1728), the "most celebrated of all American Puritans," encouraged singing schools,[64] published *The Accomplished Singer,*[65] and wrote letters ventilating the controversy. In one to Thomas Hollis, London nephew of the benefactor who endowed the first Divinity chair at Harvard, Mather wrote on November 5, 1723:

A mighty Spirit came Lately upon abundance of our people, to Reform their singing which was degenerated in our Assemblies to an Irregularity, which made a Jar in the ears of the more curious and skilful singers. Our Ministers generally Encouraged the people, to accomplish themselves for a Regular singing, and a more beautiful Psalmody.[66]

[61] Cf. Britton, p. 87. George Pullen Jackson, "The Strange Music of the Old Order Amish," in *The Musical Quarterly,* XXXI/3 (July, 1945), 285, quotes a highly ornamented traditional version of the 1100-year-old Hildebrand song current among the Amish.

[62] Symmes, *Utile dulci,* p. 44: "*Most* of the *Psalm-Tunes,* as Sung in the *Usual way,* are much more like Song-tunes, than as Sung by Rule."

[63] Britton, pp. 93–95, provides a checklist of thirty titles. Half of these span the first two decades of the controversy. Controversialists active before 1776 include Peter Thacher (1723), Josiah Dwight (1725), Valentine Wightman (1725), Timothy Woodbridge (1727), Nathaniel Chauncey (1728), John Hammett (1739), Jonas Clarke (1770), Zabdiel Adams (1771), Lemuel Hedge (1772), Joseph Strong (1773), Oliver Noble (1774), and Samuel John Mills (1775).

[64] Singing schools, the most potent force in improving American church music before 1800, started usually as private ventures. For data on Boston masters who taught "Singing Psalm Tunes" in 1714, 1739, 1743, 1751, and 1768, see Robert F. Seybolt, *The Private Schools of Colonial Boston* (Cambridge, Mass.: Harvard University Press, 1935), pp. 13, 27–28, 31, 33, and 56. Similar instruction was being given in Virginia as early as 1710.

[65] Hood, who devotes half *A History of Music in New England* to Regular Singing tracts, prints excerpts at pp. 105–112, but without identifying Cotton Mather as the author. Symmes, *Utile dulci,* p. 56, alludes to "Dr. C. Mather's *Accomplished Singer.*" On the other hand, Hood erred in assigning Mather the 1723 *Pacificatory Letter* (p. 114).

[66] *Diary of Cotton Mather 1709–1724,* in *Massachusetts Historical Society Collections. Seventh Series, Vol. VIII* (Boston: The Society, 1912), p. 693. Mather emphasizes the appeal of Regular Singing to young people.

Earlier his own Second Church had alarmed him, and on March 13, 1721, he had asked himself: "Should not something be done towards mending the *Singing* in our Congregation?" [67] A singing school then in progress offered the most obvious means, and on March 16 he preached "in the School-House to the young Musicians, from Rev. 14. 3.—no man could learn that Song." Samuel Sewall, whose musical enthusiasm remained keen despite his having resigned the precentorship in 1718, wrote of the occasion: "House was full, and the Singing extraordinarily Excellent, such as has hardly been heard before in Boston. Sung four tunes out of Tate and Brady." [68] Even with this impetus, however, Mather feared that the lessons were not coming home to his own congregation. On June 5, 1721, he confided to his diary: "I must of Necessity do something, that the Exercise of *Singing* the sacred *Psalms* in the Flock, may be made more beautiful."

Within the next three years, sophisticated Boston—now a city of twelve thousand, with eleven churches, two grammar schools, two writing schools, and three thousand houses [69]—responded so well to treatment prescribed by the musical uplifters that by 1724 Mather could consider the battle won in the city. Only country yokels still held out. A letter of his dated April 22, 1724,[70] expresses the sort of biting contempt for "a Little Crue at a Town Ten miles from the City of Boston" which was to be frequently voiced by later eighteenth-century writers, under similar provocation. The hinterland pocket of resistance to which Mather refers was so "sett upon their old Howling in the public Psalmody, that being rebuked for the Disturbance they made, by the more Numerous Regular Singers, they declared They would be for the Ch. of E. and would form a Little Assembly for that purpose."

Mather's ridicule has a proleptic ring. Through American church history, like a binding thread, was to run in succeeding centuries this same big-city contempt for backwoods music. How superior he felt becomes clearer yet in the following extract:

But, who would beleeve it? Tho' in the more polite City of *Boston,* this Design mett with a General Acceptance, in the Countrey, where they have more of the *Rustick,* some Numbers of Elder and Angry people, bore

[67] *Ibid.,* pp. 560 (Oct. 13, 1718) and 606.
[68] Sewall, *Diary,* III [1714–1729], 285.
[69] See facsimile of 1722 map, with accompanying statistics, in *Diary of Cotton Mather 1709–1724* (opposite title page). For the distinction between "grammar" and "writing" schools, see Seybolt, p. 92.
[70] *Diary,* p. 797.

zelous Testimonies against these wicked Innovations, and this bringing in of Popery. Their zeal transported some of them so far . . . that, they would not only use the most opprobrious terms, and call the Singing of these Christians, a worshipping of the Devil, but also they would run out of the Meeting-house at the Beginning of the Exercise. The Paroxysms have risen to that Heighth, as to necessitate the Convening of several Ecclesiastical Councils.[71]

Musical literacy, far from newfangled popery, was an old New England tradition, according to Thomas Symmes (1678–1725), who vouched for the printing of Harvard College musical theses as early as the 1650's.

[Singing by Note] was studied, known and approv'd of in our College, for many Years after its first Founding. This is evident from the Musical Theses, which were formerly Printed, and from some Writings containing some Tunes with Directions for Singing by Note, as they are now Sung; and these are yet in Being, tho' of more than Sixty Years standing.[72]

Only during the epoch 1660–1720 had New England lapsed into slovenly musical habits, he everywhere claims in his sermon, The Reasonableness of, Regular Singing. The first delivery of this sermon in his own rural Bradford (thirty-five miles north of Boston) brought him numerous invitations to repeat it elsewhere.

Both the 1720 sermon and the 1723 dialogue Utile dulci reveal Symmes's favorite musical theorist to have been the polymath Johann Heinrich Alsted (1588–1638). Alsted, the encyclopedist whom Calvinists revered as a latter-day Isidore of Seville,[73] enjoyed universal renown in his own century. In proof of its continuing popularity, Alsted's Templum musicum was as late as 1664 still regarded by a London publisher as a sufficiently important work to be published

[71] Ibid., p. 693.

[72] The Reasonableness of, Regular Singing, or, Singing by Note (Boston: B. Green, for Samuel Gerrish, 1720), p. 6. For comment, see Henry W. Foote, "Musical Life in Boston in the Eighteenth Century," in Proceedings of the American Antiquarian Society, XLIX/2, new ser. (Oct., 1939), 300–301. Symmes entered Harvard in 1694, aged seventeen, after preparing under the "famous Master Emerson" in Charlestown. Leverett was his Harvard tutor. He stayed two years after receiving his M.A., aided by Brattle's generosity. For further biographical data, see A Particular Plain and Brief Memorative Account of the Reverend Mr. Thomas Symmes (Boston: T. Fleet, for S. Gerrish, 1726), pp. 2–6.

[73] Neue deutsche Biographie (Berlin: Duncker & Humblot, 1952), I, 206; Alexander Chalmers, ed., The General Biographical Dictionary (London: J. Nichols and others, 1812), II, 45–46. Comenius, the Moravian educator whom Governor John Winthrop visited in 1642 while traveling in Europe and whom he reputedly invited to assume the Harvard presidency, was Alsted's most famous disciple.

in an English translation.[74] Symmes—Harvard valedictorian in 1698 [75] —knew the original Latin, if his quoting Alsted's *De musica* on the title page of *Utile dulci* is sufficient evidence. But when he adapts Alsted's account of the Guidonian syllables (*Utile dulci*, p. 36 = *Templum musicum*, pp. 35–36) or when on Alsted's authority he classifies music as a "special arithmetick" (p. 14 = p. 2), he carefully scales down the text to the capacity of the Bradford rural community of sixty families to which he ministered 1708–1725, and which knew a mere five tunes when he first transferred there from Boxford (*Utile dulci*, p. 25). Some of his flock were so misinformed as to imagine that King David himself composed St. David's psalm tune (p. 37). Others removed their hats religiously on hearing merely the textless tune of this or that psalm. Such reverence incites Symmes's queries:

Why do you take such care to put off your Hats, and put on a great *shew of Devotion* and Gravity whenever *Psalm Tunes* are sung, tho' there be not *One Word* of a *Psalm?* Are you not guilty of *Superstition* in this?[76]

Among the new tunes to which he introduced his country congregation—after taking on himself "the Trouble *of setting the Tune*" (*Utile dulci*, p. 55)—at least one was such a *dernier cri* novelty as to have made its début in print the very year that he published *The Reasonableness of, Regular Singing*. Isle of Wight, first published in *A Sett of Tunes in 3 Parts (Mostly New)* for use with Simon Browne's *Hymns and Spiritual Songs* (London, 1720),[77] gave his 250-member congregation such slippery troubles that some old-timers forthwith nicknamed it Isle of Shoals. Nonetheless, it had gained sufficient popularity in Boston for John Tufts to include it among the thirty-seven tunes in the "first American music textbook"—*An Introduction To the Singing of Psalm-Tunes* (1721: a copy of the 5th ed., 1726, is the earliest extant). In justifying a tune so extreme as to vaunt the chromaticism of $E\flat$-D-C$\sharp$ in the first phrase,[78] seven unusual

---

[74] See H. G. Farmer's article on John Birchensha, the translator, in *Grove's Dictionary*, 5th ed.

[75] Samuel E. Morison, *Harvard College in the Seventeenth Century* (Cambridge, Mass.: Harvard University Press, 1936), I, 63.

[76] *The Reasonableness of, Regular Singing*, p. 18.

[77] Lowens, "John Tufts' *Introduction to the Singing of Psalm-Tunes* (1721–1744): The First American Music Textbook," in *Journal of Research in Music Education*, II/2 (Fall, 1954), 98.

[78] Hamilton C. Macdougall, *Early New England Psalmody: An Historical Appreciation 1620–1820* (Brattleboro, Vt.: Stephen Daye Press, 1940), p. 154, prints the first two incises of the tune.

two- and three-note melismas, and (in the Tufts "G minor" harmonization *a 3*) an F♮ in the top voice against a simultaneous F♯ in bass,
Symmes contended that "*Ministers* are Debtors, not to the *Weak* only,
but to the *Strong*." Because it is their moral duty, "*Chief Musicians*
and Masters of Song must . . . set Tunes to Exercise the Gifts of the
more skilful." He himself had not balked at bringing in even "a Tune
to the 24th Psalm, which is said to be an *Indian* Tune" when the quality of the melody warranted learning it.[79]

Not only did Symmes's unusual doubling as preacher and precentor
enable him to introduce such new tunes as ISLE OF WIGHT, 24TH
PSALM = BELLA, BRUNSWICK,[80] and STANDISH (first published in
1700), but also to take the lead in abolishing the ubiquitous country
custom of lining out the psalms. One admirer of his courage wrote:

He thought it was high time that our common Custom of Reading the Line
in Singing, should be laid aside, not only because of its very much interrupt-
ing the Melody and sometimes the Sense, but because the Reason of it
now ceases, which was for the help of such as could not read, or want of
plenty of Psalm-Books; both of which may now be sufficiently remedied.[81]

As the most suitable means of teaching congregations to read the
tunes as well as the words in a book like the 1698 Bay Psalm Book
(earliest extant with a tune supplement), Symmes advocated singing
schools, meeting "Two or Three Evenings in the Week" from five or
six to eight o'clock. Ministers should take the lead in establishing such
singing schools. When the people learn to sing by note they will no
longer interpolate ornaments so lengthy as to triple the number of
notes in the original tune.

[79] *Utile dulci*, p. 54. Thomas Walter, *The Grounds,* 1721, p. 34, prints ST. JAMES'
TUNE (by Raphael Courteville, 1697; see Robert G. McCutchan, *Hymn Tune Names:
Their Sources and Significance* [New York: Abingdon Press, 1957], p. 140) and 24TH
PSALM TUNE. The latter reached print for what seems to have been the first time in
A New and Easie Method To Learn to Sing by Book (London: William Rogers,
1686), p. 102. Cf. *Hymns Ancient and Modern, Historical Edition* (London: William
Clowes and Sons, 1909), p. (80), discussing BELLA. BELLA sounded so much like
CAMBRIDGE SHORT TUNE to Joseph Hawley, a bellowing singer at Farmington, Con-
necticut, that he was fined for mixing them up on Sunday, February 19, 1725 (*New
England Historical and Genealogical Register,* X [Oct., 1856], pp. 311–312).
[80] BRUNSWICK, copied by hand in Walter's *The Grounds and Rules of Musick The
Second Edition* (Boston: B. Green for S. Gerrish, 1723), p. 24 (same page with
STANDISH), came to New England with the reputation of being King George I's
favorite tune. The twenty-four additional hand-copied tunes in Walter's *The Second
Edition,* New York Public Library copy, include "On the Divine Use of Music," for
singing the stanzas thus entitled in Symmes' *The Reasonableness,* p. [21].
[81] *A Particular Plain and Brief Memorative Account* (see n. 72 above), p. 25.
According to this account, p. 24, Symmes was an "excellently accomplished" singer
whose "introducing many new Tunes into his [Bradford] Assembly" was one of his
brightest virtues.

The way in which so hoary a common tune as SOUTHWELL (printed 1591; in Tufts [1726], p. 4, Walter [1721], p. 30) was being embellished—by English as well as New England country singers *ca.* 1686 —can best be understood from Example 8, pairing (I) the unvar-

Example 8

I. John Tufts, *An Introduction To the Singing of Psalm-Tunes,* 11th edition (Boston, Samuel Gerrish, 1744), p. 4, and
Thomas Walter, *The Grounds and Rules of Musick Explained* (Boston: J. Franklin, for S. Gerrish, 1721), p. 30
II. *A New and Easie Method To Learn to Sing by Book* (London: William Rogers, 1686), p. 101

nished traditional tune with (II) a contemporary transcript of the "Bovicelli" notes that country singers delighted in adding. The editor of *A New and Easie Method* prints the unvarnished tune, then the embellished, with this observation: "The Notes of the foregoing *Tune* are usually broken or divided, and they are better so sung, as is here prick'd." It was against such "breakings" and "divisions" that Symmes, Tufts, Walter, and their abettors inveighed from 1720 to 1760.

A quick survey of the editions of Tufts's *Introduction* shows "20 Psalm Tunes, with Directions how to Sing them" in the *editio princeps* (announced January 2/9, 1721), 28 tunes in the second (April 24/ May 1, 1721), and 18 (later amplified to 34) in the third (January 21/28, 1723). Only in the third did he begin providing basses to the trebles. The "Fifth Edition (with several excellent Tunes never before publish'd here)," announced October 17/24, 1726, contains "a Collection of Thirty Seven Tunes in Three Parts" that was to serve as model for the numerous later editions (1738, 1744, are in the Library of Congress). Tufts's letter-notation,[82] using only *mi-fa-sol-la* syl-

---

[82] See Sirvart Poladian, "Rev. John Tufts and Three-Part Psalmody in America," in *Journal of the American Musicological Society,* IV/3 (Fall, 1951), 276–277. The earliest edition of the Bay Psalm Book yielding to Tufts's innovation was the 26th (Boston: J. Draper, for T. Hancock, 1744), which ends with a twelve-page letter-notation supplement (thirty-three three-voice harmonizations, tune in treble).

lables,[83] caught on so quickly that in this very same year another "Collection of Psalm Tunes in Three Parts . . . with Letters instead of Notes" was announced at Boston. The recently composed tunes in Tufts's 1726 edition included: ISLE OF WIGHT, NORTHAMPTON, and PORTSMOUTH (this trio derive from Simon Browne's 1720 *A Sett of Tunes*), PSALM 100 NEW, PSALM 149 (William Croft, 1708), ST. JAMES (Raphael Courteville, 1697), and STANDISH [84] (*Psalm-Singer's Necessary Companion,* London, 1700). Of this group of seven novelties, only ST. JAMES had entered Walter's 1721 *Grounds.*

PSALM 100 NEW, which now rates as a likely candidate for the honor of being the sole original New England contribution to Tufts's 1726 edition, eventually garnered sufficient popularity at Boston for Benjamin Mecom in 1760 to insert it at page 17 of "Walter's Singing Book . . . With eight tunes more than usual." [85] Illustrating how loosely the term *anthem* was used at Boston in 1760, Mecom here calls it "Anthem to 100." [86] Is it coincidence that the same page shows the much more correctly written WARWICK TUNE, on which PSALM 100 NEW indeed seems to have been modeled? Only one other "new tune" was picked up from the fifth edition of Tufts (1726) by Walter's 1760 editor—PORTSMOUTH (Mecom, p. 18), which however merely echoes PSALM 113 (Tufts) = PSALM 115 (Walter, 1721).

Mecom's 1760 edition and Thomas Johnston's of 1764 bring Walter's reign to a close. The fifth edition still includes *Vater unser im Himmelreich,* but no longer the historic *Lasst uns erfreuen* (1526) that had been included in every New England collection of Psalm tunes from Ainsworth, through the Ninth Edition of the Bay Psalm Book (1698), to Tufts. So far as changes between 1721 and 1746 in *The Grounds and Rules* are concerned, Walter can be held respon-

---

[83] A2 verso: "*Mi* is the principal Note." Tufts repeats "W. L.," pp. 12–13 (see n. 60 above), who in 1719 wrote: "You are first to find out the proper place for *Mi*." See Britton, p. 177. Not until 1774 (see n. 2 above) did a psalm book appear in the thirteen colonies with an introduction publicly endorsing seven-syllable solmization (ut re mi fa sol la ci = CDEFGAB = fa sol la fa sol la mi, four-syllable system).

[84] Symmes, who had difficulty teaching his flock STANDISH, protested (*Utile dulci,* p. 25): "As to *Standish,* it has been Sung for many years, (as I'm inform'd) in the Church of *N. Hampton.*"

[85] Lowens, "John Tufts' *Introduction,*" pp. 99–100, first proposed 100 PSALM TUNE NEW as "American." Matt B. Jones, *Bibliographical Notes on Thomas Walter's "Grounds and Rules of Musick Explained"* (Worcester: American Antiquarian Society, 1933), p. 11, describes the Walter 1760 edition. James Lyon includes 100 PSALM TUNE NEW in *Urania* (1761), p. 66.

[86] So named also in Daniel Bayley's *The Psalm-Singer's Assistant* (Newbury-Port: [author], *ca.* 1764), p. 8, where the part-writing remains unchanged. In the same tune supplement, Bayley publishes NEW YORK, p. 7, and NEWBURY-PORT, p. 13. Not only the tune names but also the "forbidden" consecutives give both an American look.

sible for only those in the second edition (1723), published two years before his premature death of tuberculosis. What had started as Dorian music—PENITENTIAL HYMN (first English printing, 1562)— appears with one flat in his 1721 *Grounds,* but with two flats in the 1723. The notes of an Italian augmented-sixth chord crop up in the 1723 G minor harmonization (p. 10) as a result of the added signature flat.

"Mr. *Walter's* Sermon on Regular Singing," *The sweet Psalmist of Israel* (Boston: J. Franklin, for S. Gerrish, 1722), moulded the future of New England psalmody hardly less forcefully than did his *Grounds and Rules.* Later called "the most beautiful composition among the sermons which have been handed down to us from our fathers," this was a sermon "Preach'd at the Lecture held in Boston, by the Society for promoting Regular & Good Singing And for Reforming the Depravations and Debasements our Psalmody labours under, In order to introduce the proper and true Old Way of Singing." One purpose was to convince the opinion-makers of Boston congregationalism that three-part vocal harmonizations such as he had published the year before in *The Grounds* ought to be sung in public worship. His method was simple: he "proved" that David's psalms were thus sung in Bible times. Whereas John Tufts in his 1721 *Introduction* (and in successive issues to 1726) dared publish only the tune, Walter began at once in 1721 with all three parts, cantus, medius, bassus. In his sermon, he explains his reasons (p. 8):

The *Music* of the Temple, as it was under the Management and Direction of our *Sweet Psalmist* of Israel, was a *Chorus of Parts.* The Singers and the Players upon Instruments, were divided into THREE Sets or Quires. One for the *Bass,* another for the *Medius* or inner Parts; the third for the *Trebles* or *Altus's.* Mr. *Ford* in his Preface to his Exposition on the *Psalms,* has done to my Hand, what I might have attempted; even to prove that *Music in Parts* (in spight of popular Ignorance) is as Ancient as the Times of holy *David.*

Walter continues by approving a translation of I Chron. 15:21 and Ps. 6:1 [*hhal hassheminith*] that reads: "To a grave and low Symphony: that is, to a *Bass* Note and Key" (p. 9). Jeduthun "had the regulation of the *lower Parts.*" Heman "was the Master and Moderator of the *Altus* or highest Part," and "*Asaph* therefore was the Master of the *Medius* or middle Quire" (p. 10).[87]

[87] Walter twice quotes (pp. 12, 18) as his musical authority the Jesuit Athanasius Kircher, whose *Musurgia universalis* (Rome, 1650) he cites by its alternate title,

The upward surge of New England psalmody from 1714 to 1769 can best be seen in (1) the mushrooming of singing schools (taught by such masters as James Ivers, John Waghorne, Skiner Russell, Moses Deshon, Jacob Buckman, and John Barry [88]); (2) the rise of choral concerts; (3) the enlargement of the choristers' repertory. Already in the dedication of his 1722 sermon to Governor Paul Dudley, Walter commends "the Reverend Mr. *Brown* of *Reading*" for having addressed "a *Singing Lecture* there." Five years later, Timothy Woodbridge printed in New London a sermon preached at a "Singing Lecture." [89] This neutral name covered the public exhibitions offered by choirs at the close of a singing school. As a rule the exhibition numbers were picked from tune books peddled by the singing master who ran the school. These three factors—singing schools, culminating in graduation concerts that incorporated a repertory selected from the singing master's personally sold books—made possible the career of the first famous American composer of church music, William Billings. The careers of his numerous contemporaries and successors who were to publish between 1770 and 1800 no less than twenty-six tune books containing music composed by American natives, and by them only —Samuel Babcock (*The Middlesex Harmony,* 1795), Supply Belcher (1751–1836), Daniel Belknap (1771–1815), Jacob French (*The New American Melody,* 1789; *The Psalmodist's Companion,* 1793), Oliver Holden (1765–1844), Samuel Holyoke (1762–1820), Solomon Howe (1750–1835), Jacob Kimball (1761–1826), and Merit Woodruff (1780–1799)—rest on the same foundation.

What the singing schools did from 1720 onwards in making possible church music composition throughout New England was repeated in Pennsylvania (James Lyon's *Urania,* 1761, and the publications of Andrew Adgate's Uranian Academy, 1785–1788). In Virginia, where William Byrd of Westover mentions the movement as early as 1710, the Tidewater gentry not only accepted singing by note as

---

Ars magna consoni et dissoni. Walter's lengthy catalogue of the virtues of music and of the classical heroes who acknowledged its powers (p. 12) would do credit to a Renaissance theorist. Charles Chauncy (1705–1787), who knew Walter personally, claimed for him an "almost intuitive knowledge of everything" and rated him as one of the three most brilliant minds produced by New England Congregationalism ("Notices of the Walter Family," *New England Historical and Genealogical Register,* VIII/3 [July, 1854], 213).

[88] Cf. Seybolt, pages listed in note 64 above. John Barry, whom Seybolt equates with a schoolmaster who arrived on September 29, 1766, co-operated with William Billings in the 1769 "Singing School near Old South Meeting-House."

[89] *The Duty of God's professing people, in glorifying their Heavenly Father,* preached at Hartford, June 28, 1727. See Charles Evans, *American Bibliography,* I (Chicago: Blakely Press, 1903), item 2979.

proper for psalmody but also took up four-part singing of psalms as an accepted social diversion.[90] By 1775 only the backwoods Scotch-Irish clung to such old customs as having "the Clerk raise the tune . . . with a deep-strained Gutteral, from the last Word of the Reading." [91] A Presbyterian missionary from New Jersey who toured the Staunton region in 1775 "was agreeably entertained and surprized to hear an Irish Congregation singing universally without the Roll & Whine," but soon found the reason—a singing school begun shortly before his arrival. He mentions the son of John Trimble, a Princeton graduate, as teacher. After attending the young lad's singing school, the missionary confides to his diary: "It is beautiful, to behold the Progress of Civilization." [92]

[90] Philip Fithian, *Journal and Letters,* I (Princeton: University Library, 1900), p. 187.

[91] Fithian, *Journal, 1775–1776* (Princeton University Press, 1934), pp. 18–19. John Adams in his diary (August 21, 1771) complained of the same Presbyterian drawling. Fithian calls it their "Whine & Roll."

[92] Fithian, *Journal,* II, 140, 175. See also pp. 155–156, 177.

4

PENNSYLVANIA GERMANS

ALTHOUGH the Quakers were no great friends of music, William Penn's "Holy Experiment" [93] turned the colony (of which Charles II made him proprietor in 1681) into a haven for religious perfectionists from Germany and Holland, many of whom were musicians. Their numbers included Johannes Kelpius (1673–1708), Johann Conrad Beissel (1690–1768), and a dynasty of Moravians stretching from Jeremias Dencke (1725–1795) to Johann Friedrich Peter (1746–1813) whose careers trace a constantly rising musical trajectory.

What seems to be the earliest musical manuscript compiled in the colony was the work of Kelpius—an Altdorf University [94] graduate distinguished for his mastery of Hebrew, Greek, Latin, and English. Translated from German the title of the manuscript reads: "The Lamenting Voice of the Hidden Love at the time when She Lay in Misery & forsaken" (MS Ac. 189, Historical Society of Pennsylvania). All ten melodies scattered through the seventy leaves of this manuscript breathe the middle Baroque, and indeed four melodies with basses come from a hymn book printed at Nuremberg in 1684, only a decade before Kelpius and his disciples reached Pennsylvania (Christian Knorr von Rosenroth's *Neuer Helicon,* nos. 56, 34, 18, and 30 = Kelpius, fols. 1 [35], 9, 21 [57], and 66).[95] Three other melodies (fols. 63, 17 [56c], and 30) show affinities with German sources

[93] Penn's early travels on the Continent had given him a wide acquaintance in both France and Germany. See *Caspipina's Letters; . . . To which is added, The Life and Character of Wm. Penn, Esq.* (Bath: R. Cruttwell, 1777), II, 122–123 (France), 144–145 (Germany).

[94] Or the University of Helmstedt, according to Francis H. Williams's "John Kelpius, Pietist," in *New World* (Boston), III/10 (June, 1894), 218. Williams prints two important letters written by Kelpius from the "Wilderness of the Elect of God," the first dated December 11, 1699, the second May 25, 1706 (pp. 223–226). These explain the theological positions that drove him to Pennsylvania.

[95] Albert G. Hess, "Observations on *The Lamenting Voice of the Hidden Love,*" in *Journal of the American Musicological Society,* V/3 (Fall, 1952), 219.

dated 1690, 1693, and "before" 1718. Still another awaited 1708 for its first printing in J. A. Freylinghausen's *Geist-reiches Gesang-buch* (p. 515 [no. 333] = Kelpius, fol. 56b). Those two melodies (fols. 56a, 68) that have not yet been traced obviously belong to the same era. The rich harmonies designated in the seven melodies with basses, and the warm modulations implied by the three without, prove how responsive Kelpius must have been to all the more recent trends in German Pietist hymnody. Even if he was no composer himself, the filling up of the middle parts with chords suitable for keyboard without pedals (fol. 21 [57]) shows musical intelligence beyond the capacity of any contemporary musician in the English colonies. The errors that sometimes intrude can be debited to the copyist of the extant manuscript, who was not Kelpius but was possibly Dr. Christopher Witt (*ca.* 1675–1765), his disciple, who translated all of the perfervid poetry into English.[96] Even so, the literacy of the transcript far outruns anything by Sister Anastasia, copyist of hundreds of Beissel's original hymns.

Conrad Beissel, whose musical career earns its most sympathetic recent treatment at Thomas Mann's hands in *Doktor Faustus*,[97] was orphaned by the death of both father and mother before he was nine. Apprenticed to his father's trade of baking, he came under a master baker who played the violin. Having learned fiddling as well as baking, Beissel "had the opportunity to display his bright disposition at weddings, at which, when exhausted with playing the violin, he would betake himself to dancing." [98] After sojourns in Mannheim and Heidelberg, he emigrated to Germantown by way of Boston in 1720. Baking proving of little avail in Pennsylvania, he studied weaving with Peter Becker, a German Baptist missionary. In 1721 he moved inland to what is now Lancaster County, and on November 12, 1724, accepted Becker's baptism by immersion. Four years later he published a tract

---

[96] For facsimile of the manuscript, see *Publications of the Pennsylvania Society of the Colonial Dames of America—IV: Church Music and Musical Life in Pennsylvania in the Eighteenth Century*, I (Philadelphia [Lancaster: Wickersham Printing Co.], 1926), 21–165. The English translations face the German original. Witt's life is outlined, I, 17–18. Cf. Hess, p. 217.

[97] *Doktor Faustus* (Stockholm: Berman-Fischer Verlag, 1947), pp. 104–109; English transl. by H. T. Lowe-Porter (New York: Alfred A. Knopf, 1948), pp. 63–68; Andres Briner, "Wahrheit und Dichtung um J. C. Beissel: Studie um eine Gestalt in Thomas Manns 'Dr. Faustus,'" in *Schweizerische Musikzeitung*, 98/10 (Oct., 1958), pp. 365–369. Briner's article summarizes the previous literature on Beissel's musical interests.

[98] Brothers Lamech and Agrippa, *Chronicon Ephratense Enthaltend den Lebens-Lauf des ehrwuerdigen Vaters in Christo Friedsam Gottrecht* (Ephrata: Gedruckt, 1786), p. 3; translated by J. Max Hark, *Chronicon Ephratense* (Lancaster: S. H. Zahm & Co., 1889), p. 4.

urging seventh-day observance and in 1732 gathered a band pledged to follow him in a life of celibacy at Ephrata, sixty-five miles from Philadelphia.

During the first decade this perfectionist group sang both Pietist hymns and traditional chorales such as *Ein' feste Burg*,[99] but in 1743 the afflatus seized Beissel and during the next quarter-century he composed "thousands of pieces" [100]—hymns, whole chapters of the Old Testament, and two entire settings of the Song of Songs. Before his death, his many musical outpourings were transcribed with loving care into a series of copybooks called by Hans T. David the "most beautiful illuminated MSS executed in colonial America."

The general character of this music, which is much less varied in style than its quantity might suggest, finds apt characterization in a letter written by the "Assistant Minister of Christ's Church, Philadelphia," Jacob Duché (1737–1798), to the Lord Bishop of B——l, October 2, 1771. First published as Letter V in *Observations on a Variety of Subjects, Literary, Moral and Religious* (Philadelphia: John Dunlap, 1774), Duché's account gives a picture of Ephrata three years after Beissel's death. Although Duché found that "their society seems to be upon the decline, not exceeding one hundred members" at the time of his visit, he could not sufficiently extol their singing. He reserves a dsecription for the close of his letter (pp. 78–79):

I shall at present remark but one thing more with respect to the *Dunkers,* and that is, the peculiarity of their *music.* Upon an hint given by my friend, the sisters invited us into their chapel, and, seating themselves in order, began to sing one of their devout hymns. The music had little or no air or melody; but consisted of simple, long notes, combined in the richest harmony. The counter, treble, tenor and bass were all sung by women, with sweet, shrill and small voices; but with a truth and exactness in the time and intonation that was admirable. It is impossible to describe to your Lordship my feelings upon this occasion. The performers sat with their heads reclined, their countenances solemn and dejected, their faces pale and emaciated from their manner of living, their clothing exceeding white and quite picturesque, and their music such as thrilled to the very soul.— I almost began to think myself in the world of spirits, and that the objects before me were ethereal.

---

[99] *Chronicon,* 1786, p. 72; Hark, p. 87.
[100] Hans T. David, "Ephrata and Bethlehem in Pennsylvania: A Comparison," in *Papers Read by Members of the American Musicological Society, 1941* (1946), p. 100. As David observes, "a few of his followers wrote and composed hymns in his manner" and it is "practically impossible to distinguish between his products and those of his adherents."

Beissel's restricting his first singing school to women owed something to chance. Since his knowledge of violin did not fit him to conduct or compose, he engaged *ein Meister des Singens* named Ludwig Blum to instruct some Sisters who showed musical aptitude.[101] Their protests caused him to let Blum go after a while, but not before one or two of the Sisters had siphoned off what they could understand and had taught it all to Beissel. He thereupon began rehearsing them four hours nightly. Arrayed in "white habits, they made such a singular procession that people of quality frequently visited the school." His exacting discipline eventually wore everyone out, and only the rescue of the singing school by the devoted Sister Anastasia saved it. With the addition of two bass parts, his entire choir in its heyday reached 25 (15 women, 10 men). Many of their best effects depended on a skilful antiphony such as is required in the *Die Braut des Lamms* (printed at pp. 140–144 of *Das Gesaᵉng der einsamen und verlassenen Turtel-Taube Nemlich der Christlichen Kirche* [Ephrata: Drucks der Bruederschafft, 1747]) by the rubrics "Erster Chor," "Zweyter Chor," "Der Mittel-Chor," and "Drey Vers werden mit dem folgenden Lied Chor-weiss gesungen." This particular "antiphonal anthem"—so-called by Elizabeth S. Houck because its length forbids classing it as any mere hymn—can be seen partially transcribed in her 1956 Union Theological Seminary thesis, "Johann Conrad Beissel: His Life and Music" (pp. 42–46; complete German text, pp. 51–56; English translation, pp. 38–41).

Better to give a foretaste of heavenly harmony, Beissel on principle excludes all strong-beat dissonances, not allowing even suspensions. To show how reduced a role he wishes passing-note dissonances to play, he enjoins his copyists to transcribe them as small-note graces resembling plicas in the beautiful but extremely mannered Ephrata manuscripts.[102] Just as the Renaissance humanist insisted on favoring accented syllables with longer time values, so also Beissel wishes to wed all accented German syllables to lengthier triadic ("master") notes.

---

[101] *Chronicon*, 1786, p. 136; Hark, p. 160. Blum *verstund auch das Componiren*, and it was his own *kunstreiche Stücke* that persuaded Beissel to engage him. Although Blum departed from Ephrata in anger, Beissel invoked God's blessing on him.

[102] Carl Engel, "Views and Reviews," in *The Musical Quarterly*, XIV/2 (April, 1928), 301–303, describes the most splendid of these, a nine-hundred-page "Das Gesäng der einsamen Turteltaube" acquired by the Library of Congress in 1927. Peter Miller presented this 1746 manuscript to Benjamin Franklin, who carried it to England (p. 305). A slightly later example of superb colonial calligraphy, "The Writing-Master's Amusement," took Abdiah Holbrook (1718–1769) ten years to copy. Holbrook opened a school to teach the "rules of psalmody" at Boston in 1744.

With all his megalomanias, he is not completely insensitive to the monotony of so much consonance—great quantities of it moving in forbidden parallels and most of it eschewing minor chords. Throughout the 375 hymns copied by Sisters Anastasia [103] and Iphigenia in New York Public Library MS *KD 1747, a tunebook counterparting the 1747 *Turtel-Taube,* he seeks variety by changing keys schematically from hymn to hymn. His circle of keys includes all majors from three sharps to three flats. The infrequent minors inhabit narrower bounds, since sharp signatures are for them interdicted. To move from one key to another as lithely as possible proves a problem to Beissel—which he attempts to solve with some not altogether clear instructions in the *Turtel-Taube* preface, *Vorrede u^{e}ber die Sing-Arbeit.*[104] To a modern analyst, his naivetés presage the similar innocence of harmonic "rules" noticeable in the early works of William Billings, Daniel Read, and other New England worthies. Moreover, Beissel keeps company with the New England group active 1770–1800 when he propagates his effusions through a singing school and flatters himself into thinking them worth preservation. His avoidance of dissonant suspensions also jibes with New England practices.

On the other hand, he contrasts with the New Englanders who flourished a generation later by harping on the 6/4 chord, by making women the foundation of his choral body, by treating the men as only a more or less incidental appurtenance, by assigning much wider melodies to the top women (Middle C to high B♭), and by requiring such ungainly skips of the men as ninths and sevenths. A considerably more devious personality than any of the New Englanders, he knew how to infuse *Sehnsucht* alien to their thinking. The G minor hymn (Example 9) serves as a specimen (the text deals with Christ's wounds). Certainly no New Englander would have so prominently displayed the augmented chord as does Beissel in *Wo geh ich hin* (New York Public Library, MS *KD 1747, no. 410 = *Turtel-Taube,* p. 324), or would have conceived sequences of hymns as sets of variations (*KD 1747, nos. 344, 352, 389 = pp. 305, 308, and 320 in

103 Sister Anastasia, *née* Anna Thomen in the Canton of Basel, was not only an "excellent singer" but also Beissel's "right-hand" in the singing school and his most zealous copyist. She left a young suitor at the altar to follow Beissel's counsels of celibate perfection. Only after Beissel's death did she finally marry. *Chronicon,* 1786, pp. 139–140; Hark, pp. 163–164.

104 Facsimiles of eight pages in Julius F. Sachse, *The Music of the Ephrata Cloister; also, Conrad Beissel's Treatise on Music* (Lancaster: New Era Printing Co., 1903), pp. 59–65, 72. Cf. the translation of the "dissertation on harmony" at pp. 70–79 with Engel, pp. 303–304, who protests against serious errors in the translation. For instance, Beissel's *brechen* is rendered "train" and his comments on swerving from key to key are improperly understood.

Turtel-Taube), however primitively the variations are worked out. Of course, the very system prescribed by Beissel inflicts upon him turns of phrase repeated from one hymn to another (a scale step down followed by the drop of a fourth is a typical melodic mannerism).

Example 9   Ich werde aufs Neue

New York Public Library: MS *KD 1747, Gesa^eng: No. 354; fol. 86, and *Das Gesa^eng der einsamen und verlassenen Turtel-Taube* (Ephrata, 1747), p. 337

Other mannerisms include numerous phrases **beginning with eighth-** note upbeats and eighth-note anticipations of final chords. Although he uses nothing but cut-time signature, he casts all but his most joyous hymns in free enough rhythms to please even a Dom Mocquereau.

The copy of the *Turtel-Taube* at the Huntington Library, San Marino, California, boasts less music than New York Public Library MS *KD 1747. However, its 120 tunes (117 for soprano and alto) do enjoy the advantage of having been exhaustively analyzed in Carl T. Holmes's 1959 University of Southern California thesis, "A Study of the Music in the 1747 Edition of Conrad Beissel's *Das Gesaeng der einsamen und verlassenen Turtel-Taube,* Huntington Library 39957, Evans 5959." Without endorsing Beissel's claim that angels gave him the tunes, Holmes concludes that many can still please, and foresees that a carefully chosen anthology might well restore "a wealth of vital and dignified melodies to **American** hymnody" (pp. 85–86). Holmes's bountiful transcriptions (**pp.** 88–217) and his thematic index (pp. 219–234) sustain the thesis advanced above that Beissel frequently repeats himself. For instance, 13 of the 120 Huntington tunes start with the five-note incipit now familiar to all as the opening of Michael Haydn's LYONS (pp. 229–230). But while reveling in the upward fourth for his first interval, Beissel avoids the ascending third like the Whore of Babylon. Holmes's "Study" is the more valuable because almost every tune in the Huntington Library turns up again in the omnibus Ephrata manuscript now at the Library of Congress.

When Benjamin Franklin labeled the Ephrata manuscript given him by Peter Miller a "curiosity," he might equally well have been describing Beissel's music itself. But the compositions of Jeremias Dencke, who arrived in nearby Bethlehem in 1760; of Johann Friedrich Peter, who came a decade later; of Georg Gottfried Müller (1762–1821), who reached America in 1784; of Johannes Herbst (1734–1812), who began at Lancaster in 1786 and at Lititz in 1791; of John Antes (1741–1811), who though born in Fredericktown (Pennsylvania) spent his adult life abroad; [105] and of Jacob Van Vleck (1751–1831), who was the second American-born Moravian composer of consequence, entitle the Moravian school of sacred composers centered at Bethlehem in the latter part of the eighteenth century to first-class honors in any history of Protestant music. [106] Memorabilia of the Moravian heritage include (1) organs built by such workmen as Johann Gottlieb Klemm—who after installing an organ at Bethlehem as early as 1746 [107] plied his trade there 1757–1762, and David Tanneberger = Tannenberg, who after sixteen years in America set up an organ shop at the Moravian settlement of Lititz in 1765 that eventually won him renown as the best organ builder in

---

[105] John Bland published before 1795 three Trios for two violins and cello as Antes's Opus 3. Apparently these were completed at Cairo, Egypt, during Antes's convalescence from a beating (1779–1781). "All of Antes's sacred music is preserved only in American archives." Cf. Donald M. McCorkle, "John Antes, 'American Dilettante,' " in The Musical Quarterly, XLII/4 (Oct., 1956), 486–499.

[106] Apart from McCorkle's works, the following provide useful introductions to Moravian achievements: (1) Hans T. David's "Musical Life in the Pennsylvania Settlements of the Unitas Fratrum," in Transactions of the Moravian Historical Society, XIII/1–2 (1942); reprinted with addenda and corrigenda by Donald M. McCorkle, Moravian Music Foundation Publications, No. 6 (Winston-Salem, 1959); (2) Ruth Scott's "Music among the Moravians: Bethlehem, Pennsylvania, 1741–1816," Master of Music thesis, University of Rochester, 1938; (3) Rufus A. Grider's Historical Notes on Music in Bethlehem, Pennsylvania, from 1741 to 1871 (Philadelphia: J. L. Pile, 1873; Moravian Music Foundation Publications, No. 4, Winston-Salem, 1957).

[107] An "orgel positiv of four stops purchased from Gustavus Hesselius of Philadelphia," according to Joseph A. Maurer, "Moravian Church Music—1457–1957," in American Guild of Organists Quarterly, II/1 (Jan., 1957), 6. Klemm (1690–1762) was "one of the most important American builders at the middle of the century," according to Talmage W. Dean, "The Organ in Eighteenth Century Colonial America," University of Southern California Ph.D. dissertation, 1960, pp. 108–114. He completed the three-manual Trinity Church (New York) organ in 1741.

the English colonies; (2) *de rigueur* instrumental accompaniment for all choral singing; [108] (3) a healthy tradition not only of voluntary choir singers but of voluntary string and other instrumental players, meeting for regular rehearsals in anticipation of church services; [109] (4) an avid interest in new sacred music, whenever possible by local Moravians; [110] (5) perfect integration of even the most "artistic" concerted music (such as anthems and arias with continuo, strings, and winds) into worship services; [111] (6) intriguing extensions of such practices as polyglot singing (imported from Herrnhut, Moravian European headquarters) to include singing in as many as thirteen languages; [112] (7) foundation of a *collegium musicum* at Bethlehem

[108] Unlike New England singing school masters, who were often forced to tune their choirs with no more aid than a pitch pipe, Moravian singers from the beginning of their American settlements (Bethlehem was founded in 1741) depended on instrumental support. A *Spinett* built by a Moravian fan-maker in London, Peter Knolton, reached Bethlehem January 25, 1744, and was the next day used in church service (David, p. 14). Christian I. Latrobe, the foremost Moravian musician in England, summarized Unitas Fratrum opinion on this issue when in his introduction to *Hymn-Tunes sung in the Church of the United Brethren* he contended that the pitch of any but highly sophisticated *a cappella* singers invariably sinks during a long hymn: "so that the longer the singing lasts, the more grievous the dissonance." Some kind of instrumental support must be given; "for the firmest and most powerful voice of the Precentor is borne down by the weight of the sinking multitude" (quoted in Theodore M. Finney's "The Collegium Musicum at Lititz, Pennsylvania, during the Eighteenth Century," in *Papers Read by Members of the American Musicological Society . . . 1937*, pp. 46–47).

[109] C. I. Latrobe, *Anthems for One, Two or more Voices performed in the Church of the United Brethren* (London: n. p., 1811), p. 2. No "attempt is made to exhibit the skill of the performers by a display of extraordinary powers of execution" (p. 3).

[110] Albert G. Rau in his preface to the *Catalogue of Music by American Moravians 1742–1842. From the Archives of the Moravian Church at Bethlehem, Pa.* (Bethlehem: The Moravian Seminary and College for Women, 1938), compiled by himself and Hans T. David, writes (p. 6): "Quite naturally the large part of this mass of material consists of works composed in Europe by musicians, Moravians and otherwise, during the last half of the eighteenth and the beginning of the nineteenth centuries." The sheer bulk of the European product therefore overwhelms the "quantity of original work done by these people [i.e., Moravians] in America." But Maurer counters (*A.G.O. Quarterly*, II/1, 6) that the quality of the music composed by Moravians in America soars to far greater heights than that reached by such Europe-based Moravians as the pioneering Johann Daniel Grimm (David, p. 9) or Christian Gregor (1723–1801). Certainly, the level of the works by Grimm and Latrobe printed in 1811 (preceding note) falls below that maintained in the *Arias, Anthems and Chorales of the American Moravians, 1760–1860*, Vol. I, recorded for Columbia (ML 5427, MS 6102) under Thor Johnson's direction.

[111] Latrobe, *Anthems*, p. 3, remarks that concerted music was usually followed by congregational singing of a hymn on the same subject. Because the words of the concerted music had to be intelligible to the congregation at all times, "vocal fugues also, are not used."

[112] Joseph M. Levering, *A History of Bethlehem, Pennsylvania 1741–1892* (Bethlehem: Times Publishing Co., 1903), p. 205. On August 21, 1745, the thirteenth anniversary of missionary beginnings at Herrnhut, the Bethlehem Moravians sang simultaneously in five languages and on September 4 *In dulci jubilo* in thirteen languages (including Mohawk and Mohican).

in 1744 [113] (one at Lititz *ca.* 1765,[114] another at Salem *ca.* 1786 [115])
that before the end of the century became a playing group capable of
performing "the chamber music and the orchestral music of the
Grauns, the Hasses, the Haydns, the Stamitzes, the Bachs who were
the great figures of the period." [116]

The long neglect of the Moravians in standard histories of American music can be easily enough explained, if not justified. Augustus
Gottlieb Spangenberg (1704–1792), who was to serve as a Moravian
bishop in both Pennsylvania and North Carolina, preceded John and
Charles Wesley in Georgia. Another Moravian leader who influenced
the Wesleys even more profoundly was Peter Boehler, who came out
to Georgia on the same ship with John and Charles. Moravian musical enthusiasm, no less than their repertory of German hymns, had an
obvious effect in Wesley's epoch-making *Charlestown Collection*
(Charleston, S. C.: Lewis Timothy, 1737), sometimes called "the
first real Anglican hymnal." [117] The five German hymns in this collection include one by Count Nikolaus Ludwig von Zinzendorf (1700–
1760), whose estate at Herrnhut Wesley visited immediately after his
Aldersgate conversion. The other four reflect Moravian viewpoints
no less clearly.[118] However, the Moravians never grew into the flour-
ishing national denomination that the Methodists have become. As an
inevitable result, early Moravian feats tend to be regarded by standard
historians—reversing Paul's oft-quoted figure of speech in the address
before King Agrippa—as a "thing that hath been done in a corner."
Like Nathaniels, historians have asked: "Can there any good thing
come out of Nazareth?" (the Moravians settled at both Nazareth and
Bethlehem). Only so much of a specialist in baroque and classical
music, so competent an editor of old music, and so much of a linguist

[113] *Ibid.*, p. 172. John Christopher Pyrlaeus was the leader at the first formal meeting, on December 13, 1744. See also David, p. 15.

[114] Finney, p. 48, quoting *Church Music and Musical Life in Pennsylvania in the
Eighteenth Century* (1927), II, 190. The young men of Lititz were urged to join the
group being organized by the Reverend Bernhard Adam Grubé so that their idle
time would be spent in better diversions than card games.

[115] Donald M. McCorkle, *"The Collegium Musicum Salem: Its Music, Musicians,
and Importance,"* in *The North Carolina Historical Review,* XXXIII/4 (Oct., 1956),
484.

[116] Irving Lowens, "Moravian Music—Neglected American Heritage," in *Musical
America,* LXXVIII (Feb., 1958), 31.

[117] Winfred Douglas, *Church Music in History and Practice* (New York: Charles
Scribner's Sons, 1937), p. 235.

[118] *John Wesley's First Hymn-Book: A Facsimile with Additional Material,* ed.
Frank Baker and George W. Williams (Charleston: Dalcho Historical Society, 1964),
pp. xxii–xxiii. Wesley translated thirty-three German hymns all told, most of them
while in Georgia.

as Hans T. David possessed the necessary equipment to exhume the music lying a century disused in Bethlehem archives and to present it properly to scholars. His editions of ten sacred songs for soprano, strings, and organ by Dencke, J. F. and S. Peter, Müller, Herbst, and Antes (New York Public Library, 1939), of seven concerted anthems for chorus or double chorus and of five string quintets by J. F. Peter, and of one anthem each by Herbst, Peter Wolle (1792–1871), and Francis F. Hagen (1815–1907) at last provided in 1939 the indispensable musical documentation required by all those who believe: "by their fruits ye shall know them."

At first victory was hailed by only a select coterie. Fortunately, however, the music so perceptively edited by Dr. David was to enlist interpreters of no less distinction—especially Thor Johnson, son of a Moravian minister and sometime conductor of the Cincinnati Orchestra. His devoted direction at Bethlehem festivals drew national attention in 1950 to John Antes's third string trio, to J. F. Peter's second and sixth string quintets, and to a symphony by the early nineteenth-century Philadelphian Charles Hommann (the merits of which had not been previously foreseen [119]). In 1954 he introduced 14 *Parthien* for winds by David Moritz Michael (1751–1825),[120] an overture by Hommann, further quintets and trios by Peter and Antes, and various concerted anthems by Johann Christian Bechler (1784–1857),[121] the most prolific of the "silver age" Moravian composers in America. By 1955, when the third Moravian festival and seminar transpired at Winston-Salem (seat of Donald McCorkle's remarkable researches in Southern Moravian music), Olin Downes had become so much of a convert to the cause that in a *New York Times* Sunday edition he hailed Moravian investigations as "the most significant research ever undertaken in American music." Next year was organized the Moravian Music Foundation, under whose auspices a

---

[119] Rau and David, *A Catalogue* (1938), p. 118: "this symphony, the quality of which is not very high, was apparently written in the thirties or early forties."

[120] *Ibid.*, p. 98: "All of Michael's compositions are quite poor. They display an extreme lack of imagination." Cf. the comments in *Moravian Music Foundation Publications*, No. 6, p. 35, followed by data at p. 44 demanding a revision of this premature judgment. McCorkle was responsible for inserting the *Parthien* in the 1954 festival and for exculpating Michael from such unheeding criticism.

[121] Like Christian Gregor, Johannes Herbst, Jacob Van Vleck, and Peter Wolle, Bechler finally rose to a bishopric. All the composers in the *Music of the Moravians in America* series edited by H. T. David were clergy. Nothing comparable has been seen in the history of a Protestant denomination. In sixteenth-century Spain, Morales, Guerrero, and Victoria were priests, but never bishops. Only Bernardino de Figueroa, the royal chapelmaster at Granada who later became a bishop at Barletta (southern Adriatic port) after winning fame as Juan Bermudo's endorser, violates the rule.

fourth festival was presented in 1957. In 1958 McCorkle's "Moravian Music in Salem" (Indiana University Ph.D. dissertation) advertised Peter's North Carolina *oeuvre*—which includes 30 anthems, most of which are "full," and four soprano solos.[122]

A further milestone was soon reached with the issuing under this foundation's auspices of a Columbia record reviewed by such perceptive critics as Nathan Broder [123] and Richard Franko Goldman.[124] Broder "was particularly struck by the depth of feeling in Antes's aria for soprano *Go, Congregation, Go!* [*Music of the Moravians,* ed. David, 1939, last item in No. 1] and the smooth melodic portion in Michael's *Hearken! Stay close to Jesus Christ.*" Though unwilling to cry up the Moravian music at the expense of other valid American church music (by Billings, for instance), he did commend the repertory for "another quality, which is rare and precious, the quality of utter sincerity, of unquestioning faith in the efficacy of musical prayer." Goldman wrote:

Unlike their contemporaries in New England at the end of the 18th century, these Moravian composers were all professionally trained and artistically skilled. They are not "primitives" like Billings or [Andrew] Law, *dilettanti* like [Francis] Hopkinson, or merely second-rate talents like Reinagle or Hewitt. They are beyond question the first real composers to work on American soil. . . . It is a tragedy for American music that their work was never known beyond the limits of the small communities in which they lived.

In assessing the stature of the pieces by Herbst, Antes, Peter, Michael, and E. W. Leinbach (1823–1901) chosen for recording, Goldman wrote (by way of summary): "They are extraordinarily interesting, not only from the standpoint of antiquarianism, or from the bias of national or local pride, but as genuinely moving and deeply felt expressions of a culture that was musical as well as religious."

J. F. Peter, already rated in Gilbert Chase's *America's Music* (1955) as "the chief member of the group," [125] seems not to have been more performed in his own time than Herbst. However, his six ingenious quintets for two violins, two violas, and 'cello give him entrée into the modern concert hall denied the other composers tran-

---

[122] Lowens, "Moravian Music," p. 124. McCorkle, "Moravian Music in Salem," pp. 135–142, 323–362.

[123] *High Fidelity,* X/6 (June, 1960), 57–58.

[124] *The Musical Quarterly,* XLVI/4 (Oct., 1960), 547–548.

[125] Cf. Albert G. Rau's pioneering article, now subject to many corrections, "John Frederick Peter," in *The Musical Quarterly,* XXIII/3 (July, 1937), 308.

scribed in David's pace-setting edition. The anthems deserve no paler encomiums. Throughout Peter's sacred works a definite development can be observed. In his first American year he composed a delicious solo with strings and organ, *Leite mich in Deiner Wahrheit* (July 13, 1770). But the ingenuous part-writing cannot be compared with such harmonic niceties as the ingenious German augmented-sixth chords reserved for "es sey vor Ihm stille" in the moving *Der Herr ist in Seinem heiligen Tempel* (November 13, 1786) that belongs to his North Carolina decade. Even in the mass of music that he chose to copy, he made a clear advance on American soil. His growth, like that of J. S. Bach, responded to suggestions read out of the various masters' works that he was constantly transcribing. This copying habit, acquired while he was still at school in Germany (between 1767 and 1770 he transcribed numerous symphonies and chamber works by C. F. Abel, J. C. F. Bach ["Bückeburg"], Stamitz, and Haydn [126]), persisted throughout life—culminating in the parts for the first American performance of Haydn's *Creation* at Bethlehem in 1811.[127] Nor was he averse to copying and recopying his own compositions, in the process improving them. By doing so, he keeps company with the prolific Herbst, who likewise in his last years completely rewrote several early anthems—meanwhile turning them into truly "exceptional" works.[128]

Peter's *Unto us a Child is born* in the improved final version (David ed., No. 5) vies worthily with Handel's *Messiah* chorus, many characteristics of which it self-consciously appropriates.[129] The larger conceptions of Peter's later years not only exploit more instruments (two flutes, two horns, bassoon added to strings and organ in *Unto us*) but also *cori spezzati*. The brilliant antiphonal play in *Lobet den*

[126] David, *Musical Life*, pp. 20–22. In 1766 Peter copied Haydn's Symphony No. 17. His transcript, now at Winston-Salem, was made "the same year in which the work first appears in the Breitkopf and Sigmaringen catalogues," and antedates "by about fifteen years the surviving European copies listed by Robbins Landon in *The Symphonies of Joseph Haydn* (London, 1955)." See Jan LaRue, "English Music Papers in the Moravian Archives of North Carolina," in *The Monthly Musical Record*, 89/995 (Sept.–Oct., 1959), p. 186.

[127] M. D. Herter Norton, "Haydn in America (before 1820)," in *The Musical Quarterly*, XVIII/2 (April, 1932), 327–328.

[128] Rau and David, pp. 89–92. The title pages carry *Di Johs Herbst vermehrt u. verbessert* or some such legend. Herbst's best work seems to date from his sixties and seventies. Like César Franck, whose reputation rests on compositions dated from his fifty-seventh year onward, Herbst "arrived" late.

[129] *Ibid.*, pp. 42–43; "As a composition by Peter with German words [*Uns ist ein Kind geboren*] appears in the Salem catalogue it is quite possible that Peter composed that earlier version there." Against thirty-nine works with German text, Rau and David catalogued only four by Peter with English (pp. 39, 42–43, 47), and these date from his last years.

Herrn, and for that matter the antiphony of paired voices in *Unto us,* provides especially welcome relief to choral writing from which fugues are excluded. So far as form is concerned, the anthems commence with the concise instrumental statement of a subject that is at once repeated by voices with instruments. Following a sharpward [130] thrust, Peter places the initial subject in dominant, next pleasantly involving himself in altered chords.[131] He thence returns to the tonic, restating material gleaned from the first bars. He rounds out the anthem with a brief instrumental epilogue to frame what may best be thought of as a monogenic concept.[132] In length, his anthems compare with a four-stanza hymn. Never ostentatious or "learned," they exploit only the resources at Peter's immediate command—even compensating for the men drawn off to play instruments by doubling the tenor part an octave higher in second soprano.

Because Peter knows so well how to wring dry the expressive possibilities of even a single German word ("stille" in *Der Herr ist in Seinem heiligen Tempel*), adaptation of his German anthems to English texts [133] poses all the problems deplored by Latrobe in the preface to *Anthems for One, Two or more Voices performed in the Church of the United Brethren* (London, 1811). Still another roadblock prevents easy present-day access to Peter's and Herbst's anthems: the obtaining, at least in a church, of a proper instrumental cadre. The famous trombone choir (treble, alto, tenor, bass) that announced "weddings, christenings, pageants, funerals, church and community affairs" [134] with different music cuing the age and sex of those for whom the announcement was being made, does not enter his accom-

---

130 In minor anthems—such as the beautiful *Die mit Thränen säen*—he moves to relative major. Peter, the first composer in America to master the new Viennese "sonata-allegro" principles, deferred to his era by casting all six string quintets in major keys (D, A, G, C, Bb, Eb).

131 Rau, *MQ* 1937, pp. 312–313, tabulates various harmonic felicities in the anthems. Simon Peter, Johann Friedrich's brother, reveals like sensitivity in a profoundly wrought solo with strings, *O Anblick, der mirs Herze bricht* (David ed., I, vii).

132 Anthems with "a contrasting middle section" (*Make a Joyful Noise,* Rau and David, p. 39) or "in two parts, the second of which introduces a new melody and a different tonality" (*Jesus, unser Hirt, ibid.,* p. 50) disobey the rule. Although Peter copied and presented such works as Mozart's 1788 Eb Symphony, he comes much closer to Haydn, who could make an entire first movement of one "theme," than to Mozart. The six quintets prove this. None of the anthems in David's edition lapses into Johann Daniel [Henry] Grimm's old-fashioned *da capo* structure (Latrobe, *Anthems,* 1811).

133 Carleton Sprague Smith adroitly translates the German of nine solos (*Ten Sacred Songs,* ed. Hans T. David [C. F. Peters, 1954: No. 6084]).

134 Donald M. McCorkle, "The Moravian Contribution to American Music," in *Notes of the Music Library Association,* sec. ser., XIII/4 (Sept., 1956), 599.

paniments. But *Da werdet Ihr singen* for double chorus does bespeak horns, clarinets,[135] flutes in pairs, bassoon, and organ.[136] To these, he adds a second bassoon and two trumpets in *Singet Ihr Himmel.*[137]

[135] In his *Autobiography* (1788), Franklin recounts having visited the Moravian church at Bethlehem in 1756, "where I was entertain'd with good Musick, the Organ being accompanied with Violins, Hautboys, Flutes, Clarinets, &c." This would have been five years before Jeremias Dencke's arrival in America and is too soon for the clarinet (McCorkle, "The Moravian Contribution," p. 600). However, at nearby Philadelphia a "Mr. Hoffmann, junior" played a "Solo upon the Clarinet" at the "first 'composers-concert' given in our country," November 16, 1769 (O. G. Sonneck, *Early Concert-Life in America* [Leipzig: Breitkopf & Härtel, 1907], p. 73).

[136] In the Moravian church at Bethlehem organ solos were avoided until the installation of the Jardine organ (December, 1873). See Maurer, p. 32. The *pièce de résistance* at the dedicatory "Grand Organ Concert" in January, 1874, was Rossini's *William Tell Overture* played by G. W. Morgan (1823–1892), sometime organist of both St. Thomas's and Grace Episcopal Churches in New York City. Such an organ part as David provides for Peter's *Leite mich* (I, v) can be compared with the unfigured bass of the original manuscript (facsimile in Rau and David, Plate F). Even a short undoubled organ passage (*Singet Ihr Himmel* [David ed., IV, p. 12]) is quite rare.

[137] Rau and David, p. 40; "Obviously he never again had an opportunity to use as large an orchestra."

⚮ 5 ⚮

NATIVE-BORN COMPOSERS IN THE
MIDDLE ATLANTIC COLONIES

WHO was the first native American composer? O. G. Sonneck, answering this query, wrote:

As our knowledge stands today, it was not the tanner and psalmodist William Billings of Boston (1746–1800). Though public and historians have worshipped this eccentric but remarkable man, whose crude utterances contain a spark of genius, as the Father of American Composers for well nigh a century, the title belongs to either James Lyon of Newark, N. J. (1735–1794), or Francis Hopkinson (1737–1791).[138]

Despite having chosen for the text of his first dated composition, "An Anthem from the 114th Psalm," 1760, three verses from the prose of the Authorized Version (Ps. 114:5–7), the youthful Hopkinson trips it as delicately over the trembling earth in his maiden anthem as does Dr. Arne on similar prompting. This anthem, for two sopranos, bass, and continuo (in addition to text, the bass line carries figures), comes at pages 180–181 in a large oblong manuscript book [139] compiled by Hopkinson while a student at the newly founded College (later University) of Pennsylvania. The first entry in the manuscript points to a teacher who arrived in Philadelphia in the 1750's and gave his first public concert January 20, 1757—Giovanni Palma.[140] Enamoured of vocal display, Palma shows his mettle with thirty-nine notes for "da" in the second line of his *Di render mi la calma* (p. 1 of Hopkinson's MS). "Glo-"ry in Nahum Tate's "While Shepherds

---

[138] *Francis Hopkinson, the First American Poet-Composer (1737–1791) and James Lyon, Patriot, Preacher, Psalmodist (1735–1794): Two Studies in Early American Music* (Washington: H. L. McQueen, 1905), p. 77.

[139] Library of Congress, ML 96.H83. Described in *Francis Hopkinson*, pp. 32–34.

[140] George Washington attended Palma's concert of March 17, 1757, his tickets costing him 52*s.*6*d.* See O. G. Sonneck, *Early Concert-Life in America (1731–1800)*, p. 65. Four years later Lyon published Palma's setting of the Christmas hymn by Nahum Tate that is nowadays always sung to a tune arranged from the soprano aria with which Handel closes Act II of his opera *Siroe* (1728).

watch'd y˙ Flocks by Night" (Palma's first Anglican composition is in both the Hopkinson manuscript [LC, ML 96.H83, p. 125] and Lyon's *Urania* [pp. 192–194]) revels in a run of no less than sixteen notes. With Palma's example to guide him, Hopkinson assigns thirty-two notes to "trem"-ble.

In his "Anthem from the 114th Psalm," dated 1760, just as in his presumably earlier song "My days have been so wondrous free," [141] Hopkinson adopts three emphatic quarter-notes moving stepwise to the tonic as the characteristic tag-ending for nearly every phrase. His Tate-Brady *The 23rd Psalm* (MS, p. 179) exploits the same cadential descending three-note figure (here made even more emphatic because in half-notes). This twenty-third psalm in retorted cut-meter obviously enjoyed the most immediate popularity of all Hopkinson's work. James Lyon, the Princeton B.A. 1759, M.A. 1762 who made musical history with *Urania, or A Choice Collection of Psalm-Tunes, Anthems, and Hymns, From the most approv'd Authors, with some Entirely New; In Two, Three, and Four, Parts* (1761) includes it at pp. 50–51 as one of the "entirely new" works in *Urania*. He makes only a few small changes, such as dispensing with the instrumental epilogue, adding a fourth voice ("counter") to Hopkinson's three, and suppressing any hint of figured bass.

Lyon addressed his collection "To The Clergy of every Denomination in *America*." Consequently, he had to forgo figured bass, and also such instrumental interludes as he was advantageously to insert under the title of "symphonies" in the first, second, and fourth choruses of his incidental music for the "Commencement, held in Nassau-Hall, New Jersey, September 29th, 1762" (*The Military Glory of Great Britain* [Philadelphia: William Bradford, 1762]). Hopkinson had never tried appealing to "every denomination." When he published his *23ʳᵈ Psalm* anew in *A Collection of Psalm Tunes with a few Anthems and Hymns Some of them Entirely New for the Use of the United Churches of Christ Church and S. Peter's Church in Philadelphia,* 1763 (plate XX), he therefore felt free to figure the bass and to revert to his original three voices. [142] The figured bass implies keyboard accompaniment—which in at least St. Peter's was available from 1763 (the year in which Philip Feyring built an outstanding organ).

[141] Facsimile in *Francis Hopkinson*, p. 79. Sonneck dates it 1759 because of its appearing at p. 63 of LC ML 96.H83.

[142] The four-part *Urania* arrangement of Hopkinson's "23ᵈ. Psalm *Tune*" came back into print in John Stickney's *The Gentleman and Lady's Musical Companion* (Newbury-Port: Daniel Bayley, 1774), p. 195.

The nonconformist ministers to whom the young Presbyterian minister-to-be James Lyon principally addressed himself did not begin approving of church organs until much later. The following brief summary shows what roadblocks had prevented the acceptance of organs in colonial dissenting churches.

In 1713 the rich Boston merchant Thomas Brattle had bequeathed an organ to the church in Cambridge that he had helped found, and of which his brother was pastor. Dissenting principles prevented its being accepted —whereupon the Anglican church in Boston (now King's Chapel) gratefully received it, importing for £30 annual salary and "other Advantages as to Dancing, Musick, etc." the London organist Edward Enstone to play it.[143] In 1742 Trinity Church, Newport, another Anglican church, obtained the second organ in New England. By 1754 the Dutch Reformed church in New York already owned "a small Organ" and about 1760 there was "an Organ erected in Nassau Hall [Princeton] for the use of Scholars at public prayers" (taken away before 1785).[144] Not until July 8, 1770, however, did an organ first sound "in a dissenting presb. Chh. in America . . . or Great Britain"—that day being the Sunday when a gift organ of 200 pipes secretly installed during June in the First Congregational (now Unitarian) Church of Providence, Rhode Island, was "for the first time . . . played upon in divine Service." To cite usages in another famous Providence church: First Baptist though founded by Roger Williams eschewed all instrumental music until 1804, countenanced a bass viol as sole accompaniment 1804–1834, and admitted an organ for the first time as late as 1834.[145]

Episcopalian churches boasting organs made Entertainment, not Edification, their prime goal—or at least so argued the dissenters until at least 1800. For evidence from an outside authority, they could quote the musically knowledgeable Marquis de Chastellux. After visiting Philadelphia he wrote (*Travels in North-America, in the Years 1780–81–82* [New York, 1828 ed.], p. 136): "The service of the English church [January 10, 1781] appeared to me a sort of *opera,* as well for the music as the decorations:

[143] Henry Wilder Foote, *Annals of King's Chapel* (Boston: Little, Brown, and Co., 1882), I, 208–214, quotes the documents for the introduction of the first organ into the English colonies. In New Mexico, organs were a commonplace a century earlier. See Agustín de Vetancurt's *Teatro Mexicano,* IV (*Menologio Franciscano*), first published 1698 (Madrid: José Porrua Turanzas, 1961), pp. 113, 271; Lota M. Spell, "Music Teaching in New Mexico in the Seventeenth Century," in *New Mexico Historical Review,* II (1927), 29–31; Lincoln B. Spiess, "Benavides and Church Music in New Mexico in the Early 17th Century," in *Journal of the American Musicological Society,* XVII/2 (Summer, 1964), 151.

[144] *The Literary Diary of Ezra Stiles, D.D., LL.D.,* ed. Franklin B. Dexter (New York: Charles Scribner's Sons, 1901), I, 58. See also Joyce E. Mangler, "Music in the First Congregational Church, Providence, 1770–1850," in *Rhode Island History,* XVII/1 (Jan., 1958), 2.

[145] William Dinneen, "Music in the First Baptist Church, Providence, 1775–1834," in *Rhode Island History,* XVII/2 (April, 1958), 41–42.

a handsome pulpit placed before a handsome organ; a handsome minister in that pulpit, reading, speaking, and singing with a grace entirely theatrical; . . . a soft and agreeable vocal music, with excellent sonatas, played alternately on the organ; all this, compared to the quakers, the anabaptists, the presbyterians, &c. appeared to me rather like a little paradise itself, than as the road to it."

A German noble officer, visiting Boston for an Episcopalian service held on March 19 of the same year (1781), wrote no less frankly than the Marquis de Chastellux (*The Revolutionary Journal of Baron Ludwig von Closen 1780–1783*, translated and edited by Evelyn M. Acomb [University of North Carolina Press, 1958], p. 73): "The Preacher frisked about in the pulpit like the Devil in a fount of holy water; sometimes he read a chapter, and sometimes he intoned a hymn in which the congregation joined on all sides. I must admit that the singing was very harmonious, and that the accompaniment and preludes of the organist were even more pleasing to the ear."

But music that pleased and tickled the ear was no more what the dissenters wanted than it was what Augustine wanted within church walls. Organs, opera, and opulence therefore remained whipping-boys of Presbyterian and Congregational divinity until at least 1800 in frontier America. To add weight to their arguments, the dissenting apologists never tired of citing the patristic aversion to all instruments. Lest the dissenters' position be too lightly dismissed, James McKinnon's 1965 Columbia University Ph.D. dissertation, "The Church Fathers and Musical Instruments," should be read. In the dissertation, and in the résumé, "The Meaning of the Patristic Polemic Against Musical Instruments" (*Current Musicology,* Spring, 1965, pp. 69–82), McKinnon amply proves that the Puritan position on any church use of instruments duplicates unanimous Patristic thought.

Not even Lyon with his youthful enthusiasm had the courage to attack such historic sentiments as these against organs. Instead, he felt that he had gone as far as it was prudent to go when he announced *Urania* in the Philadelphia press (May 22, 1760) as the "first Attempt of the kind to spread the Art of Psalmody, in its Perfection, thro' our American Colonies." Certainly, Lyon was the first to emphasize boldly the "Entirely New" compositions: three psalm tunes (pp. 44, 50, 63), two anthems (pp. 125–132, 165–169), and a hymn tune (p. 194). To this band of six novelties he might also have added "Jehovah reigns" (pp. 133–141, "An Anthem taken out of the 97th Psalm") by William Tuckey (1708–1781), appointed clerk at Trinity Church, New York, in 1753.[146] Tuckey, the first to conduct

---

[146] Andrew Law identified LIVERPOOL = *Jehovah reigns* = *An Anthem taken out of the 97th Psalm* as "a composition by William Tuckey." See Sonneck, *Francis Hop-*

a reasonably complete *Messiah* in America (January 16, 1770), roams through five keys, changes meter five times, and shifts frequently from solo voices and duets to full chorus. Lyon's most ambitious original contribution to *Urania,* "Two Celebrated Verses by Sternhold & Hopkins," veers from duet to full chorus, exploits the antiphony of answering voices, includes some vocal flourishes that would tax any singer's virtuosity, and divides into sections to be sung at contrasting speeds. On the other hand, the Lyon of *Urania* betrays himself an American (in contrast with Tuckey, whose excellent organ at Trinity, New York, could always be relied on to keep the pitch up [147]) by modulating no further afield than the dominant. In his "An Anthem taken from the 150th Psalm," Lyon proves himself similarly reluctant to modulate, except from A to E.

Tuckey's Tate-Brady "Jehovah reigns" (lacks vss. 9–11), Lyon's "The Lord descended from above" (= "Two Celebrated Verses by Sternhold and Hopkins" [Ps. 18:9–10]), and Lyon's Tate-Brady "Let the shrill trumpets" ("An Anthem taken from the 150th Psalm" [vss. 3–4]) continued to be choral *pièces de résistance* for a generation. Already in 1769 "Let the shrill trumpets" was popular enough in New England for Daniel Bayley to class it among the "Favourite Hymn Tunes and Anthems" by the "Latest and most Celebrated Authors" and to publish it that year at Newburyport in *The American Harmony, or Universal Psalmodist* (pp. 60–61). On May 4, 1786, Andrew Adgate conducted Lyon's three *Urania* anthems at "the Reformed Church, in Race Street" (Philadelphia). A chorus of 230 singers accompanied by 50 instrumentalists drew an audience of one thousand. A reviewer in the *Pennsylvania Packet,* May 30, again called them "the *celebrated* anthems." The next year Adgate revived another Lyon anthem—"Friendship," to Isaac Watts's lyrics. More ambitious harmonically than Lyon's anthems to Sternhold-Hopkins and Tate-Brady texts, "Friendship" had first reached print in John Stickney's *Gentleman and Lady's Musical Companion* (1774, pp. 17–22), probably because it had not been composed by 1760. In this same 1774 collection Stickney had followed Bayley's example when he reprinted "Let the shrill trumpets" (pp. 160–161).

---

kinson, p. 174. Law endorsed Lyon, to at least a degree (*ibid.,* p. 189), but not the type of fuging tune in *Urania* at pp. 42–43, 48–49 (5th and 15th Psalm Tunes) or the elaborate imitations at pp. 38–39 (CRANLEY), 46–47 (THE 12TH PSALM TUNE).

[147] Concerning the twenty-six-stop Trinity organ built by Johann Gottlieb Klemm of Philadelphia and installed in 1741, see Dean (n. 107 above), pp. 103–104, 108–113. Advertised for sale in 1763, this organ was one of the largest in the colonies. It included at least two mixtures (cornet and "sesqui alto") but followed English tradition in lacking pedal stops.

As late as Elias Mann's *Massachusetts Collection of Sacred Harmony* (1807), Lyon's "Friendship" continued in sufficient demand for Mann to include it (pp. 170–174). In the preface Mann lambasted fuging tunes and excoriated the erratic bounciness of the Billings school. Andrew Law (1749–1821), another frequent opponent of the fuging company, did not disdain to include Lyon's Psalm 19 in *The Rudiments of Music*. Some of the qualities that gave Lyon so enduring a cachet can be easily listed: (1) he never constructs an imitative point involving text-conflict; (2) for textural relief, he prefers antiphony; (3) his vocal writing includes brilliant shakes and runs, but always in musical illustration of scriptural words such as "fly," "rode," "trumpets," "harps," "organs." Like most early Americans, his part-writing will strike a Victorian as execrable. However, as a mitigating attraction, the individual parts can be quite grateful. This is particularly true of such an anthem as "Two Celebrated Verses by Sternhold and Hopkins" published at pages 126–132 of *Urania* and reprinted at Philadelphia so late as 1808 in Nathan Chapin and Joseph L. Dickerson's *The Musical Instructor* (pp. 78–81), but with the title "Anthem. From Psalm 18," and now in shape notes.

In 1774 Philip Fithian met Lyon in Cohansie, New Jersey. On April 22 "that great master of music, Mr. Lyon . . . sung at my request, & sing with his usual softness & accuracy." On April 23 Fithian spent the morning copying "some of Mr Lyons Tunes" and the afternoon and evening visiting with him:

He sings with great accuracy   I sung with him many of his Tunes [*he is about publishing a new Book of Tunes which are to be chiefly of his own Composition*] & had much Conversation on music, he is vastly fond of music & musical genius's   We spent the Evening with great Sattisfaction to me.[148]

Both were, of course, Princeton men. In histories of early American music so much more attention has heretofore been accorded Harvard graduates than Princeton ("Nassau-Hall") that their role is easily forgotten. But no less than a quarter of the first edition of *Urania* went to faculty, alumni, and students of the New Jersey college. President Samuel Davies signed for four copies. The spread of the copies is told in the list of subscribers' names. Sonneck, inventorying only

---

[148] *Journal & Letters of Philip Vickers Fithian, 1773–1774*, ed. Hunter D. Farish (Williamsburg: Colonial Williamsburg, 1943), p. 135. Cf. Sonneck, *Francis Hopkinson*, p. 186. The American Revolution dampened numerous publication projects, and Lyon's original tunes of 1774 were apparently a war casualty.

those that survive in the northeastern states (p. 137), makes no mention of the copy that went to Antigua in the Leeward Islands. Jack W. Broucek's 1963 dissertation, "Eighteenth Century Music in Savannah, Georgia" (pp. 213–214), locates another copy unknown to Sonneck, now among the Telfair Family Papers, Georgia Historical Society.

In the bicentennial year of *Urania,* Princeton University (founded 1746), the Westminster Choir College (moved from Ithaca in 1932), and the Princeton Theological Seminary combined to make the town a musical cynosure. But in 1961 even native Princetonians did not always remember that their tradition of countrywide musical leadership is at least two centuries old—and therefore one of the nation's proudest.

ᘒᘒ 6 ᘒᘒ

THE SOUTH BEFORE 1800

VIRGINIA, the oldest colony, remained a wholly agricultural economy throughout the 169 years from the founding of Jamestown (1607, burned 1676 during Bacon's Rebellion, Statehouse destroyed 1698) to the Declaration of Independence. Jefferson in his "Notes on Virginia," written 1782–1783, recorded that even Williamsburg (capital, 1700–1780) had never exceeded 1800 inhabitants and that Norfolk, the largest place, never rose above 6000.[149] Nevertheless, Virginia gentlemen visited London and discussed the relative merits of Cuzzoni, Faustina, and Senesino in *The Virginia Gazette* (November 6, 1736), and congratulated Handel on making £1500 from a single night's oratorio performance (July 28, 1738).[150] That slaves as well as masters played the violin appears from such notices as: "a likely young Negroe Man . . . plays very well on the Violin" (December 5, 1745), and "a Negro Man, named Harry . . . plays upon the Fiddle" (March 27, 1746). Important collections of secular music reached Virginia, including works by Handel, Hasse, Purcell, Rameau, and their less celebrated English contemporaries (in 1755 [151]), and by such composers as Stamitz, Richter, Gasparini and Vivaldi ["cuckoo concertos"] (1766–1776).

As early as 1710 William Byrd II recorded the birth of the singing-school movement in Virginia. On the afternoon of December 15, 1710, he "went with the two colonels to hear the people sing Psalms and there the singing master gave me two books, one for me and one for my wife." Next afternoon he had a quarrel with his wife "about learning to sing Psalms, in which she was wholly in the wrong,

[149] *The Writings of Thomas Jefferson* (Washington: Thomas Jefferson Memorial Association, 1903), II, 147–148.

[150] Albert L. Stoutamire, "A History of Music in Richmond, Virginia, from 1742 to 1865," Ed. D. dissertation, Florida State University, 1960, p. 9.

[151] John W. Molnar, "A Collection of Music in Colonial Virginia: The Ogle Inventory," in *The Musical Quarterly*, XLIX/2 (April, 1963), 158–161.

even in the opinion of Mrs. Dunn who was witness of it." The day
before Christmas he went to church, where "we began to give in to the
new way of singing Psalms." On January 25, 1711, "my two boys,
Bannister and G-r-l, began to learn to sing Psalms," presumably
according to the new book-method imparted by the singing master.[152]

Philip Pelham became organist of Bruton Parish Church in November, 1755, and in 1774 the singing of four-part hymns and anthems
in a country house was an accepted diversion—such are the next
landmarks in the history of sacred music in Virginia.[153] Philip Fithian
vouches for the latter in his diary entry for Monday, June 27, 1774:

Evening at Coffee the Colonel [Councillor Robert Carter of Nomini Hall
(downstream from Mount Vernon in Westmoreland County)] shew'd me
a book of vocal Musick which he had just imported; it is a collection of
psalm-Tunes, Hymns & Anthems set in four parts for the Voice; He seems
much taken with it & says we must learn & perform some of them in their
several parts with our voices & with instruments.

But it was South Carolina with populous Charleston—the largest
city south of Philadelphia in 1775—that took the lead in importing
organs and organists, in installing expensive rings of bells, in attract-
ing printers such as Lewis Timothy who published John Wesley's first
hymnbook in 1737, and in developing before the close of the century a "school" of church composers.[154] The original church edifices
of St. Philip's and St. Michael's (the senior Anglican parishes) date
from 1682–1690 and 1751–1763,[155] and it was in these two that the
early church musical life of South Carolina found richest expression.

The organist at St. Philip's from 1737 to 1750 was Charles Theodore Pachelbell (1690–1750), son of the famous predecessor of

---

[152] *The Secret Diary of William Byrd of Westover 1709–1712*, ed. Louis B. Wright
and Marion Tinling (Richmond: Dietz Press, 1941), pp. 272, 276, 292.

[153] Molnar, p. 156 (Peter Pelham), and n. 90, above. The secular bias makes allu-
sions to secular music in the colony easier to find than references to sacred. Norman
Arthur Benson, "The Itinerant Dancing and Music Masters of Eighteenth Century
America," University of Minnesota Ph.D. dissertation, 1963 (*Dissertation Abstracts*,
XXV/4 [October, 1964], p. 2551), places Pelham among the seven principal masters
to whom the 1740–1780 epoch owed its polish—the other six being Stagg, Dering,
Victor, Christian, Stadler, and Hartley.

[154] George W. Williams, "Charleston Church Music 1562–1833," in *Journal of
the American Musicological Society*, VII/1 (Spring, 1954), p. 38, col. 2. Williams
begins with the Huguenots, who sang *Les Pseaumes de David* from a copy preserved
in the exceedingly rich Manigault family (facsimile of title page in *Transactions of
the Huguenot Society of South Carolina*, No. 4 [Charleston: Walker, Evans & Cogs-
well, 1897], opposite p. 57). In *Transactions*, No. 7 [1900], p. 49, Daniel Ravenel
specified what the Huguenots sang in colonial Charleston.

[155] Williams, *St. Michael's, Charleston, 1751–1951* (Columbia: University of South
Carolina Press, 1951), pp. 4, 15.

J. S. Bach, Johann Pachelbel.[156] Born at Nuremberg, Charles Theodore composed a *Magnificat â 8 Voci con Continuo ex C* [157] before
leaving Europe for Boston at about the age of forty. From 1733 to
1735 he served as the organist of Trinity Church, Newport, Rhode
Island, where he played the new English instrument donated by the
metaphysician George Berkeley. After exhibiting himself as a harpsi-
chordist in two New York City concerts (January 21 and March 9,
1736), he relinquished the North in favor of Charleston. In 1737—
the year that Wesley gave his first hymnbook to the press at Charleston—Pachelbell at last felt securely enough placed to marry, and
also gave his first public concert in South Carolina.[158] Twelve years
later he began to suffer from "lameness in his hands" and thought for
a time of abandoning the organ bench in favor of a singing master's
livelihood. However, death intervened in September, 1750. His will
itemizes "Sundry books of Musick, paper and Crow Quills, 1 small
spinnet, and 1 Clairchard" (= clavichord) valued at £21 in a total
estate of £579.14.9.

This sum was slightly in excess of the £528 St. Michael's paid in
1768 for the two-manual Johann Snetzler organ that by virtue of
its size took second place in America to only the Trinity Church,
New York, organ by the same maker (imported in 1764 and destroyed by fire in 1776 [159]). As if to compensate for having the sec-
ond-best organ, the ring of bells "of remarkable sonority . . . cast at
the famous foundry of Rudhall, Gloucester, England" that was installed at St. Michael's before 1750 (and not destroyed until 1865),
took second place to none in America. Only the eight bells landed at
Boston in 1745 costing Christ Church £560 (with a tenor weighing
1400 pounds) could in any way compete.[160]

From 1782 to 1803 St. Michael's had for its rector Dr. Henry Purcell (1742–1802), himself an amateur composer who encouraged

---

[156] Virginia Larkin Redway, "Charles Theodore Pachelbell, Musical Emigrant,"
in *Journal of the American Musicological Society*, V/1 (Spring, 1952), 33. All subsequent biographical details are extracted from this definitive article.

[157] Edited by Hans T. David (New York [Public Library Series]: C. F. Peters,
1959). For comment, see *Die Musik in Geschichte und Gegenwart*, X (1962), 552.

[158] Announced in *The South Carolina Gazette* of November 5, 1737, for St.
Cecilia's Day (November 22), this was a "Vocal and Instrumental Concert" with a
Cantata "suitable to the Occasion." See Redway, p. 34.

[159] Williams, *St. Michael's, Charleston*, p. 204: "This Snetzler organ was an instrument second to none in quality on this continent, matched only by its peer at Trinity,
New York." See also pp. 218–233, and corresponding notes, pp. 354–356.

[160] Arthur H. Nichols, "Christ Church Bells, Boston, Mass.," in *New-England
Historical and Genealogical Register*, LVIII/1 (Jan., 1904), 63, 66. Nichols, pre-
eminent authority on early American church bells, lists those cast by Paul Revere
of "midnight ride" fame (LVIII, 155–157).

the congregation to sing original hymn and psalm tunes by the St.
Michael's organist, Peter Valton (*ca.* 1740–1784),[161] and Jervis
Henry Stevens (1750–1828);[162] these rank among the earliest sacred
compositions produced in the South and are invariably "genteel"
music. As an example of the Rev. Dr. Purcell's own muse, his setting
of Psalm 89 [163] is extracted from the Eckhard MS, which it enters at

Example 10   *Hereford*

Jacob Eckhard Choirmaster's   Henry Purcell (1742–1802)
Book (Library of Congress
MX33), no. 25

161 "Jacob Eckhard Choirmaster's Book," manuscript presented to St. Michael's in
1946 [microfilm MX–33, Library of Congress], nos. 1 (ST. PETER'S), 2 (ST. PHILIP'S),
3 (ST. JOHN'S NEW), 4 (ST. MICHAEL'S), 5 (ST. ANN'S NEW), 34 (ST. PAUL'S),
35 (ST. ANDREW'S), 36 (ST. JOHN'S OLD), 78 (ST. MARK'S). For facsimiles, see
George W. Williams, "Eighteenth-Century Organists of St. Michael's, Charleston,"
in *South Carolina Historical Magazine,* LIII/4 (Oct., 1952), 214–217. Biography,
pp. 212–216.

162 Eckhard MS, nos. 20 (HACKNEY), 24 (CHURCH STREET). Facsimiles, *South
Carolina Historical Magazine,* LIII/4, 217–218, with accompanying biography.

163 Authorized Version numbering. In the Eckhard MS, Purcell's "Ps. 23" has
nothing to do with the A. V. Ps. 23 (S. M. in Tate-Brady) but refers instead to the
L. M. psalm numbered 23 in the selection of psalms from Tate-Brady published at
Charleston by Robert Smith and Henry Purcell in 1792. Purcell's "Ps. 23" is the
PSALM X of the 1789 Prayerbook (Philadelphia: Hall and Sellers).

No. 25 with the title HEREFORD (Example 10). The figures for the harmony are his; he places these between the two outer parts in the manuscript. The L. M. text was printed at pp. 15–16 in *A Selection of Psalms with Occasional Hymns* (Charleston: W. P. Young, 1792)[164] after the rectors of St. Philip's and St. Michael's found that the Prayerbook adopted by the Protestant Episcopal Church in 1789 had expunged the musical supplement, reduced the hymns from 51 to 27, and rejected all the condensed psalms of the "Proposed" (never adopted) Prayerbook of 1786.[165]

Since South Carolina lacked a vigorous music publishers' industry of the sort fostered in New England by the singing school movement, composers active in Charleston before 1800 remained unknown outside aristocratic circles. Even their hymn tunes, which should have been their most popular product, failed to circulate. True, the one American-composed eighteenth-century hymn tune now universally known to all Protestants—CORONATION (1793)—is credited to a "South Carolina" composer in Samuel Eliot Morison's *The Oxford History of the American People* (New York: Oxford University Press, 1965, p. 292). However, the composer of this C. M. tune, sung always today with the text of Edward Perronet (1726–1792) beginning "All hail the power of Jesus' Name," was the Massachusetts-born carpenter, Oliver Holden (1765–1844), who after the Battle of Bunker Hill made Charlestown in the Bay State his home, not Charleston, South Carolina.

Elegant eighteenth-century Charleston boasted instead of a Peter Valton, who before arriving in October of 1764 had already won his spurs in London "as deputy organist to Dr. Boyce, Dr. Nares, and Mr. Keeble, at the King's Chapel, Westminster Abbey and St George's Hanover Square which shews (though so young a gentleman) his being long conversant in Church Musick." Four years later Valton could advertise his Opus 1 in the *South Carolina Gazette* as *Six Sonatas for Harpsichord or Organ, with Violin Obbligato*. Catches, glees, anthems, and odes made to the measure of the best British taste flowed from his pen. None of Valton's scented glove, swallow tail musical proprieties bothered the carpenter turned general-store keeper, when Holden sat down to harmonize his CORONATION. For that matter, not until after Lowell Mason had spent fifteen years in another Southern out-

---

[164] Facsimile reprint with introduction by Leonard Ellinwood, *The Charleston Hymnal of 1792* [*Publications of the Dalcho Historical Society of the Diocese of South Carolina*, No. 10] (Charleston: Diocesan House, 1956).

[165] Francis Hopkinson supplied the "Proper Tune for Ps. 96th . . . 7th Metre" with which the Musical Supplement of 1786 closes (p. 8).

post equally subservient to the latest European trends—Savannah, Georgia, 1815–1827—did a native musical leader arrive in Boston who could write a piece of music as enduring as CORONATION, but "correctly" harmonized. Margaret Freeman LaFar describes "Lowell Mason's Varied Activities in Savannah" in *The Georgia Historical Quarterly,* XXVIII/3 (September, 1944). However, this is to anticipate. First, we must study the generation of Billings and Holden. Only then will it be apparent why Andrew Law called so much of their music faulty, and why Mason returning from Savannah with such tunes as HAMBURG and MISSIONARY HYMN in his traveling bags could look on his task of sweeping away the last crudities of the old New England music as in itself a divine mission.

❧ 7 ❧

SINGING-SCHOOL MASTERS
IN THE NEW REPUBLIC

IN CONTRAST with Charleston, where such "correct" English composers as Boyce, Nares, and Kelway were considered the brightest lights of church music in the 1780's, New England during the same decade basked in rays shed by Britishers who moved outside the cathedral orbit. The favorites of the New Englanders included:

(1) Aaron Williams, whose *The Universal Psalmodist* (London: Joseph Johnson, 1764) was "calculated to promote and improve the most excellent Part of Social Worship, and thereby render it both useful and delightful in all Country Choirs," [166]

(2) Joseph Stephenson, the third edition of whose *Church Harmony Sacred to Devotion* had appeared as early as 1760 [167] with a fuging tune, "Thru all the changing scenes" [Ps. 34], that was to be reprinted frequently in New England, beginning with

---

[166] Lowens and Britton, "Daniel Bayley's 'The American Harmony': A Bibliographical Study," in *Papers of the Bibliographical Society of America*, XLIX/4 (1955), 343, list a 1763 edition as the first, 1765 as the third, and two more editions in 1770. They discuss the uses to which Bayley put Williams on pp. 341–342. On the title page of the fifth edition, Williams designated the work as suitable for "Country Choirs" in *"Great Britain, Ireland, and America."*

[167] Lowens, "The Origins of the American Fuging Tune," p. 50, shows the facsimile of Stephenson's "Thirty-Fourth" (first English publication of which he assigns to approximately 1755) as republished in Daniel Read's *Supplement to the American Singing Book*, New Haven, Connecticut, 1787. Stephenson's "34th" (*Church Harmony*, 4th ed., dated *ca.* 1775, pp. 44–45) and two other fuging psalm tunes "are extraordinarily close to the American idiom in formal structure and general character, and as two of the three [Stephenson fuging psalm tunes] were published in American tune books during the 1760's, it is quite likely that they served as actual prototypes for Billings's work and perhaps for that of other early American composers as well" (Lowens, p. 51). Edwin H. Pierce erred in making Billings "the originator of the Fugue-tune" ("The Rise and Fall of the 'Fugue-Tune' in America," in *The Musical Quarterly*, XVI/2 [April, 1930], 217). Alexander W. Thayer, Beethoven's biographer, published as early as 1879 his opinion that the fuging tune was "brought to Boston from England" and that "the oldest known . . . give the name of Stephenson as composer" (*Dwight's Journal of Music*, XXXIX/1007 [Nov. 22, 1879], 186, col. 3).

Daniel Bayley's *The American Harmony, or Universal Psal-modist* [Newbury-Port, 1769] [168]—thereby setting the fashion for a huge American output in the fuging-tune vein before 1810, and

(3) William Tans'ur, whose *The Royal Melody Compleat* had already by 1740 given him the reputation of being one of the "best Authors . . . of the present Age." [169]

It is especially easy to document Tans'ur's early influence on William Billings (1746–1800) [170]—whose début publication, *The New-England Psalm-Singer: or, American Chorister* (Boston: Edes and Gill, 1770), begins with an Introduction adapted from Tans'ur's "New Introduction to the Grounds of Musick" [171] and whose *Singing Master's Assistant* (Boston: Draper and Folsom, 1778) contains a glossary (pp. 23–27) copied from Tans'ur.[172] Even more crucially Tans'ur's influence can be detected in Billings's musical praxis. Tans'ur in *A New Musical Grammar* (London: Jacob Robinson, 1746, p. 119) decreed that "two *Fifths,* or two *Eighths* (and no more) may be taken together in *Three,* or more *Parts* (when it cannot be well avoided) rather than spoil the Air." Billings, whose "greatest asset was his unerring feeling for melody," [173] embraced Tans'ur's dictum with such wholehearted abandon that scarcely one of his

---

[168] Lowens and Britton, pp. 347–348, analyze the *editio princeps,* of which the Huntington Library owns a copy (bound with Tans'ur's *Royal Melody Complete* [Boston: W. M'Alpine, 1767]). In Bayley's 1771 *The American Harmony, or Universal Psalmodist* Stephenson's PSALM 34TH is at p. 48, but with such changes to meet the American taste as the intrusion of an escaped dissonance in the top voice (last beat, meas. 2), elimination of the trill on the first note, top voice, meas. 20, which has been changed from C to B in order to avoid a suspension (suspensions were never congenial to early American taste; cf. J. Murray Barbour, *The Church Music of William Billings* [East Lansing: Michigan State University Press, 1960], p. 66).

[169] John Arnold, *The Compleat Psalmodist* (London: A. Pearson, 1740), Bk. III, p. 188. Ralph T. Daniel's "English Models for the First American Anthems," in *Journal of the American Musicological Society,* XII/1 (Spring, 1959), 54–55, analyzes Tans'ur's influence upon the American anthem composers of the late eighteenth century. He does the same for Aaron Williams, pp. 56–57, and Joseph Stephenson, pp. 57–58. Tans'ur's *Jubilate Deo* subtitled "A Morning Service" and published at Newbury-Port in 1769 (pages 76–77 of Bayley's *The American Harmony*) takes pride of place as the first "service" music published in the colonies.

[170] Barbour, pp. 57 (Tans'ur's melismas), 113 ("forbidden" parallels), 119 (choosing notes), 129 ("Tans'ur's *Chesterton* also has the pattern of these Billings tunes"); Lowens and Britton, p. 341 ("Tans'ur was in actuality Billings' mentor in the art of composition"). The Italian terms which Barbour praises Billings for using correctly (p. xiii) duplicate those in Tans'ur, *The New Harmony of Sion,* Bk. 3 (London, 1766).

[171] Cf. *The New-England Psalm-Singer,* p. (13), chap. v and pp. (14–15) with Tans'ur's *Royal Melody Complete* (Boston: W. M'Alpine, 1767), pp. [4–5], p. [10].

[172] Britton, "Theoretical Introductions," p. 134.

[173] Barbour, p. 43.

257 psalm tunes or 47 anthems lacks parallel octaves and/or parallel fifths. Two typical passages (shown in Examples 11a and 11b) from *The Royal Melody Compleat . . . . The Third Edition* (London: R. Brown, 1764), pp. 240 (last four bars of "O praise the Lord of Heaven") and 246, third bar (on the word "peace"), show how freely

Example 11a   Example 11b

Tans'ur, when composing, availed himself of the license he had granted as a theorist [174]—a license that Billings and his New England confrères later turned into law.

Among other New England style traits, 1780–1805, one of the more noticeable is the lack of suspensions. This again is a hallmark of the Tans'ur repertory as well. The "country" composers in both England and New England seem to have missed the formal training in counterpoint needed by anyone who wishes to write "4th species" involving several parts. Even if they could have done so, the hearty bluff tread of their typical product left no room for enervating suspensions, colorful chromaticisms, subtle modulations, and the like. Charles II, who came to the throne in 1660, liked church music to which he could tap his foot; the rustic subjects of his kingdom a century later can scarcely be blamed for having had no better taste.

Examination of the native music makes it quite apparent that the basic elements of the peculiar idiom in which it is written are derived from British sacred choral music of the previous one or two generations. . . . Aside from its archaic aspect,[175] American music may be recognized by two general features. In the first place, it seems to be more closely allied with

[174] Israel Holdroyd, "A Complete Introduction to the Grounds of Music," p. 26 (*The Spiritual Man's Companion* [London: Robert Brown for J. Hinton, 1753]), wrote: "N.B. That two Fifths or two Eighths may be taken together in four Parts, rather than spoil the Air of the Tunes; but let it be between one of the upper Parts and the Bass, by reason of the Tenor's being between the *upper* Parts and the Bass, it will be easier tolerated." John Arnold, *The Compleat Psalmodist. In Four Books.* (London: A. Pearson, [1746]), Bk. 1, p. 24, said the same. Tans'ur merely echoed the general sentiment voiced by "country church" composers. Even Christopher Simpson, erudite forbear of the psalmodists, endorsed covered fifths and, occasionally, parallel fifths (*A Compendium: or Introduction to Practical Musick,* 4th ed. [London: W. Pearson, 1706], pp. 33, 100–101).

[175] Whatever the cultural transplant, whether the Spanish *romance* in New Mexico (investigated by Aurelio Espinosa) or the English folk song in North Carolina (collected by Cecil Sharp), American manifestations have had a habit of appearing conservative when compared with their European congeners.

folk music. For instance, there is a greater use of the natural minor scale, especially in gapped varieties, and much more irregularity of phrase. All American music has a strong rhythmic pulse, a characteristic only occasionally to be sensed in the earlier English music. In the second place, American music displays a far greater number of what to the musician's eye seem to be harmonic inepitudes.

These were Allen P. Britton's conclusions in "The Musical Idiom in Early American Tunebooks," a summary written after examining the "more than 130 tunebooks (collections of unaccompanied three- and four-part choral music for use in churches) . . . published in the United States by the close of the year 1800" (*Journal of the American Musicological Society,* III/3 [Fall, 1950], p. 286). Twenty-six of the 130 tunebooks studied by Britton contain contemporary music by American composers and sixteen "are devoted to the compositions of single composers."

William Billings, the earliest and most prolific of the singing masters to publish only original compositions, issued his first collection, *The New-England Psalm-Singer* (1770), when he was only twenty-four. However, he soon discovered that many of the pieces were "never worth my printing" and returned eight years later with a second publication, *The Singing Master's Assistant,* in the preface to which he wrote: "therefore in order to make you ample amends for my former intrusion, I have selected and corrected some of the Tunes which were most approved of in that book, and have added several new pieces which I think to be very good ones." LEBANON (Example 12) is a sample of a tune from 1770 "corrected" in 1778 (reprinted in the emended form the next year). The corrected form adjusts the prosody, doubles note-values but under a retorted signature moving the 1778 half-note at the gait of the 1770 quarter-note, and limns a bolder harmonic outline involving three cross-relationships (flat versus sharped leading-tone). Even in so short an exercise as a psalm tune, Billings thus shows the self-consciousness of an artist rather than a mere artisan.

Another psalm tune (but of diametrically opposed sentiment) "improved" in his 1778 *SMA* is the delightful Christmas carol to the folkish melody BOSTON (*NEPS,* p. 23, *SMA,* p. 2) shown in Example 13. AFRICA (14 = 4), AMERICA (1 = 5), AMHERST (48 = 7), BROOKFIELD (7 = 4), DORCHESTER (78 = 9), MARBLEHEAD (71 = 14), NEW HINGHAM (59 = 15), and PUMPILY (60 = 24) exemplify the same trend toward "self-improvement"—sometimes in the principal melody itself (always confided to the tenor), occasionally

Example 12   *Lebanon.* C.M.

The New-England Psalm-Singer: William Billings (1746–1800)
or, American Chorister (Boston:
Edes and Gill, 1770), p. 95

The Singing Master's Assistant,   [Billings]
or Key to Practical Music (Boston:
Draper and Folsom, 1778), p. 14
[*Music in Miniature* (Boston: The
Author, 1779), p. 9]

in the bass, but most often in the two upper voices, and in the third phrase.

His willingness to change time-signatures when revising his pieces (AMHERST, DORCHESTER, PUMPILY) should prepare us for his skill as a writer of variations. Barbour draws attention to the meter change in the middle of the delightful Christmas carol, SHILOH (Example 14). Upon shifting from $\frac{4}{4}$ to $\frac{6}{4}$ Billings contrives a "clever variant of the first melody" [tenor]. On a larger scale, he devised the anthem *Lamentation over Boston* ("By the rivers of Watertown") published in *The Singing Master's Assistant,* pp. 33–38, as a "chaconne." [176]

---

[176] Barbour, pp. 47 (SHILOH), 110, 134 (*Lamentation over Boston*).

Example 13   *Boston.* C.M.

The New-England Psalm-Singer,   [Billings]
p. 23

The Singing Master's Assistant, p. 2

Billings, whose favorite poets were Isaac Watts (1674–1748, revealed an Arian in his later writings) [177] and James Relly (*ca.* 1722–1778, Universalist [178]), set his own poetry at least three times—in

[177] Robert M. Stevenson, *Patterns of Protestant Church Music* (Durham: Duke University Press, 1953), pp. 107–110.
[178] Barbour, p. 1.

Example 14   *Shiloh*

The Suffolk Harmony (Boston: Billings
J. Norman, 1786), pp. 1–2

CHESTER, his patriotic hymn [179] given a fresh lease on life by William Schuman (in his *New England Triptych,* 1956 [Bryn Mawr: Merion Music, 1957], pp. 31–47), and in BOSTON and SHILOH.[180] Even better than in his verse, his literary penchant shows to advantage in his lively prefaces. His "Dialogue, between Master and Scholar," pp. xii–xxxiv of *The Continental Harmony* (Boston: Isaiah Thomas and

[179] For attribution of the CHESTER text to Billings, see Daniel Read, *The American Singing Book* (New Haven: The Author, 1785), p. 41, who sets it as a fuging tune. Billings's own setting: *NEPS,* p. 91, *SMA,* p. 12, *Music in Miniature,* p. 12. The militant forthrightness of Billings's tune did not prevent Samuel Holyoke (1762–1820), a Harvard graduate, from wedding it anew to a poem beginning "Jesus, my love, my chief delight For thee I long, For thee I pray," in *The Christian Harmonist* (Salem: Joshua Cushing, 1804), p. 16 [No. 12]. Holyoke designed this collection "for the Use of the Baptist Churches in the United States." Some years earlier (1791), Holyoke gave "a nasty dig at Billings's fugue-tunes" (Pierce, "The Rise and Fall of the 'Fugue-Tune' in America," p. 223).

[180] For testimony to Billings's authorship of the SHILOH text, see *The Suffolk Harmony, consisting of Psalm Tunes, Fuges, and Anthems* (Boston: J. Norman, 1786), p. 1.

Ebenezer T. Andrews, 1794), contains the famous encomium of fuges that has been quoted to prove him fonder of the fuging tune than of any other variety of music.[181] Although recent research denies Billings the honor of having published more fuging tunes than did such less famous men as Samuel Holyoke, Daniel Read, Stephen Jenks, and Jacob French, at least he still retains his laurels as the first American to publish specimens of the genre.[182]

The vicissitudes of the fuging tune can best be understood by showing in their original form and in their later transformations two tunes by composers whose fuges far outdistanced any of Billings's in the public favor—Edson [183] and Read. LENOX (1782), the *succès fou* of Lewis Edson (1748–1820), appears in Example 15, first in its primitive state,[184] then in the fumigated form published by the famous composer of TOPLADY ("Rock of Ages"), Thomas Hastings (1784–1872).[185] Not shown, but easily accessible, is the still staider version considered appropriate for *The Army and Navy Hymnal* (New York:

[181] Ananias Davisson, *Kentucky Harmony,* 2nd ed. (Harrisonburg, Va.: The Author, 1817), p. 14; also 4th ed. (1821), p. 14. Pierce, p. 221, quotes *The Continental Harmony,* p. xxviii (facsimile reprint, ed. by Hans Nathan [Cambridge: Belknap Press, 1961]). Pierce, p. 222, also transcribes GILEAD, Billings's fuging tune at p. 82 of *The Continental Harmony* with "words by Dr. Watts," but mixes up the text in the soprano at mm. 10–11 and 12–13.

[182] Lowens, "The Origins of the American Fuging Tune," p. 44; *Music and Musicians,* p. 238 ("the first American-composed specimen appeared in print in William Billings's *New-England Psalm-Singer* [1770]"). Lowens, who has studied the "more than 1000 fuging tunes which appeared between 1761 and 1810," certifies five other fuging-tune composers as having been more popular with compilers: Daniel Read, Oliver Holden, Joseph Stone, Lewis Edson, and Elisha West (p. 51; p. 248 [n. 10]). Billings "may not have been the strong force in 18th-century American Music that he had formerly been thought to be," concludes Marvin C. Genuchi in "The Life and Music of Jacob French (1754–1817), Colonial American Composer," Iowa State University Ph.D. dissertation, 1964 (*Dissertation Abstracts,* XXV/2 [Aug., 1964], 1248).

[183] Barbour disparages "the tomtom beat of Edson's *Lenox*" (p. 99) without denying that LENOX mesmerized many of Billings's younger contemporaries. Read's SHERBURNE (*The American Singing Book,* 1785, p. 53) and Jeremiah Ingalls's NORTHFIELD (1800), two hardly less successful fuging tunes, pulse with the same healthy vigor.

[184] Lowens, "Origins," p. 50, prints a facsimile of the Daniel Read version (1787), which duplicates Andrew Law's *Rudiments* version (1783), except for the "choosing" notes in the penultimate chord. Apart from the alto E at [1], bass A at [2], and bass E at [3], Ananias Davisson repeats the Law-Read verson [F♯ in alto, measure 2, corrected to natural] in the extremely popular *Kentucky Harmony.* See 2nd and 4th eds., p. 17. John Wyeth's *Repository of Sacred Music,* printed at Harrisburg, Pa., as late as 1834 duplicates at p. 47 the 1787 version, omitting only the F♯ and changing the bass at [2] to F.

[185] *Church Melodies,* "the first hymnal in this country to have words and the appropriate tune printed on the same page" (Mary B. Scanlon, "Thomas Hastings," in *The Musical Quarterly,* XXXII/2 [April, 1946], 274), disdains all other fuging tunes. Pierce, pp. 225–226, transcribed the Hastings arrangement. *The Hymnal* (Philadelphia: Presbyterian Board of Publication, 1900), no. 395, still preserved the fuging entries.

Example 15   *Lenox*

Andrew Law, *The Rudiments of*   Lewis Edson (1748–1820)
Music (Cheshire [Conn.]: William
Law, 1783), p. 16, and
*Supplement to The American Singing
Book* (New Haven: Daniel Read,
1787), p. 1

Thomas Hastings, *Church Melodies*
(New York: A. D. F. Randolph,
1858), p. 230 (no. 703)

The Century Co., 1920, p. 73 [no. 82]) and *The Methodist Hymnal* (1935, no. 211).[186]

Read's RUSSIA, because in minor, has proved less attractive to denominational hymnbook editors. Isaac B. Woodbury (1819–1858), who made a "purified" arrangement of RUSSIA for *The Dulcimer* (1850), started life a blacksmith—just as Billings began a tanner, Daniel Read (1757–1836) a comb maker,[187] and Oliver Holden (1765–1844) a carpenter.[188] But Woodbury visited Europe, and, like Lowell Mason (1792–1872), William B. Bradbury (1816–1868), and George F. Root (1820–1895), came back a "scientific" musician. He therefore footnotes his arrangement of RUSSIA (shown with Read's original in Example 16) thus:

We insert a few of these Continental tunes at the earnest request of many old and venerated people, who in their younger years were wont to perform them in the house of God with perhaps *as much devotion and religious effect* as more modern choirs now sing the music of the day. The Melodies and Bases have always been retained, when consistent with the rules of counterpoint, and in order to do this several licenses have been taken in the arrangements.

Woodbury implies that in the northeast fuging tunes had already passed their popularity peak before 1800. The date for the passing of their vogue comes later elsewhere. For their decline and fall, Andrew Law, Elias Mann, and (after 1820) Lowell Mason and his tribe can take considerable credit. But another important factor not to be forgotten was the role of the Methodist Episcopal Church.

[186] Except for some slight rhythmic adjustments, the Methodist version copies W. Howard Doane's (*The Baptist Hymnal* [Philadelphia: American Baptist Publication Society, 1883], p. 124). Doane (1832–1915), one of the most successful gospel hymn composers, eschewed the fuging—thus still further denaturing the original. He, Mason, and Isaac B. Woodbury are the only native-born Americans whose hymn-tunes crossed the water to gain sanctuary in any edition of *Hymns Ancient & Modern*. See Maurice Frost, *Historical Companion to Hymns Ancient & Modern* (London: William Clowes & Sons, Ltd., 1962), pp. 603 (RESCUE) and 669 (Doane).

[187] Lowens, "Daniel Read's World: The Letters of an Early American Composer," in *Notes of the Music Library Association,* sec. ser. IX/2 (March, 1952), 234. This essay, pp. 233–248, should be read for the light it throws on Read's later "silent" years. Like many other active composers of his era, he lived into the new "scientific" epoch of Lowell Mason and Thomas Hastings. In old age Read repudiated "the native American idiom he had been instrumental in developing" (p. 243). Lowens emphasizes the often overlooked fact that Read and others of his ilk did not design their publications for church use (p. 245).

[188] David W. McCormick's "Oliver Holden, Composer and Anthologist," D. S. M. dissertation, Union Theological Seminary, 1963, provides exhaustive coverage of the composer of CORONATION ("All hail the power of Jesus' Name"). Like Read and others, Holden far outlived his vogue.

Example 16   *Russia*

Supplement to The American Singing   Daniel Read (1757–1836)
Book, p. 13

The Dulcimer: or The New York
Collection of Sacred Music, ed. by
I. B. Woodbury (New York:
F. J. Huntington, 1850), p. 25

From the minutes of the Baltimore Christmas Conference of 1784 through the 1852 edition, *The Doctrines and Discipline of the Methodist Episcopal Church* invariably contained a section against congregational singing of "fuge-tunes." Typical was the entry in Chapter 1, Section 24, "Of the Spirit and Truth of Singing," published at page

42 of *The Eighth Edition* (Philadelphia: Perry Hall, 1792). The fifteen rules read in part:

9. Recommend our tune-book.
11. Sing no hymns of your own composing.
13. When the singers would teach a tune to the congregation, they must sing only the tenor [later editions add here in brackets, "the air"].
15. Let it be recommended to our people, not to attend the singing-schools which are not under our direction.
N. B. We do not think that fuge-tunes are sinful, or improper to be used in private companies: but do not approve of their being used in our public congregations.

So revered were the precepts of Bishops Thomas Coke and Francis Asbury, under whose eyes these singing rules were devised, that when *The Doctrines and Discipline of the African Methodist Episcopal Church* were first drawn up and printed at Philadelphia (Richard Allen and Jacob Tapsico, 1817), precisely the same singing rules were repeated in Chapter 1, Section 16—including the disapproval of "fuge-tunes" for congregational singing.

But if fuge-tunes proved such a "stone of stumbling, and a rock of offence" to some churches and to many musicians in the young republic, what of the other genres popular in New England before 1800?

If length measures importance, the pre-1800 New England singing masters poured their best selves not into the fuging tune but into the anthem—and their anthems are indeed the only Revolutionary genre thus far considered a sufficiently significant topic for a Harvard doctoral dissertation (Ralph T. Daniel's "The Anthem in New England before 1800" [1955]). Such terms as *ode, dirge, poem,* and *chorus,* though also used in New England for through-composed choral pieces lasting some five minutes or so, usually denoted occasional music commemorating a specific event. On the other hand, the *anthem,* composed for mixed choir *a 4* rather than for congregational singing, and set to unversified Scripture, could be used as the commencement piece for any singing school. As a matter of record, "graduating" exercises from such schools and not church services did almost invariably offer the first opportunity to display a new anthem in any given community.

In New England from 1764 to 1800 so great did the demand for this class of music grow to be that Daniel found some three hundred instances of anthem publication in his period. To summarize his comments on the native American product:

Billings, the foremost composer, published forty-seven anthems. These vary from two to twelve minutes in performance time, with the average running five minutes. His earlier anthems tend to be the more diffuse, the more markedly sectional, the more slow-paced. Even the later ones are always multisectional, however. As in a Josquin motet, the sections reflect breaks in the text. *A cappella* works *a 4,* they call for instruments only twice—in PEACE ("God is the king"), a twelve-minute work dated August, 1783, and in "O Thou to whom all creatures bow" (*The Continental Harmony* [1794]). Only one of his forty-seven anthems hews throughout to the same time signature and tempo, frequent changes to fit the shifting sentiments of the text being his usual practice. Just as his sense of formal balance improved in his later anthems, so also his handling of speech rhythms, his part-writing skills, and his feeling for complete chords. Chary of ornaments, he endorsed the "grace of transition" (discretionary short passing-note between long melody notes a third apart) in his 1770 *NEPS,* but even then frowned on promiscuously added trills. His later anthems exhibit fewer dynamic markings than his earlier, and lean ever more heavily on textural contrasts for variety. Octave-doublings of upper parts ravish his senses with their sweetness in his later anthems, rather than graces and dynamics. "O God Thou hast been displeased" (*CH,* 1794) roams through keys so far apart as those with four flats and with none; but as a rule he forbears modulating. Indeed, Daniel finds true modulations in but two of his anthems. So much a child of the late eighteenth century as to eschew all modes except major and minor, Billings sets an American pace when he insists on solid accents even in slow pieces, when he prefers fast harmonic rhythm no matter what the time unit, and when in company with others of his era he closes always with an authentic cadence rather than the more churchly Amen of a plagal cadence. Among the "endearing young charms" of his anthems is the frequent "tunefulness" of the tenors. At times, his folkish tunefulness inspires him to write whole sections in four-bar phrases.

With 47 anthems, Billings alone accounts for more than a third of the 117 anthems by native Americans published in New England before 1800. This ratio is the more interesting because Daniel finds 21 native composers. Amos Bull, born in 1744, published 12 original anthems at Worcester in *The Repository,* 1795. Nine of these set Prayerbook rather than King James versions of the psalms, thus suggesting that Bull wrote for Episcopal choirs. Even so, he requires only two trebles, tenor, and bass—leaving out the usual filler voice between the leading tenor and the sopranos.

Oliver Holden, composer of twelve anthems in nine eighteenth-century publications, deliberately omits the fuging passages so much beloved of Billings. His reason, given in *The Union Harmony,* 1793, echoes an objection at least as old as the Council of Trent: the difficulty of understanding the words in imitative points. As an example of Holden's non-fuging style, Daniel transcribes "The Lord is good to all" (A CONCLUDING ANTHEM FOR THANKSGIVING DAY, *The American Harmony,* 1792, pp. 30–32). A recurrent refrain lends this anthem an over-all unity not often found in the Holden repertory. In further contrast with Billings, Holden limited half of his anthems to only three voices: treble, tenor, bass (counter omitted).

Jacob French (1754–1817), a composer whose dates have been established by Genuchi, trails after Holden with some nine or ten anthems published in the period. If accidentals in *New American Melody,* 1789, are accepted at face value, French painted with a more varied harmonic palette than did either Billings or Holden, even permitting himself such chords as the Italian augmented-6th ("O sing unto the Lord," meas. 5). Lowens finds French "one of the most musically sensitive of the early New England tunesmiths" and gives his THE HEAVENLY VISION; AN ANTHEM pride of place in a pioneer recorded anthology of pre-1800 native music (*The American Harmony,* released in May, 1961, by Washington Records [418]). Originally published in Isaiah Thomas's *Laus Deo, or the Worcester Collection of Sacred Harmony,* 1786, this anthem typifies its epoch so far as its centonized text is concerned. Six verses from Revelation make up the text, but in the following order: 7:9, 4:8b, 8:13, 6:15–17. Even so, the Scriptural verses are not quoted with scrupulous exactness. Further discussing it, Lowens remarks: "An anthem of this sort was frequently used as the climax of the singing-school 'concert' in which pupils demonstrated to all who would hear the mastery they had achieved after a few weeks of study."

Daniel Read, six of whose anthems were published seventeen times before 1800, specified an optional instrumental accompaniment for his "O be joyful in the Lord" (*Columbian Harmonist, No. 3,* 1795). This anthem is one of three in Daniel's chosen epoch to close with a plagal instead of authentic cadence; it also violates the norm of its epoch by resorting to so un-American a device as a suspension. Like Handel, two of whose *Messiah* choruses enter the same collection ("Glory to God" with a new introduction apparently by Read himself), our Connecticut Yankee precedes the last two bars of his "O be joyful" anthem with a rest in all parts. Read, who named one of his own sons after the Halle master, later capitulated entirely to the vogue of "better" European music. His 1795 anthems show him already on the road leading from his rough-hewn fuging-tune RUSSIA to the polished niceties of such a "Beethoven" hymn-tune as GERMANY.

At the bottom of the list, so far as number of published anthems is concerned, comes the celebrated breeder of a horse that bears his name, Justin Morgan (1747–1798). "Known to have composed less than a dozen tunes" of any type, Morgan endowed one of these—AMANDA—with sufficient distinction for Lowens to call it a "stark and bitter" expression "undoubtedly inspired by the death of his wife after the birth of a child in 1791." "Hark, you mortals, hear the trumpet," Morgan's one anthem published before 1800, effectively exploits opposing vocal registers. Even more singular than the textural contrasts is the harmonic scheme. Thrice he shifts without warning from E minor to Eb major. No cushioning modulation separates these alien keys. For Beethoven to have plunged from C minor into E major at the beginning of the second movement in his Opus 37 was a stroke of genius, but for ears habituated to conventional harmonic usage, Morgan's unprepared shifts border on crudeness. Nonetheless, reprintings of this *Dies irae* anthem (published in Asahel Benham's *Federal Harmony,* 1795) guarantee its acceptability to numerous generations of singing-school graduates. For example, a decade after Morgan's death the vogue of his "Hark, you mortals" had spread so far afield that Nathan Chapin and Joseph L. Dickerson could make it the culminating piece in their hundred-page anthology, *The Musical Instructor* (Philadelphia: W. M'Culloch, 1808). Moreover, they went to the trouble of transcribing it into the seven-shape notation that they had devised along lines suggested by the Little and Smith four-shape system invented *ca.* 1798. Once in character notes, it enjoyed an assured future as a frontier favorite.

∽ 8 ∾

THE HALF-CENTURY PRECEDING
THE CIVIL WAR

DISDAINED even in its own time by such college-bred composers as Andrew Law (1749–1821, honorary M.A., Yale, 1786)[189] and Samuel Holyoke (1762–1820, A.B., Harvard, 1789),[190] the fuging tune with its dispersed harmony lost ground steadily in New England after Billings's death. European professors of "scientific" music such as the Danish Hans Gram (1754–1804)[191] and the English Dr.

---

[189] Richard Crawford and H. Wiley Hitchcock, *The Papers of Andrew Law* (Ann Arbor: [University Library], 1961), p. 9. Law was one of the earliest compilers of American sacred music to become embroiled in lengthy complaints against pirates. Isaiah Thomas was the most famous printer whom he accused of "pillaging my books." See Lowens, "Andrew Law and the Pirates," in *Journal of the American Musicological Society*, XIII/1–3 (1960), 214; also "Copyright and Andrew Law," in *Papers of the Bibliographical Society of America*, LIII/2 (1959), 150–159.

In 1965 Crawford completed a brilliant 460-page University of Michigan Ph.D. dissertation surveying Law's entire output, "Andrew Law (1749–1821): The Career of An American Musician." A precursor of the genteel tradition, Law has now been more thoroughly dissected, both professionally and personally, than any musician active before 1800 (pp. 383–384, viii). Still useful, especially for such conveniences as the tune incipits in Law's publications, is the 1950 Union Theological Seminary thesis, "Andrew Law: Intellectual Musician," by Charles Leroy Hickman.

[190] Holyoke, *Harmonia Americana* (Boston: Isaiah Thomas and Ebenezer T. Andrews, 1791), Preface [p. 4]: "fuging pieces are in general omitted. But the principal reason why few were inserted was the trifling effect produced by that sort of music; for the parts, falling in, one after another, each conveying a different idea, confound the sense, and render the performance a mere jargon of words." This disclaimer did not prevent his yielding to popular sentiment when publishing *The Christian Harmonist* (see n. 179 above). For Holyoke's career, see J. Lawrence Willhide, "Samuel Holyoke, American Music-Educator," University of Southern California Ph.D. dissertation, 1954. Nor did a Harvard degree deter another compiler—Jacob Kimball—from including numerous fuging tunes in *The Rural Harmony* (Boston: Thomas and Andrews, 1793). Kimball's INVITATION and WOBURN (John Wyeth's *Repository, Part Second*) enjoyed the cachet of Southern approval. See Glenn Wilcox, "Jacob Kimball, Jr. (1761–1826): His Life and Works," University of Southern California Ph.D. dissertation, 1957.

[191] McCormick, "Oliver Holden," reveals much new biographical data on Gram (pp. 75–82; supporting documents, pp. 170–171). Born into an affluent family at Copenhagen, March 20, 1754, he became secretary in 1781 to the governor of St. Croix, Danish West Indies, moving four years later to Boston where he at once

George K. Jackson (1745–1823)[192] so deprecated the native school that by the time Elias Mann's *The Massachusetts Collection of Sacred Harmony* (Boston: Manning and Loring, 1807) appeared with the famous preface warning against "those wild fugues, and rapid and confused movements, which have so long been the disgrace of congregational psalmody"—LENOX, SHERBURNE, RUSSIA, and NORTHFIELD were no longer welcome on the soil that gave them birth. In their place, sedate pieces by Dr. Samuel Arnold (1740–1802), William Selby (1738–1798, organist at King's Chapel, Boston, from 1777), and other "correct" composers now enjoyed seats of honor. James Hewitt (1770–1827), organist at Trinity Church, Boston, 1812–1816,[193] included nothing by Billings, Holden, French, Ingalls, Edson, Read, or any of their tribe in his *Harmonia Sacra* (Boston: Joseph T. Buckingham, 1812)—instead advertising the collection quite rightly on the title page as "selected and adapted from the works of Handel, Luther [OLD HUNDRED is mistakenly attributed to Luther at p. 113], Ravenscroft, J. Clark, Drs. Croft, Arnold, Howard, Boyce, &c. &c. with which are interspersed a number of new tunes composed expressly for this work" by himself.

K. P. E. Bach enters Hewitt's collection at page 62 with a tune dubbed EMANUEL. The English doctors include, in addition to those named on the title page, Greene, Hayes, Madan, Miller, and Wainwright. So far as the character of these borrowed tunes is concerned, Hewitt bows to the spirit of the times when he anthologizes only twelve tunes in minor keys compared with ninety-five major. What other compilers had been doing can be seen from the following statistics:

Elias Mann's *Massachusetts Collection* (1807): 110 major tunes, 52 minor.
Daniel Read's *American Singing Book* (4th ed.: 1793): 29 major, 18 minor.

---

married Jane Burdick. Around 1789 financial reverses drove him to music teaching and a short term as music editor for the Isaiah Thomas–Ebenezer Andrews combine. In 1791 Billings placed 200 unpublished pages in Gram's hands, and Andrews's letter of June 23, 1791 (American Antiquarian Society, Worcester) mentions Billings's "9 or ten tunes which Gram has played on his Harpsichord and thinks quite good" (McCormick, p. 78). The same year Gram became the first in America to publish in full score an original orchestral composition—*The Death Song of an Indian Chief.* He died in the Boston Public Alms House, April 28, 1804, leaving four children.

[192] H. Earle Johnson, *Musical Interludes in Boston, 1795–1830* (New York: Columbia University Press, 1943), pp. 201–220; also *The Musical Quarterly*, XXIX/1 (Jan., 1943), 113–121 (omits the bibliography of Dr. Jackson's compositions).

[193] John Tasker Howard, "The Hewitt Family in American Music," in *The Musical Quarterly*, XVII/1 (Jan., 1931), 28.

Read's *The Columbian Harmonist No. 1 Containing . . . A Choice Collection of New Psalm Tunes of American Composition* (New Haven: The Editor, 1793): 16 major, 16 minor.[194]

Anthem [195] collections published in New England about the time of the War of 1812 show the same curious "anti-American" trend. *A Volume of Sacred Musick containing Thirty Anthems selected from the works of Handel, Purcel* [196] [sic], *Croft and other eminent European authors* (Newburyport: E. Little & Co., 1814) ranges as widely as Elizabethan literature for William Byrd's "Bow thine ear" (pp. 28–33) [197] but includes nothing from the compiler's compatriots— unless William Selby, who emigrated to New England *ca.* 1771, qualifies as an American. John Hubbard (1759–1810), the Dartmouth College professor who selected the anthems, provided in this predominantly *a cappella* collection a set of anthems suitable for so "refined" a group as the Harvard University choir; [198] still, there must have been enough less cultivated buyers to make commercial publication profitable. Other New England collections shared in the same

[194] All the early New Englanders who mention the emotions aroused by major and minor agree on happiness and sadness. Billings claims that men find major and minor equally pleasing but that nine out of ten women prefer minor. The "happy-sad" dichotomizing of major and minor goes back to Zarlino, if not further (Robert W. Wienpahl, "Zarlino, the Senario, and Tonality," in *Journal of the American Musicological Society,* XII/1 [Spring, 1959], 28; Billings, *The Continental Harmony,* pp. xxiii–xxiv).

[195] For Billings's definition of an anthem, see *The Continental Harmony,* p. xxxii. Daniel, "English Models," p. 51, summarizes the characteristics of English anthems published in America before 1800. "The Anthem in New England before 1800," Daniel's definitive Ph.D. dissertation (Harvard, 1955), deserves especially high praise because of the author's success in tracing English precedents.

[196] Only one of the three anthems attributed to Purcell is authentic—"O give thanks" (pp. 64–72). No hint of an instrumental accompaniment is given, but four years later, in the *Old Colony Collection of Anthems* (Boston: James Loring, 1818), an instrumental ritornello does appear, p. 7. Cf. Franklin B. Zimmerman, *Henry Purcell 1659–1695: An Analytical Catalogue of His Music* (London: Macmillan & Co., 1963), pp. 31–32 [no. 33]. The other two anthems, extracted like "O give thanks" from Aaron Williams's *Royal Harmony or the Beauties of Church Music* (London: [1765]), must be classed as spurious or doubtful; see Zimmerman, pp. 432, *S16* = Hubbard, p. 26, and 405, *D2* = Hubbard, p. 51.

[197] Adapted from Byrd's *Ciuitas sancti tui (Liber primus sacrarum cantionum Quinque vocum,* 1589, p. xxi), "Bow thine ear" is the only unaccompanied anthem *a 5* in the Hubbard collection. Byrd's round for three voices, *Non nobis Domine* (Playford, *Musick and Mirth,* 1651), appears at p. 116 of the *Old Colony Collection,* Vol. II (1819). Lowell Mason, *The Boston Anthem Book* (Boston: J. H. Wilkins and R. B. Carter, 1839), p. 284, again reprinted this popular round.

[198] H. Earle Johnson, p. 20. For Hubbard's biography, see Frank J. Metcalf, *American Writers and Compilers of Sacred Music* (New York: Abingdon Press, 1925), pp. 109–110. Anthem XXVI, "Thy mercy, O Lord, is in the heav'ns" [Ps. 36], published at pp. 97–98 in Hubbard's *Thirty Anthems,* is identified in Nathaniel Gould's *Church Music in America* (Boston: A. N. Johnson, 1853), pp. 65–66, as having been composed by Hubbard himself. Gould knew Hubbard personally.

trend: for instance, the *Old Colony Collection,* Volume I (1818), included Mozart's *O Isis und Osiris* arranged as a four-voice anthem ("Almighty God, when round thy shrine"), and Volume II (1819) included the Kyrie and Gloria of the disputed Mass, K. Anh. 233 (Köchel-Einstein, *Chronologisch-thematisches Verzeichnis,* 3rd ed. [Ann Arbor: J. W. Edwards, 1947], pp. 875–876, 1047), adapted to English text. The *Old Colony Collection,* Volume II, included also two lengthy choruses from *Christus am Ölberge,* Beethoven's Opus 85 (composed in March 1803 and published in 1811 by Breitkopf und Härtel)—the more popular of the two choruses proving to be "Hallelujah to the Father" = *Welten singen Dank und Ehre,* final piece in the oratorio.[199]

With all these "better music" influences at work, Lowell Mason found a ready-made public waiting for such tunes as the six ascribed to Beethoven in his "epoch-making" *Boston Handel and Haydn Society Collection of Church Music* (Boston: Richardson and Lord, 1822).[200] Taking his cue from William Gardiner (1770–1853), the British stocking manufacturer whose *Sacred Melodies* (1812–1815) contained numerous adaptations of the Viennese classicists,[201] Mason included the following traceable Beethoven excerpts: VIENNA (28 = Andante Scherzoso of Violin Sonata, Op. 23), WESTON (48 = Adagio of Trio for clarinet, 'cello, and piano, Op. 11), GANGES (186 = violin Romance, Op. 40), and HAVRE (207 = Adagio of Piano Sonata, Op. 2, No. 1).[202] An even larger number of selections flow from the pen of the formidable czar of Boston "good taste," Dr. George K. Jackson, whose favorable recommendation induced the Handel and Haydn Society to publish this 320-page collection made by a mere bank clerk working in Savannah, Georgia. Between 1822 and 1858 twenty-two editions appeared—netting Mason a profit

[199] This chorus "was frequently performed in the years that followed and with marvellous rapidity it spread over the whole country, rivalling in popularity Handel's Hallelujah Chorus"; see Otto Kinkeldey, "Beginnings of Beethoven in America," in *The Musical Quarterly,* XIII/2 (April, 1927), p. 234.

[200] On the genesis of this collection, see Johnson, pp. 214–215, 235–237; and Arthur L. Rich, *Lowell Mason, "The Father of Singing among the Children"* (Chapel Hill: University of North Carolina Press, 1946), pp. 8–11.

[201] Kinkeldey, "Beginnings of Beethoven in America," pp. 218–219, 235. Carl Engel, "Beethoven's Opus 3—An 'Envoi de Vienne'?" in *The Musical Quarterly,* XIII/2 (April, 1927), 273, argues for 1794 as the year when Gardiner first heard Beethoven. Mason met Gardiner on May 26, 1837, and was "sorry to hear profane expressions from the composer of *Sacred Melodies*" (Daniel G. Mason, "Some Unpublished Journals of Dr. Lowell Mason," in *New Music Review and Church Music Review,* IX/108 [Nov., 1910], 580).

[202] Kinkeldey, p. 236. For more recent attempts to identify "Beethoven's" most famous hymn tune, GERMANY, see Leonard Ellinwood, *The Hymnal 1940 Companion* (New York: Church Pension Fund, 1951), p. 305.

from this one collection alone estimated at from \$10,000 to \$30,000. Dr. Jackson died, however, in 1823, and from the ten selections tactfully included in the first edition his representation slips in the next decade to nothing—while Mason from a mere three lines at page iv of the 1822 preface moves up to the title page as sole editor.

Mason learned the precepts of correct German harmony from F. C. Abel,[203] an immigrant whose settlement at Savannah was as fortunate for the young bank clerk as was Hermann Kotzschmar's later settling in Portland an advantage for the young John Knowles Paine (1839–1906). It was Abel who set Mason on the track he was to follow throughout his long teaching and composing career of always turning to German treatises and German musical practice for the only true and "scientific" [204] models. Mason's enormously successful *Manual of the Boston Academy of Music* (Boston: J. H. Wilkins & R. B. Carter, 1834 [8th ed., New York: Mason Bros., 1861])—which according to the preface boasted an "essentially different" approach to music instruction from any other known in America—claimed to derive from the "system of Pestalozzi"; but was in reality a mere annotated translation of G. F. Kübler's *Anleitung zum Gesang-Unterrichte in Schulen,* published at Stuttgart in 1826.[205]

---

[203] If A. W. Thayer was right in making F. C. Abel "a member of the well-known family of that name" (*Dwight's Journal of Music*, XXXIX/1007, 186 [see n. 167 above]), Abel may profitably be compared with C. T. Pachelbell. Rich, p. 8: "While studying with Abel, Mason compiled a book of psalm and hymn tunes using as a model William Gardiner's *Sacred Melodies.*" The manuscript is catalogued in Joel Sumner Smith, "Lowell Mason Library of Music, Yale University," 1918, p. 400, no. 2085 (Library of Congress, ML 136. N48 Y3). At p. vi of the 1822 edition Abel boasts that "the Base is correctly figured, and in no instance are the laws of counterpoint and Thorough Bass violated, as is the case in most American musical publications." ALSEN, Abel's hymn tune at p. 178, 1822 ed., shows some parallel fifths between outer voices that Mason seeks to correct with "choosing" notes at p. 220, 1832 ed.

[204] This catchword appears everywhere in the pro-Mason literature of the period, and even in the writings of the older generation trying to catch up. See Lowens, "Daniel Read's World," pp. 243–244. For typical uses of the term by Lowell Mason himself, see *Musical Letters from Abroad* (New York: Mason Brothers, 1854), pp. 41, 65, 96, 140. The highest praise that Thomas Hastings could bestow on Crotch, in his *Dissertation on Musical Taste* (Albany: Webster and Skinner, 1822), p. 186, was that he "is probably one of the most scientific musicians now living."

[205] Howard Ellis, "Lowell Mason and the *Manual of the Boston Academy of Music,*" in *Journal of Research in Music Education*, III/1 (Spring, 1955), 3–10. Ellis summarizes (p. 10): "Mason published the *Manual* under his own name as author. He described his sources of information in such a way as to conceal the fact that the *Manual* was in fact a translation of Kübler's *Anleitung,* reedited for American consumption." According to A. W. Thayer, who had every right to know, Mason could not read in the original any of the "works of Mattheson or Marpurg," the purchase of which turned the Lowell Mason collection of those German theorists into the world's "finest and completest" outside the Royal Library at Berlin (*Dwight's Journal*, XXXIX/1008, 196).

PLATES

FIGURE 1

FIGURE 1. Although the first edition of John Tufts's *An Introduction To the Singing of Psalm-Tunes, In a plain & easy Method* appeared at Boston in January of 1721, the earliest surviving copy is dated 1726, fifth edition. Nevertheless, Irving Lowens was able to deduce from contemporary newspaper advertising the format and contents of the lost first edition and to determine the changes made in the lost second through fourth editions; see pages vii–viii of a fifth edition facsimile issued in 1954 (Philadelphia: Albert Saifer for Musical Americana [Harry Dichter]).

The Library of Congress copy, from which pages 1–2 are here reproduced in facsimile, belongs to the tenth edition, 1738. Since so much of Protestant church music history has in America been tied to attempts at a simpler music notation, Tufts's book is a highly appropriate document with which to begin the study of that history. Tufts places the congregational tune in the Cantus. Of the six tunes here shown, WESTMINSTER was composed by Orlando Gibbons (first published, 1623), YORK is a Scottish tune (1615), HACKNY (=HACKNEY), OR S. MARY'S a Welsh tune (1621). S. DAVID'S first appeared in Ravenscroft's *Whole Booke* (1621), WINDSOR dates back to William Daman's *The former Booke* (1591), and CANTERBURY to Thomas Est's *Whole Booke* (1592).

Maurice Frost reprints the originals of these six tunes in *English & Scottish Psalm & Hymn Tunes c. 1543–1677* (London: Oxford University Press, 1953), at pp. 70, 275, 429, 256, 407, 161 (item 19 = CANTERBURY, 234 = S. DAVID'S, 362a = WESTMINSTER, 205 = YORK, 333 = HACKNY, OR S. MARY'S, 129 = WINDSOR).

FIGURE 2

FIGURE 2. In 1732, Conrad Beissel organized a community of German Seventh-Day Baptists at Ephrata, nineteen miles southwest of Reading, Pennsylvania. Although its members were pledged to celibacy, the enrollment rose to 300 before Beissel's death in 1768. For community use, hymnals were printed at both Philadelphia and Ephrata, but the amount of music composed by Beissel and his adherents outran the capacity of any colonial press. The music was therefore copied by hand in margins of printed hymnals or gathered into manuscript anthologies, of which the most luxurious is the 935-page "Die Bittre Gute . . ." now at the Library of Congress.

This manuscript (19 x 24.5 cm.), of which p. 457 is shown here in facsimile, adheres to the Ephrata custom of spreading music across an entire opening. The titles as well as the music cannot be read successfully except from a facsimile of two facing pages. The hymn text in the first system reproduced in facsimile begins: "Ich hab wied'r einen Schritt gethan auf denen *schmalen Himmels-Wegen: die enge rauhe Creutzes"* (printed text in the 1747 *Turtel-Taube*, p. 215 [40]). Text for the second hymn begins: "Grosser Gott . . . *vollem Hertzens-Grund* . . ." (p. 201 [33]). The last hymn starts: "O Jesu! reine Lebens-Quell, thu Dich in mich *ergiesen, damit in mir Geist, Leib und Seel mo^{r}g gantz* in Dir zerfliessen . . ." (p. 254 [66]).

Peter Miller, Beissel's successor, gave the manuscript in question to Benjamin Franklin, who in turn left it with the then Lord Mayor of London, John Wilkes (1727–1797), in April, 1775. After a century and a half, the manuscript was sent back from London for auction in the United States. See the *Report of the Librarian of Congress . . . 1927* (Washington: U. S. Govt. Printing Office, 1927), pp. 109–112, for an account of the history of this monument of colonial calligraphy.

FIGURES 3–6. James Lyon (1735–1794), after marking six compositions in the Index to his *Urania* (Philadelphia: William Bradford, 1761) with a star, explained in the right margin that "All Tunes marked with an Asterism [Asterisk] are New." His second starred item is Francis Hopkinson's "The 23^d. Psalm Tune." The accompanying facsimiles show: first, this item as it appears *a 3* at p. 179 of "Francis Hopkinson His Book," a 206 page manuscript copied by him (Library of Congress ML 96.H83; Plate 3); second, a page of this same psalm as printed in *Urania* with an added Counter voice-part (Plate 4). Hopkinson two years later republished the same psalm at pl. XX of *A Collection of Psalm Tunes with a few Anthems and Hymns Some of them Entirely New*. O. G. Sonneck's *Francis Hopkinson The First American Poet-Composer (1737–1791) and James Lyon Patriot, Preacher, Psalmodist (1735–1794)* (Washington: H. L. McQueen, 1905) shows at p. 92 a facsimile of the 1763 version *a 3* with figured bass and at page 180 the opening bars of the *Urania* version *a 4*.

Another item in *Urania* that can be identified from a concordance in "Francis Hopkinson His Book" is Giovanni (John) Palma's CHRISTMAS. This turns up in the manuscript (p. 125) with "Del Sign.^{r} Palma" written in the upper left margin (Plate 5). The same piece is in *Urania* at pp. 192–194 (Plate 6). Sonneck identified Palma as the emigrant Italian who gave a concert "at the Assembly Room in Lodge Alley" (Philadelphia) on January 25, 1757, tickets one dollar each. On March 17 Palma returned with a second concert, made notable by the attendance of George Washington. Palma's CHRISTMAS owes its text to Nahum Tate (1652–1715), Purcell's librettist for *Dido and Aeneas*.

FIGURE 3

FIGURE 4

FIGURE 5

FIGURE 6

FIGURE 7

FIGURE 7. The frontispiece of *The New-England Psalm-Singer* (Boston: Edes and Gill, 1770) links three famous names: (1) William Billings (1746–1800), making his début in print; (2) Mather Byles (1707–1788), Harvard A.B. 1725, University of Aberdeen D.D. 1765, notable preacher and *littérateur;* (3) Paul Revere (1735–1818), of midnight ride fame. Revere's versatility enabled him to combine silversmithing, copper engraving, and bell casting with distinguished service as a patriot. However, it was Dr. Byles (nephew of Cotton Mather and one of the foremost figures in Boston before the Revolution) whose collaboration in 1770 meant most for the success of *The New-England Psalm-Singer.* Further to emphasize the great man, Billings inserts at page 10 a sixteen-line ode *On Music* by "the Rev. Dr. Byles." A quarter-century later this ode was still sufficiently popular for Supply Belcher to include it in *The Harmony of Maine* (Boston: Isaiah Thomas and Ebenezer Andrews, 1794)—but now abridged and anonymous, because during the Revolution Byles had proved a notable Tory.

Belcher matches Byles's poetry with a delightful floral ornament encircling a mandolin and herald's trumpet. In general, the plain taste of young America dispensed with flowery title pages. But the penchant for graceful oval designs did inspire unusually attractive frontispieces in two now neglected imprints: Walter Janes's *The Harmonic Minstrelsey* (Dedham: H. Mann, 1807) and Israel Terril's *Vocal Harmony. No. 1 Calculated for the use of Singing Schools, and Worshiping Assemblies. . . . Engrav'd Printed and Sold by the Author* (New Haven: 1805).

FIGURE 8

FIGURE 8. First published at page 6 of *The Singing Master's Assistant* (Boston: Draper and Folsom, 1778), William Billings's JUDEA enjoys a present-day popularity known to but few eighteenth-century American pieces. The easy divisibility into four-bar phrases and the folkish flavor make it a Christmas favorite. As the facsimile shows, the singers themselves had the duty of fitting text to music. The :S: signs prescribe repetition of the last four bars. Billings enriches his harmony with "choosing notes" in both bass and soprano; also the two inner parts are to be doubled *ad libitum:* the tenor by women's voices on the part at written pitch and the viola-clef part with men's voices sounding an octave below written pitch. Interestingly enough, the only written accidental (B♮ in the tenor, measure 4) serves no modulatory purpose. To modern ears the Burgundian cadence can prove more attractive, however, than "correct" functional harmony.

What distinguishes the harmony of the Billings generation of American composers are not the gaucheries of consecutives—these were, after all, rife in the English models most admired in the colonies. Instead, it was their constant violation of the laws of chord progression, as understood in Europe, that sets them apart from their European contemporaries and gives them an archaic sound. In 1794 (*The Musical Primer; or the First Part of the Art of Singing* [Cheshire, Connecticut], p. 8), Andrew Law lamented that the Billings-Swan-Read crudities "are actually preferred, and have taken a general run, to the great prejudice of much better music, produced even in this country, and almost to the utter exclusion of genuine European compositions." Law was but the first of a long line of would-be musical czars intent on plowing under the American past in favor of up-to-date European elegance.

FIGURES 9–10. One of the earliest to cry up European music at the expense of the homegrown product was the Connecticut-born and Brown-educated Congregational preacher, Andrew Law (1749–1821). Primarily a compiler of thirty musical publications and a singing-school teacher in eleven states, he began as early as 1794 proclaiming that "American music is extremely faulty." Unfortunately, his European models were not always first-raters but were more often minor Englishmen like the divine Martin Madan (1726–1790), better known today as an advocate of polygamy than for his DENMARK and other tunes with mannered appoggiaturas at cadences. Law also liked Edward Miller and John Wall Callcott, but he quoted Handel as saying that "he would give all his oratorios, if he might be the author of OLD HUNDRED." Among his voluminous papers at the William L. Clements Library, University of Michigan, are the two letters addressed to him by Elkanah Kelsay Dare (1782–1826) and Lucius Chapin (1760–1842). Dare took exception to Law's constant berating of American music, and in his letter from Wilmington, Delaware, dated June 25, 1811, protested:

> I freely acquiesce with you that the European teachers & authors (as well as their manufactures, &c) have had a longer experience than we have— that their compositions & especially those of Madan, Handel, Randel, Arne &c. have met with general approbation & applause—but that *their* composition only, is elegant & suitable for divine worship I cannot admit. We can claim a Billings, a Morgan, a Swan, a Hall, &c. which claim no small share of merit. I know few tunes which excel in solemnity, Billings' "Brookfield"— Morgan's "Amanda" Swan's "China"—& Hall's "All Saints, New."— Nor are those all that can be produced.—As to *gay* music, it does not meet my approbation for a Church, otherwise I would name the compositions of a Holden, a Holyoke, a Jenks, &c. but they, too, have their admirers. My "Wilmington" partakes too much of this kind of composition to meet my own approbation. The Babylonian Captivity pleases me much more.

Both Dare and Chapin had been repeatedly urged to sell Law's books, but while importuning them to serve as salesmen Law showed no interest in their tunes, nor did he print even the Shenandoah Valley tunes sent by John Logan without making the captious changes that he deemed necessary to improve the musical grammar. Chapin's letter from Fleming County, Kentucky, dated March 9, 1812, adopts a conciliatory attitude toward the "great man" Law, but confesses ill success in a three-year campaign to sell Law's books.

> Yet after labouring more than three years, find but few who will either lern, or sing those tunes with pleasure. I do not, however, despair, but hope a more refined taste will succeed the bad one yet prevalent.

Chapin assures Law that the tunes sent by Logan please the local singers, and names several of the most popular in the evident hope that Law will publish them. He continues:

> Had I money to advance, I would send on for Hundreds of books, & I think, with the help of some teachers with whom I might have some influence, much might be done, to facillitate the accomplishment of the important

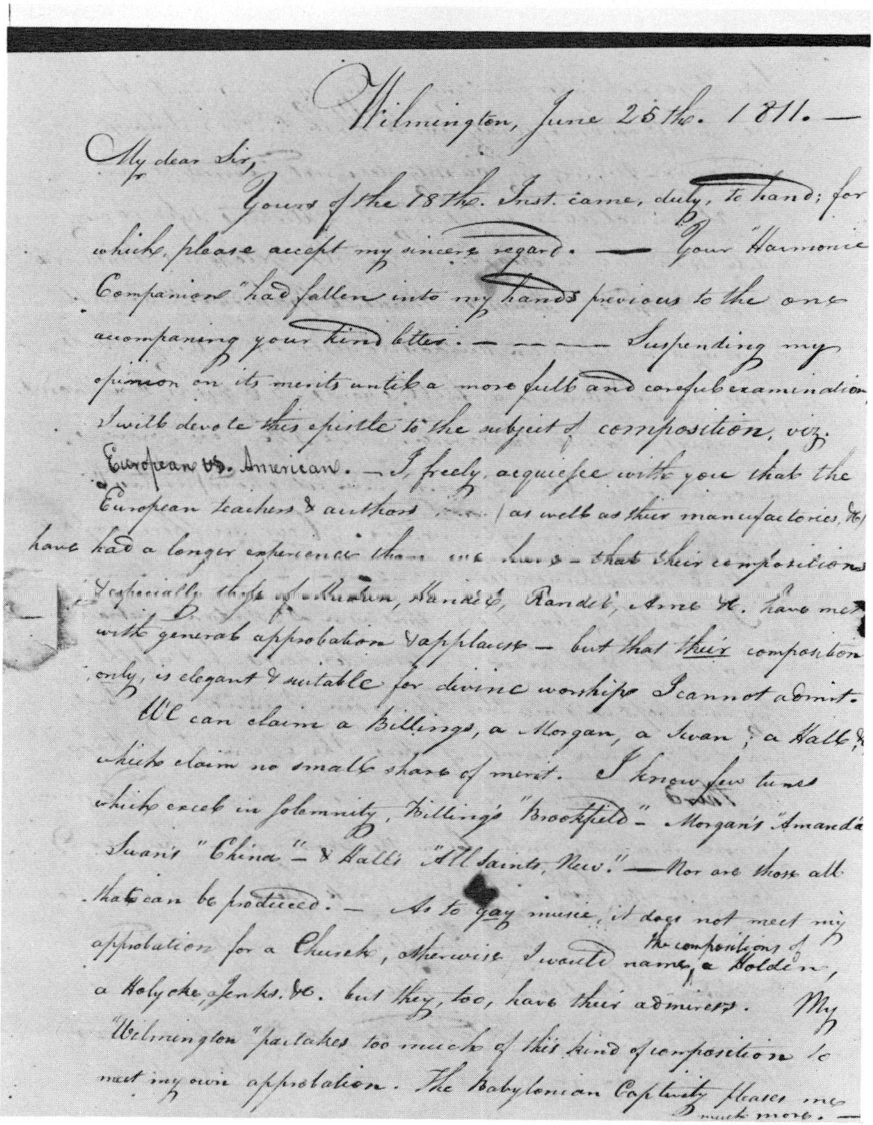

FIGURE 9

object you have in view. "The poverty of the poor, is their destruction."
Be assured of my best wishes, & endeavours, for your success.

But later in 1812 when the tunes suggested by Logan were sent back so heavily corrected by Law as to be but shadows of themselves. Logan protested in a letter dated September 9, 1812, from Augusta, Virginia. Convinced that Law would never condescend to meet the West even halfway, Chapin wrote him again (May 3, 1813) advising him to stay in Philadelphia because for the time being Kentuckians do not plan to change their "views & feelings."

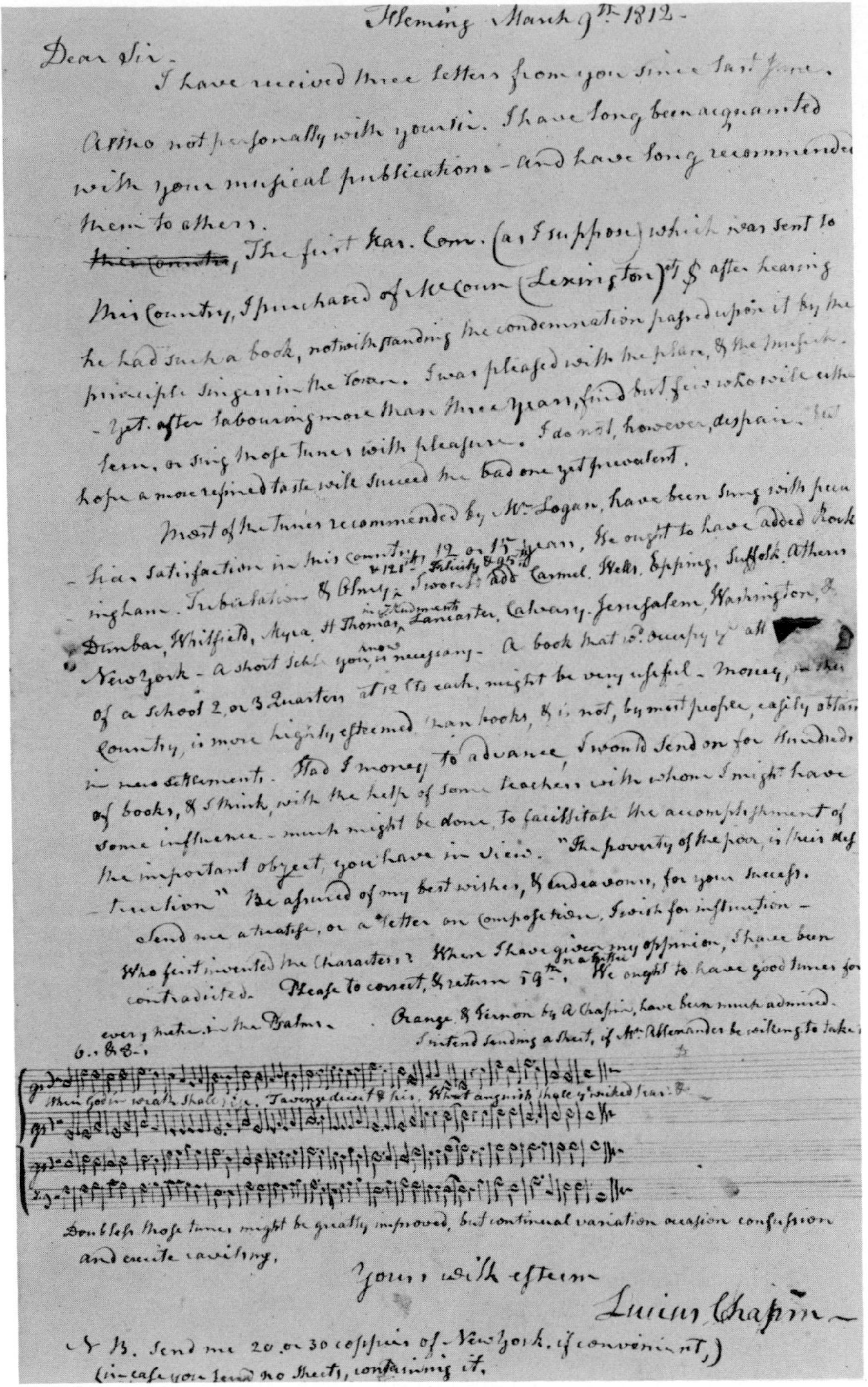

Fleming March 9th 1812 -

Dear Sir -

    I have received three letters from you since last June. Altho not personally with your tin. I have long been acquainted with your musical publications - And have long recommended them to others. ~~this country,~~ The first Kar. Com. (as I suppose) which was sent to this Country, I purchased of McCoun (Lexington) &c &c after hearing he had such a book, notwithstanding the condemnation passed upon it by the principle singers in the town. I was pleased with the plan, & the Musick - Yet, after labouring more than three years, find but few who will either learn, or sing those tunes with pleasure. I do not, however, despair. Still hope a more refined taste will succeed the bad one yet prevalent.

    Most of the tunes recommended by Mr Logan, have been sung with peculiar satisfaction in this country, 12 or 15 years, He ought to have added Rockingham, Tribulation & Olney, & 121st, Felicity & 95th & 90th add Carmel, Wells, Epping, Suffolk, Athens, Dunbar, Whitfield, Myra, St Thomas, in judgements, Lancaster, Calvary, Jerusalem, Washington, & New York - A short scale more is necessary - A book that would occupy ye all of a school 2, or 3 Quarters at 12 Cts each, might be very useful - Money, in this country, is more highly esteemed, than books, & is not, by most people, easily obtained in new settlements. Had I money to advance, I would send on for hundreds of books, & I think, with the help of some teachers with whom I might have some influence - much might be done, to facilitate the accomplishment of the important object, you have in view. "The poverty of the poor, is their destruction" Be assured of my best wishes, & endeavours, for your success.

    Send me a treatise, or a letter on Composition, I wish for instruction - Who first invented the Characters? When I have given my opinion, I have been contradicted - Please to correct, & return &c. We ought to have good tunes for every metre in the Psalms. Orange & Sermon by A Chapin, have been much admired. I intend sending a sheet, if Mr Alexander be willing to take it.

6. 8.8 -

Then Gods wrath shall rise, Avenging death & his, What anguish shall ye wicked seize &

Doubtless those tunes might be greatly improved, but continual variation occasion confusion and excite cavilling.

    Yours, with esteem
           Lucius Chapin -

N B. Send me 20 or 30 coppies of New York, if convenient, in case you send no sheets, containing it.

FIGURE 10

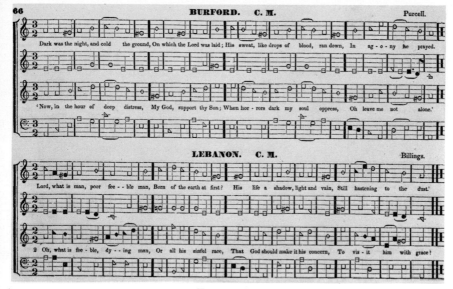

FIGURE 11

FIGURE 11. Although opposed on principle to shape notes, Lowell Mason and his brother Timothy B. Mason so far unbent as to allow *The Sacred Harp or Eclectic Harmony* (Cincinnati: Truman and Smith, 1835), an oblong 230-page anthology, to appear "in patent notes (contrary to the wishes of the Authors) under the belief that it will prove much more acceptable to a majority of singers in the West and South" (Publisher's Advertisement, dated at Cincinnati, September, 1834 [p. iv]). Nonetheless the Masons insisted that *The Sacred Harp* contained a "variety of beautiful subjects from the works of Haydn, Mozart, Cherubini, Méhul, Weber, Rossini, and other celebrated authors; all of which have been arranged and harmonized *expressly for this work,* and are now for the first time published."

The spectacle of Mozart riding the Western plains in a shape-note disguise shows what varied cultural influences were let loose on the frontier during the Age of Jackson. The facsimile gives BURFORD, ascribed to Purcell, and below it Billings's LEBANON, "purified" of harmonic errors. Franklin B. Zimmerman. *Henry Purcell 1659–1695, An analytical catalogue of his music* (London: Macmillan, 1963, p. 77, item 125), documents the lateness of the BURFORD ascription —1718.

FIGURE 12

FIGURE 12. Lowell Mason, ever faithful to the classics as he understood them, first attempted mating the second part of Isaac Watts's Psalm 98 (1719) with Handelian music in an elaborate set piece published at pages 350–354 of *The Boston Handel and Haydn Society Collection of Church Music, Fifth Edition* (Boston: Richardson and Lord, 1827). In 1836 he scrapped any allegiance to more than an opening four-note motto "from Handel" and published in *Occasional Psalm and Hymn Tunes* (Boston: J. H. Wilkins and R. B. Carter, p. 70) the carol that has now become one of the most popular pieces of American Christmas music. As the facsimile shows, first publication was in E Major, open score, with a different second ending for the third strophe. In calling it ANTIOCH, he may have been referring to the custom of antiphonal singing first introduced at Antioch—or, at any rate, so suggests Robert G. McCutchan, *Hymn Tune Names,* page 42. In *The Modern Psalmist* (same publishers, 1839), Mason transposed ANTIOCH down to D (p. 144) and gave it the close-score guise that it has worn ever since. Among Mason's twenty-five most popular tunes, ANTIOCH is unique because of its rhythmic variety and bounciness, the word-repeats (last line), and of course the vocal antiphony at the end of each stanza (Arlene E. Gray, "Lowell Mason's Contribution to American Church Music," Eastman School of Music thesis, 1941, p. 223).

FIGURE 13

FIGURE 13. *Ka Lira Hawaii: he mau leomele no na ekalesia o Hawaii nei* (Honolulu: Mea paipalapala a na misionari, 1844) heads a long list of missionary musical publications in the fiftieth state. The accompanying facsimile shows page 66. Here the 1844 *Ka Lira Hawaii* (copy in the William L. Clements Library) pairs Lowell Mason's exceedingly popular OLIVET—composed for Ray Palmer's hymn, "My faith looks up to Thee" (Mason's *The Choir*, 1832, p. 274)—with Timothy Swan's *succès fou*, CHINA. The 1848 edition of *Ka Lira Hawaii* (copies in the Library of Congress and The New Public Library, Music Division) pairs Mason's OLIVET with AMERICA (published in *The Choir*, 1832, p. 273, with the now universally known text beginning "My country 'tis of thee," by the twenty-four-year-old Samuel F. Smith [1808–1895], then preparing for the Baptist ministry).

The quick spread of missionary hymnals around the world carried American tunes like CHINA, but more especially the tunes of Mason and his successors, to the four corners of the world. Irrespective of their value as music, the tunes in missionary hymnals deserve the closest attention of Americanists because it was in this medium that American music spread to Argentina, Brazil, and Chile, Afghanistan, Burma, and Ceylon, a century before jazz and the jukebox.

FIGURE 14

FIGURE 14. Horatio W. Parker (1863–1919) completed the scoring of his masterpiece, the oratorio *Hora Novissima,* Opus 30, to a text from the twelfth-century Benedictine, Bernard of Cluny, in May, 1892. The facsimile shows the last page of the full score (204) in Parker's autograph, deposited by him at the Library of Congress. Although "Gran Cassa, Piatti" can be read before the tenth staff, he does not repeat either the key signature (here E Major) nor the names of the instruments from page to page. The English text goes in red ink beneath the Latin, which on this page reads *Cui sua pars Deus* (English alternate: "Their portion forever"). The first bracketed pair of staves above the chorus is the organ part, which is however an optional instrument throughout. Parker's German training peers out of the autograph when he lapses into *Posaunen* for trombones or when he writes the performing directions in German (p. 167 of autograph score).

FIGURE 15. George W. Chadwick (1854–1931), a leader of the Boston school in his generation, composed prolifically in the anthem vein during his long service as a church organist. Standing somewhat above his numerous yeoman contributions to the church literature, his splendid *Noël: A Christmas Pastoral* (New York: H. W. Gray, 1909, 103 pp.) calls for soli, chorus, and orchestra. The facsimile shows page 94 of the autograph full score (Library of Congress), equivalent to page 45 of the printed edition. Serving as an epilogue to a tonal fugue, the passage here illustrated brilliantly climaxes No. 6 of the twelve numbers that comprise the cantata.

FIGURE 15

The same Kübler's name appears on the title page of *The Boston Academy's Collection of Church Music . . . with many beautiful pieces, tunes and anthems selected from the Masses and other works of Haydn, Mozart, Beethoven, Pergolesi, Righini, Cherubini, Romberg, Winter, Weber, Nägeli, Kübler, and other distinguished composers* [206] *arranged and adapted to English words expressly for this work* (Boston: Carter, Hendee & Co., 1835; 11 later editions).

Of course no one denies that this essentially pro-German *Boston Academy's Collection* does make a few polite bows to the early American repertory as well—bows which were completely lacking in Mason's maiden publication of 1822. For instance, Billings (pp. 105, 130), Holden (128), Law (91), and Read (49, 92) each enjoy at least token representation. But with the harmonies retailored in Mason's shop, Billings's LEBANON now dons the harmonic habits of a polite chorale from Mendelssohn's *St. Paul* (1836). Similarly, Read's WINDHAM,[207] when newly decked out with a different time signature and with numerous added accidentals, speaks in as proper a German textbook accent as do any of the hymns of J. G. Nägeli (1773–1836) on pp. 45, 70, 135 in the same collection.

Read was himself still alive when Mason published the first edition of the *Boston Academy's Collection* (he died the next year, 1836). Not only he, but also Supply Belcher, the "Handel of Maine" (1751–1836), Timothy Swan, whose CHINA was the "most unscientific tune" ever penned (1748–1842), Oliver Holden, and Stephen Jenks (1772–1856)[208] thus shared the misfortune of much outlasting their glory. What was their reaction to Mason, his new "scientific"

---

[206] The other distinguished composers include Hasse (294), Graun (231), and Koželuch (219). Friedrich Silcher, whose musical examples Mason's *Manual* fails to acknowledge, was to win belated mention in *Carmina Sacra: or Boston Collection of Church Music* (Boston: J. H. Wilkins, 1841 [2nd ed.]) as the composer of the pieces at pp. 217, 260–261, 262–263, 284–286, 310–312.

[207] *The American Singing Book* (New-Haven: Daniel Read, 1785), p. 55. Mason converts $\circlearrowright$ to $\frac{3}{2}$, a meter not unknown to Read, who specifies it at pp. 27 and 40 of the 1785 imprint. In Mason's extremely interesting letter dated May 24, 1841, and published in H. T. Hach's *Musical Magazine; or, Repository* (Boston: Geo. P. Reed, 1841), III, 170–171, he not only vindicates Daniel Read's composition of WINDHAM —which the editor of this magazine wished to ascribe to Luther—but also praises it thus: "It is a tune we may well be proud of; it has been sung for half a century, and it will probably continue to be sung longer than any other piece of music that has ever yet been composed on this side the Atlantic." Cf. Metcalf, *American Writers and Compilers,* p. 99, who falls victim to Hach's trap. See also WINDHAM in George Pullen Jackson, *Down-East Spirituals* (New York: J. J. Augustin, 1943), p. 120.

[208] Data in Metcalf, *American Writers and Compilers,* pp. 83–85, 103–107, 154–157.

music, his wholehearted endorsement of organs and choirs,[209] his distrust of the casual singing school, and his obeisance to Germans? Read's opinions survive in a letter written when he was seventy-one. He acknowledges the harmonic sins of his youth, and to correct his errors has studied J. L. d'Alembert, A. F. C. Kollmann (1756–1829), and other theorists. After "carefully examining the system of harmony exhibited in Handel's *Messiah,* Haydn's *Creation* and other similar works," [210] and after trying the "allowed and forbidden" progressions, his "ideas on the subject of music have been considerably altered"— so much so that his own unpublished "Musica Ecclesia," finished in 1832, repudiates everything in his long bygone past that is now recognized as distinctively Read.

Mason headed a bandwagon that proved irresistible in his own epoch, and a century later the force of his personality is not spent. No American has ever written so many hymn tunes that have endured. Fifteen lyrics in *The Hymnal* (Presbyterian Board of Publication, 1935) join his tunes; he was the composer or arranger of nine tunes in *The Hymnal 1940*; and *The Methodist Hymnal* (1935) depended more largely upon him than on any other composer. The kind of favor that he has enjoyed at Methodist hands deserves underlining if only because such approval implies success with millions. Within six years of his death, Mason garnered more than double the credits of his nearest rival in the *Hymnal of the Methodist Episcopal Church with Tunes* (New York: Nelson & Phillips, 1878). With an indexed 46 original tunes and 22 arrangements to his credit in this 1878 official book, he even exceeds the combined totals of the second, third, and fourth most frequently indexed tune-composers. In second place comes William B. Bradbury with 16 entries, in third and fourth two Massachusetts-born composers—George Kingsley (1811–1884)

[209] Mason, *Address on Church Music* (Boston: Hilliard, Gray and Co., 1826), pp. 15–18 (virtues of trained choirs contrasted with the defects of unrehearsed congregational singing), 20–31 (necessity of continuous instrumental accompaniment). Never in his long career did Mason endorse untutored congregational singing—which indeed he could tolerate only when choir and organ take the lead (*Musical Letters,* p. 139). He always contended that choirs should be mixed, and even after visiting English cathedrals he continued an enemy of boys' voices (*ibid.,* p. 129).

[210] Lowens, "Daniel Read's World," p. 244. Read censured the Mason-Hastings penchant for "scraps" cut out of Handel, Haydn, and Mozart, "patched up and altered to make metre of them," and he was not alone in making such an objection (cf. H. T. Hach, *The Musical Magazine; or, Repository,* III, 155–156). On the other hand, John S. Dwight—the high priest of Boston music—defended such use of the "sublime" works of Mozart and Beethoven. Dwight's classing only great music as "sacred" gave the arrangers *carte blanche.* See his "Address, delivered before the Harvard Musical Association, August 25th, 1841," in *The Musical Magazine; or, Repository,* III/69, 70 (Aug. 28, 1841), 257–272; especially p. 259.

with 12 credits, and Joseph P. Holbrook (1822–1888) with 11 original tunes and six arrangements. Kingsley (sometime music supervisor in the Philadelphia public schools) and Holbrook (a music editor of the 1878 book) are now all but completely *passé*. Mason as late as the 1935 *Methodist Hymnal* still stood up triumphing with 32 entries in the composers' index—his nearest rival being the indomitable John Bacchus Dykes (1823–1876), Church of England priest, with 28 entries.

If this is sufficient documentation to prove that an unusually large Mason repertory still resists the ravages of time, it may also be worth recalling that he remained always true to himself, so far as his concept of "devotional" style is concerned, never violating it to win transitory successes. Both he and his New York rival Thomas Hastings believed that they were together creating a unique devotional style, and that it far transcended any such style known contemporaneously in Europe. Hastings witnessed to their common belief as early as 1837; in a letter dated November 1, 1837, to his Detroit banker-brother Eurotas P. Hastings (Mary Evelyn Durden Teal, "Music Activities in Detroit from 1701 through 1870," University of Michigan Ph.D. dissertation, 1964, II, 467), he wrote:

Europe has no style *strictly devotional* that compares at all with what we are cultivating in this country. Mr. Mason says the same—others also concur in the statement. This places us in a most responsible attitude.

Of course, Hastings was only human enough to resent ever and anon Mason's belief in his superiority because he was based at Boston, hub of the universe. "Deliver me from such teaching as I heard him put forth in all the vehemence of up and down dogmatism," Hastings confided to his Detroit brother in a letter of July 4, 1848 ("Music Activities in Detroit," II, 456). Also, Hastings fancied from time to time that Mason was about to lose his grip on the public, and in the same Independence Day letter took no little pride in the fact that:

A multitude of Mason's old adherents have become our patrons. This no doubt galls him, but we cannot help it. If his next publication is no better than the two preceding ones, he will I should think, about use himself up.

To compensate for a possible loss of Boston, Hastings was sure in 1848 that:

Friend Lowell will use every exeration to establish himself in the west, and will in his own opinion do good much in proportion as he can multiply and sell books.

But however right he may have been in seeing "Friend Lowell" as an overly energetic entrepreneur of his own books, a do-gooder determined to make every good deed pay dividends, a high pressure salesman invading the West when he could no longer bend Boston to his will, Hastings surely erred when he fondly imagined in 1848 that Mason was "petering out." Evidence available today proves exactly the contrary.

What particularly strikes a student is Mason's ability to keep turning out "hit" hymn tunes throughout the entire span of his creative activity. Of the seven representative tunes chosen by Seth Bingham for chorale-prelude elaborations (*Seven Preludes or Postludes on Lowell Mason Hymns* [New York: H. W. Gray, 1945], WESLEY ("Hail to the Brightness") was published in *Cantica Laudis,* 1850; BOYLSTON ("Blest be the tie that binds") in *The Choir; or Union Collection of Church Music,* 1832; MISSIONARY HYMN ("From Greenland's icy mountains") in *The Boston Handel and Haydn Society Collection,* 7th ed., 1829; WATCHMAN ("Watchman, tell us of the night") in the same collection, 1830 edition; LABAN ("A Charge to keep I have") in 1830; HENLEY ("We would see Jesus") in *The Hallelujah,* 1854; and WORK SONG = DILIGENCE ("Work for the night is coming") in *The Song-Garden,* 1864. His HAMBURG ("When I survey the wondrous cross") was published in 1825, OLIVET ("My faith looks up to Thee") in 1834, but BETHANY ("Nearer my God to Thee") not until 1859 in *The Sabbath Hymn and Tune Book.*

Mason preached these requisites for a good congregational tune: simplicity of intervals and rhythm; range not exceeding an octave or ninth, with D as the preferable upper limit and nothing ever above E.[211] J. S. Bach's chorale harmonies he considered utterly unsuited to congregational hymnals: "Congregations might as well undertake to sing Beethoven's Mass No. 2, as these chorals, with all sorts of complicated and difficult harmony parts."[212] When introducing unfamiliar German chorales to his American public, Mason therefore leaned on harmonizations by the discreet Conrad Kocher (1786–

---

[211] Mason, *Musical Letters,* pp. 163, 167, 170, 294.

[212] *Ibid.,* p. 301. He appealed to Leipzig for his justification: "In his church, the St. Thomas', all the people sing the melody, and the parts are sung (when at all) by the choir."

1872), not Bach. Even in so ambitious a book as his *Carmina Sacra* he kept "the harmony as simple as possible" because "the knowledge and taste of the public cannot be forced." [213]

He justified his fifth large miscellany—the 350-page *Carmina Sacra*—with the motto *Excelsior*. "Every well organized choir, if kept up with interest, must have a constant succession of new music; without this there will be no advancement," he claimed in his preface. Fortunately for him, no copyright laws prevented his carrying as much European grist as he pleased, and thus keeping his American mills continuously active. But, once having adapted a foreign tune, he could prove extremely jealous of "property rights" in his own country. A group of three rather chilly letters to his rising rival, William B. Bradbury (1816–1868), dated July 21, August 20, and October 10, 1861, culminate in the warning that "this property extends both to music and to words or poetry." [214] He also claimed property rights in the lengthy pedagogical introductions that were a prime buying attraction of such works as the *Carmina Sacra*—teaching how to sing, defining 276 musical terms, and explaining the principles of chant. His *Carmina Sacra,* after going through thirteen editions in the 1840's and '50's, alone sold half a million copies. The income—plus that from such prior successes as the *Handel and Haydn Society Collection* (1822), *Choir; or Union Collection* (1832), and *Modern Psalmist* (1839)—brought him eventually to such affluence that he could purchase the estate of Silver Spring at South Orange, New Jersey, gather the finest private musical library in America of his day, have the best musical helpers in the country, and indulge in such acts of largesse as underwriting Alexander Wheelock Thayer's third and final trip to Europe.[215]

[213] See the review of Mason's *Carmina Sacra* [1841] in *The Musical Magazine; or, Repository,* III, 307–309.

[214] Library of Congress, ML 95.M185 (gift of Herbert R. Main, 1916). Bradbury —somewhat more sentimental than Mason or Hastings—leaves us WOODWORTH (1849), now known to millions as the tune for "Just as I am," SHEPHERD (1859, "Saviour, like a Shepherd lead us"), CONSECRATION (1860, "Sweet hour of prayer"), and AUGHTON (1864, "He leadeth me"), as tokens of his immortality. A Baptist, Bradbury is represented by thirty-six tunes in *The Baptist Praise Book* of 1871, a collection "richer in the precious gems of hymnology than any other volume extant."

[215] *Dwight's Journal,* XXXIX/1008 (Dec. 6, 1879), 196. Thayer had attacked Mason in an injudicious article. Without referring to the article, Mason invited the young musicologist to make free use of his library and loaned him "a handsome sum of money, to be repaid at convenience without interest" for his further Beethoven researches in Europe. Mason was not always so successful in turning enemies into friends. See G. W. Lucas's scathing *Remarks on the Musical Conventions in Boston* (Northampton: The Author, 1844), including the charge that Mason rigged his conventions [pp. 4, 17], was jealous of his able assistant George J. Webb (1803–1887), composer of WEBB (1837, "Stand up, stand up for Jesus") [p. 7], and

To justify Mason's generosity, Thayer became America's foremost nineteenth-century musicologist. Unfortunately, Mason himself has thus far failed to attract the attention of any scholar equal to Thayer. The only facets of his career studied painstakingly to date are his pioneer labors as a music educator. How much of his long career yet remains *terra incognita* can be illustrated by referring to a single sample publication—*The Boston Anthem Book; being a Selection of Anthems, Collects, Motetts, and other Set Pieces* (Boston: J. H. Wilkins and R. B. Carter, 1839). This was but one of his books including "Set Pieces." As late as 1869 his *Boston Academy of Church Music* reverted to the term, which meant for Mason a through-composed piece as opposed to a piece in which the same music serves for successive strophes. In the 1839 book he includes such familiar hymn texts as Charles Wesley's "Hark! the herald angels sing" and Isaac Watts's "When I survey the wondrous cross," but with new music for every stanza, thus entitling them to be called "Set Pieces."

For prior use of the term in this sense, Mason could look back to such eighteenth-century authorities as Arthur Bedford (1668–1745), who took it to mean something through-composed (*New English Dictionary,* ed. James A. H. Murray [Oxford: Clarendon Press, 1914], VIII, 549, col. 1, letter d), or to John Chetham, who explained the term similarly in his *A Book of Psalmody, containing Variety of Tunes . . . in Four Parts, Within such a Compass, as will most naturally suit the Voices in Country-Churches* (London: Joseph Lord, 1752). However, Mason envisioned much more sophisticated singers for many of his "Set Pieces" than did John Chetham in 1752, or for that matter than did Timothy Swan in 1801 (*New England Harmony. Containing A variety of Psalm Tunes, in Three and Four Parts, Adapted to all Metres: Also, a number of Set Pieces, of Several Verses each, Together with a number of Anthems* [Northampton, Mass: Andrew Wright]), or Stephen Jenks in 1805 (*The Delights of Harmony; or, Norfolk Compiler. Being a New Collection of Psalm Tunes, Hymns and Anthems; with a variety of Set Pieces* [Dedham, Mass.: H. Mann]); not to mention numerous later compilers of "Set Pieces" active in New York, New Jersey, Pennsylvania, Maryland, and Virginia.[216]

---

refused to invite Hastings to Boston for fear of competition [p. 12]. Hood's history was mere Mason party propaganda, according to Lucas, and George F. Root was guilty of "cowardly and contemptible conduct" [pp. 16–17, 11].

[216] Listed in W. Thomas Marrocco's "The Set Piece," in *Journal of the American Musicological Society,* XV/3 (Fall, 1962), 349. This article forgoes any account of

Mason's *Boston Anthem Book* of 1839 even includes through-composed selections from the first great master of Baroque oratorio, Giacomo Carissimi (1605–1674), from Handel's predecessor at the court of Hanover, Agostino Steffani (1654–1728), and from the Venetian patrician whose *50 Psalmi* comprise one of the most ambitious musical publications of the late Baroque, Benedetto Marcello (1686–1739). Four psalm-sections from Marcello's monumental Venetian edition (8 volumes, 1724–1726) enter Mason's 1839 compilation, Englished—the first being part of Psalm 8 (*Estro poetico-harmonico,* I, 1724, 121–123 = 1839, pp. 28–32), the last being part of Psalm 42, A.V. numbering (VII, 1726, 118–122 = 1839, pp. 127–129). How little Mason's labors in behalf of the historic repertory are remembered comes to light when an Italian firm can now record the identical Psalm 8 of Marcello (*Odi che lodi,* Angelicum LPA 5950) for distribution in the United States, blithely presuming the Marcello psalms never before to have reached American ears.[217] Many like instances might be adduced showing how feebly known among the present generation are Mason's far-ranging endeavors. Were enough space available, each of his major publications could indeed be here shown to offer research possibilities no less exciting than those posed by the Renaissance anthologies so often favored for dissertation topics in our graduate schools.

By virtue of the spell cast over Northern church music for at least a half-century, Mason and Hastings give their names to the 1825–1875 epoch. However, when Boston and New York became too refined[218] to sing any longer the native American repertory, other

---

the long use to which such terms as "Set Tune," "Set Service," and "Set Piece" had been put in prior English publications. Richard Crawford, "Andrew Law (1749–1821): The Career of an American Musician," p. 26, defines a *set piece* as a through-composed version of two or more strophes from a poetic text; p. 25, an *anthem* as a through-composed prose selection from Scripture. Law's set pieces consistently show less textural contrast than his anthems (p. 26, n. 22), but in both set piece and anthem word repetition is allowed.

217 Mason followed London fashion when introducing Mass-movements and Psalm-excerpts from Italian composers. Sir John Hawkins, *A General History of the Science and Practice of Music* (London: T. Payne, 1776), V, 234, bitterly assailed the fad. Nowadays "there are persons that will give a boy half a guinea to sing" Marcello's Psalm 8, he complained. This is of course the very psalm that Mason was to give pride of place in 1839.

218 The editor of the *Boston Courier* lamented in January, 1848, that "the good old days of New England music have passed away, and the singing-masters who compose and teach it, are known only in history as an extinct race." The good old tunes, Billings's MAJESTY, Read's SHERBURNE, Edson's LENOX, could once "fill a meeting house quicker than the most eloquent preacher in the country," but all their glory is vanished like Ichabod while instead pompous "professors" now pum-

sections of the country fell heir to it, and built upon it. The stigmata of all the more characteristic tune books circulating in the South and West in the forepart of the nineteenth century were the shape notes introduced in William Little and William Smith's *The Easy Instructor* (1801).[219] In their new invention the "four singing syllables" take each a different shape: "*Fa* is a triangle, *Mi* a diamond, *Law* an oblong square, and *Sol* the usual form [circle]." The advertisement appearing in the August 22, 1801, *Philadelphia Repository and Weekly Register* continued: "It is evident that their different characters, indicating at sight the names of the notes, will greatly aid the student of Sacred Harmony."

I ess than a year after Little and Smith's 1801 *Easy Instructor* was advertised, Andrew Law—who had pioneered with such other innovations as placing the "tune" in the top part instead of the tenor (1793), making the half-note the basic unit of all time signatures, and reducing the number of moods [220]—patented his markedly similar "New Plan of Printing Music." This called for "four kinds of characters" to "denote the four singing syllables; and the learner will immediately learn the notes with great facility." [221] Like Little and

---

mel the ears of their pupils with precepts that profane the sanctuary. See *The Boston Musical Gazette,* III/1–2 (Jan. 31, Feb. 14, 1848), 4–5, 11–12 ("Ancient Psalm Tunes," "Old American Tunes").

[219] Lowens, "Andrew Law and the Pirates," in *Journal of the American Musicological Society,* XIII/1–3 (1960), 218; *Music and Musicians,* p. 81. For an extended discussion of the Little and Smith system, see Lowens and Britton, "*The Easy Instructor* (1798–1831): A History and Bibliography of the First Shape-Note Tune-Book," in *Journal of Research in Music Education,* I/1 (Spring, 1953), 28–55; or Lowens, *Music and Musicians,* pp. 115–137. Cf. also Lowens, "A Postscript on Shape-Notes," in *Wyeth's Repository of Sacred Music, Part Second* (New York: Da Capo Press, 1964), pp. xv–xvi.

[220] Britton, "Theoretical Introductions," pp. 254–256, 306. The moods (including C, $\mathvarphi$, $\mathcal{O}$, 3, $\frac{3}{2}$, $\frac{3}{4}$, $\frac{3}{8}$) were a subject dear to the hearts of the eighteenth-century English psalmodists, as well as to their American followers. "Time signatures" served as tempo markings, C indicating "a slow, grave movement, C "brisk," $\mathcal{O}$ or $\mathvarphi$ "very quick." Tunes marked 3 at the beginning "are sung about One Third swifter than Common Time" [C], according to John Tufts, the first American psalmodist to publish instructions in the art. William Tans'ur, *A Compleat Melody: or, The Harmony of Sion* (4th ed.; London: A. Pearson for J. Hodges, 1738), devoted his entire Chapter IV (pp. 10–17) to the "moods." Reprinted as late as *The American Harmony,* 8th ed. (Newbury-Port: Daniel Bayley, 1773), this chapter specified quarter-note motion at what would now be called M.M. 60 for C. Timothy Swan was even more precise in his *New England Harmony,* 1801, p. vii, when he allotted 4 seconds, 3, 2, and 1½ to the bar in C, $\mathcal{\phi}$, $\mathcal{O}$, and $\frac{2}{4}$ respectively; 3 seconds, 2, and 1⅓ to the bar in $\frac{3}{2}$, $\frac{3}{4}$, and $\frac{3}{8}$; and 4 seconds and 2⅔ to the bar in $\frac{6}{4}$ and $\frac{6}{8}$.

[221] Lowens, "Andrew Law and the Pirates," p. 217, quoting from Law's notice in the Boston *Columbian Centinel,* Dec. 24, 1803.

Smith, Law reserved the round note for *sol,* interchanging however their triangle and square, and dispensing with the five-line staff. The Little and Smith, Law, and other schemes toward simplifying music notation introduced by such eighteenth-century precursors as John Tufts and Benjamin Dearborn (*A Scheme for Reducing the Science of Music to a More Simple State* [Portsmouth, N. H., 1785]) [222] all had one object: making written music "so simple as scarcely to perplex the youngest child who can read." These printing innovations require attention in a history of American church music because the announced purpose was always to bring sacred song to the common folk and the earliest books always contained sacred texts exclusively.

Hastings—whose name is today kept alive with his three tunes, ORTONVILLE (1837, "Majestic sweetness sits enthroned"), TOPLADY (1830, "Rock of Ages"), and ZION (1830, "Guide me, O thou great Jehovah")—voiced the sentiment of the entire "better music" battalion when he labeled the most successful and enduring of these notation reforms, the Little and Smith shape system, as no more than "dunce notes." [223] If so, they were exactly the teaching aid needed by Ananias Davisson and the Chapins when they moved west and south.

From the start, these "dunce-note" publications specialized in the early American repertory. For instance, Little and Smith's *Easy Instructor* (New York: G. & R. Waite, 1802 [no less than 27 re-editions, 1805–1831]) [224] pitted only five European tunes against a hundred by unscientific Americans. Of the 156 tunes in John Wyeth's frequently reprinted *Repository of Sacred Music* (Harrisburg, 1810 [at least eight later editions: 1811–1834] [225]) nearly half are plagiarized from the *Easy Instructor*'s American list. The slightly later *Repository of Sacred Music, Part Second,* published by Wyeth (1770–1858) at Harrisburg in 1813 and reissued in 1820, contains a group of thirteen new items by Elkanah Kelsay Dare (1782–1826), a Methodist minister active in Delaware, who also wrote on music; [226] and of seven by (Lucius) Chapin (1760–1842),

[222] Louis Pichierri, *Music in New Hampshire, 1623–1800* (New York: Columbia University Press, 1960), Chap. XII (pp. 175–182), assembles the Dearborn data.

[223] Lowens, "A Postscript," p. xvi, and *Music and Musicians,* p. 118, n. 2 (quoted from *Musical Magazine,* I [July 1835], 87).

[224] Lowens and Britton, "*The Easy Instructor,*" Table VIII on page 55.

[225] Lowens, "John Wyeth's *Repository,*" p. 116.

[226] *Ibid.,* p. 122. Crawford and Hitchcock call attention to Dare's important 1811 letter in the Law Papers (William L. Clements Library, Ann Arbor) "enclosing a tune of his own composition" and discussing "the difference between American and European music" (*The Papers of Andrew Law,* p. [10]). In the preface to the *Repository, Part Second,* p. 9, Dare defends combining two unprepared intervals

a Yankee singing master who worked forty years in Kentucky;[227] that were to be constantly copied by later Southern tunebook compilers.

The Repository of Sacred Music, Part Second not only served as quarry for later compilers, but also was one of the earliest collections to emphasize melodies of folkish cast. "Many of the folk hymns which emerged in print for the first time in *Part Second* are to be found in modern anthologies of American folk hymnody"[228] such as George Pullen Jackson's *White Spirituals in the Southern Uplands* (1933), *Spiritual Folk Songs of Early America* (1937), *Down-East Spirituals* (1943) and Annabel Morris Buchanan's *Folk Hymns of America* (1938). Even the melodies ascribed to such named composers as Chapin in *Part Second*—NINETY-THIRD (24 = Ananias Davisson's *Kentucky Harmony,* 26 = William Walker's *Southern Harmony* [1847 ed.], 7), ROCKBRIDGE (95 = 16 = 257), and VERNON (21 = *SH,* 34), for instance [229]—bear folkish trademarks.

---

that are consonant with the "air" but dissonant with each other, D-A and A-C, for instance. He illustrates with bar 9 of his own DISMISSION (p. 47 = Lowens, p. 126, ex. 4).

[227] What George Pullen Jackson wrote on Amzi Chapin in *White and Negro Spirituals* (New York: J. J. Augustin, 1943), p. 284, has been expanded and corrected by Charles Hamm in "The Chapins and Sacred Music in the South and West," *Journal of Research in Music Education,* VIII/2 (Fall, 1960), 91–98. However, the "two-voice setting of *Sophronia* by Lucius Chapin" in Hamm, p. 96, came out in *Philadelphia Harmony . . . selected by Adgate and Spicer* (Philadelphia: Westcott & Adgate, 1788), p. 53, a tone lower; also in *A Selection of Sacred Harmony* (Philadelphia: W. Young, 1788), pp. 82–83. Adgate attributes it to [Robert] King (member of the royal band, 1680–1728). In *The Village Harmony,* 4th ed. (Exeter: Henry Ranlet, 1798), p. 198, the heading reads: "An Elegy on Sophronia, who died of the Small-Pox, 1711." Andrew Wright transposes SOPHRONIA in *The American Musical Miscellany* (Northampton, 1798), pp. 184–185, to Chapin's key, E minor. Lucius Chapin, one of seven Chapins active in the sacred music of the period, reached Kentucky in 1794 via the Shenandoah Valley, where he had begun teaching as early as 1787. Born in Springfield, Massachusetts, he nobly typified the Yankee singing masters who fanned out into the South and West after the Revolutionary War.

[228] Lowens, "John Wyeth's *Repository*," p. 120.

[229] Lucius Chapin taught in Rockbridge and Rockingham counties of Virginia and lived in Vernon forty years. These geographical coincidences argue for his composition of the tunes; cf. Hamm, p. 94. For the three tunes, NINETY-THIRD, VERNON, and ROCKBRIDGE, in modern reprints (with annotations), see Jackson, *Down-East Spirituals,* pp. 156 (no. 146), 35 (no. 19), and *Another Sheaf of White Spirituals* (Gainesville: University of Florida Press, 1952), p. 127 (no. 204). The harmonies, not printed by Jackson, lean so heavily on fourths as consonances that such a hymn as ROCKINGHAM (*Repository, Part Second,* 97 = *Kentucky Harmony,* p. 35 = *Southern Harmony,* 269 [= *Down-East Spirituals,* 158]) assumes the look of organum. But Chapin was not so conceited as to imagine his harmonizations faultless. In a letter to Andrew Law dated March 9, 1812, from Fleming County, Kentucky, he encloses a harmonization and asks, "Please to correct, and return." He also pleads, "Send me a treatise, or a letter on Composition. I wish for instruction." See Crawford, "Andrew Law," p. 338.

When such a folkish five-note tune as GLASGOW appears in *Part Second*, 1813 (42), labeled as a "new" composition by Dare, and with a different harmonization in *Kentucky Harmony*, 1815/6 (45), as a "new" piece by Davisson, the obvious explanation is that both worked with an already existing folkish melody. Similarly, Chapin's UNITIA (*Part Second*, 97 [230]) is in all likelihood his harmonization of an already existing melody. The willingness of these singing masters to cull the folk repertory assures their collections an appeal less class-conscious than that of the modish Mason manuals.

Who all these Western frontiersmen were has also begun to be investigated recently. For example, Ananias Davisson—too obscure for mention in the long list of tunesmiths prepared by W. S. Pratt and C. N. Boyd for the American Supplement to *Grove's Dictionary* (New York: Macmillan Co., 1920, pp. 386–391)—has yielded to George Pullen Jackson's research: [231] Davisson (1780–1857) grew up a staunch Presbyterian like the Chapins, with one of whom—"a teacher of the first eminence" who had been "teaching for fifteen years"—he seems to have studied after 1794. When Davisson reached Tennessee, the *Knoxville Register* for May 26, 1818, carried his typical announcement [232] of a new edition ready to sell (*Kentucky Harmony*, 2nd ed.), his general invitation to "all young people taught by [Capt. R.] Monday [233] to spend Saturday, June 20 singing," and his special invitation to Archibald Rhea, a precentor of the First Presbyterian Church who had previously taught at Lebanon, five miles away, to attend. The very homeliness of the beginnings along the frontier guaranteed that the music would stay close to the people.

---

[230] Tune in Lowens, "John Wyeth's *Repository*," p. 131, who says that it "seems to be derived from English folk song." Fortunately Lowens calls for the repeat of the last eight bars, as specified in the original. Jackson when reprinting often suppressed such repeats—thus blurring the tune structure, ABB.

[231] *White Spirituals in the Southern Uplands* (Chapel Hill: University of North Carolina Press, 1933), pp. 26–31. *Kentucky Harmony*, 2nd ed., 1817, is in the Library of Congress (M2116.D263). As in the fourth, the title page reads *Kentucky Harmony. Or, A Choice Collection of Psalm Tunes, Hymns, and Anthems; in Three Parts*. But the entire collection is in four-part harmony.

[232] Quoted in Emma K. Crews, "A History of Music in Knoxville, Tennessee, 1791 to 1910," D. Ed. dissertation, Florida State University, 1961, p. 8.

[233] *Ibid.*, p. 12. Davisson, *A Supplement to the Kentucky Harmony* (3rd ed., 1825), prints Monday's delightfully folkish tune KNOXVILLE. George Pullen Jackson, *Another Sheaf of White Spirituals*, p. 166 (no. 296), picked it up not from Davisson but from John B. Jackson's crudely printed *The Knoxville Harmony* (Madisonville, Tenn., 1838)—in which collection it is unattributed, arguing for it a close relationship with the Welsh air, *Y Glomen*. Davisson attributes TRANQUILITY to Monday = Munday, *The Kentucky Harmony*, p. 43. An equally folklike tune appeared with the same title in the pioneer Northern collection of folk hymns, Jeremiah Ingalls's *The Christian Harmony* (Exeter, N. H., 1805). Cf. *Another Sheaf*, p. 109 (no. 166).

Just as Little and Smith had disdained such enervating comforts as accidentals, so also Davisson and his frontier ilk "never were stopt by the interposition of an accidental flat, sharp, or natural, either to sink half a tone, raise half a tone, or make any primitive restoration."[234] Bare fourths and fifths, unalloyed diatonicism (often with modal flavor), abounding "prohibited" consecutives, a repertory favoring the old Yankee tunes (especially fuges), an invincible fondness for the shape notes invented by Little and Smith—these were the characteristics of the music system carried west and south by the Chapins, Davisson, and their followers.

In *America's Music,* Gilbert Chase summarizes George Pullen Jackson's remarks on such later "fasola folk" as James P. Carrell (1787–1854), who with David L. Clayton issued *The Virginia Harmony* (Winchester [Va.]: Samuel H. Davis, 1831 [LC M2117.C61 V5 1831]);[235] William Walker (1809–1875), whose *Southern Harmony* sold 600,000 copies[236] (four editions published 1835–1854 [LC M2117. W18 S5 1847]); and William Hauser (1812–1880), whose last publication, *The Olive Leaf* (Wadley, Jefferson Co., Ga.: Hauser and Turner, 1878), bridges the gap between revival and gospel song.[237] The musical examples in Chapter

[234] *The Kentucky Harmony,* 2nd ed., p. 5.

[235] Possessor of an imperfect second edition copy, Jackson thought no other copy of any edition survived (*White Spirituals in the Southern Uplands,* p. 35). The Library of Congress has both first and second (Winchester: Robinson & Hollis, 1836) editions. Robert G. McCutchan, *Hymns of the American Frontier* (New York: G. Schirmer, 1950), reharmonizes several tunes from *Virginia Harmony,* among them: "Blow ye trumpet, blow" = PORTSMOUTH, NEW (100), "Love divine, all loves excelling" = LOVE DIVINE (122), and "I want a principle within" = DEVOTION (35). The last tune, correctly ascribed by Clayton and Carrell to I. J. Pleyel (1757–1831), enters Lowell Mason's *Boston Handel and Haydn Society Collection* [1832 ed., p. 93] with BRATTLE STREET for its name. Another correctly ascribed Pleyel hymn in *Virginia Harmony,* p. 110, CONDOLENCE (theme from String Quartet, Op. 7, No. 4 [*ca.* 1782]) had already appeared in Bartholomew Brown's *Bridgewater Collection* (Boston, 1802), p. 27, in *The First Church Collection of Sacred Musick* (Boston: Thomas & Andrews, 1802 [2nd ed.], p. 61, and frequently thereafter. Lowell Mason, who arranged at least seven "Pleyel" hymns, enters *The Virginia Harmony,* 2nd ed., with WATCHMAN, p. 146, and SABBATH ("Safely through another week"), p. 177. "The Last Rose of Summer" enters the 2nd ed., p. 192, as ST. DENNIS. Chase reprints Carrell's DYING PENITENT (*Virginia Harmony,* 50 = Jackson's *Down-East Spirituals,* pp. 18–19 [no. 4] = Chase, pp. 192–193), but falls victim to Jackson's arbitrary changes of the original. Jackson identifies the folk sources for Carrell's tune in *Spiritual Folk-Songs of Early America* (New York: J. J. Augustin, 1937 [2nd ed., 1953]), p. 88 [no. 54].

[236] *White Spirituals in the Southern Uplands,* p. 63. Chapter VI tells Walker's story.

[237] *The Revivalist,* published by Joseph Hillman, Troy, New York, 1868, specialized in "choruses" like CANAAN (424 = *Hymns of the American Frontier,* 6), O HOW I LOVE JESUS (456), OLD SHIP ZION (375), among a total of 226 such refrain-songs. See *Spiritual Folk-Songs of Early America,* pp. 7–9. The verse-and-refrain pattern of the revival song joins with Sweet Adeline harmonies to make the gospel song. The

X of Chase's standard text sketch the profile of the rural music. At its most characteristic, the "air" of any given hymn sounds as if it should have been collected by Cecil J. Sharp and edited by Maud Karpeles.[238]

Charles Seeger, who studied the part-writing indigenous to the Southern fasola books ("Contrapuntal Style in the Three-Voice Shape-Note Hymns," in *The Musical Quarterly*, XXVI/4 [October, 1940], pp. 483–493), borrows WONDROUS LOVE from John Mc-Curry's *The Social Harp* (Philadelphia: S. C. Collins, 1868) for John A. and Alan Lomax's *Folk Song U. S. A.* (New York: Duell, Sloan and Pearce, 1947), pp. 348–349. This same folk hymn appears in Hauser's *The Olive Leaf*, p. 371, and may serve as an earnest of that immense repertory of folk melody recorded for posterity in nineteenth-century Southern shape-note books.

---

typical gospel song is a copyrighted commercial package designed for the quick dollar—or at least so contended Jackson in *White and Negro Spirituals*, pp. 273–274. Among the revival songs in *The Olive Leaf* the best known today are perhaps "Shall we gather at the river," p. 312 (words and music by Robert Lowry, 1864), "Pass me not, O gentle Saviour," p. 382 (words by Fanny Crosby, 1879, music by W. H. Doane), and "I will sing you a song of a beautiful land," p. 374 (words by Ellen H. Gates, music by Philip Phillips [*Hallowed Songs*]). "Christian, up! the day is breaking," words and music by Charles H. Gabriel "of Wilton Junction, Iowa, May 16th, 1878," p. 317, is the only example in the book by a composer whose successes in the gospel song arena were to match those of Irving Berlin in the commercial.

[238] Jackson outlines his system for detecting the secular originals in *Spiritual Folk-Songs*, pp. 17–21. See also *White and Negro Spirituals*, Chapter V, "The Carnal Lover is Plundered of His Tunes." If the tunes are so rarely original in the rural books from which Jackson extracted them, the question then arises: Is there anything distinctively "American" in William Moore's HOLY MANNA tune (*Columbian Harmony* [Cincinnati, 1825, but compiled in Wilson County, Tennessee]; *Southern Harmony* version reprinted in Barbour, *Church Music of William Billings*, p. 94, with comment), or in J. C. Lowry's PISGAH (*The Virginia Harmony*, 41), or in the ninety-six other folk hymns the tunes of which Jackson transcribes in *Spiritual Folk-Songs of Early America*, pp. 87–166? Similar questions arise so far as the many examples copied from Jackson in Chase's *America's Music*, Chapter X, are concerned.

9

NEGRO SPIRITUALS: ORIGIN AND PRESENT-DAY SIGNIFICANCE

In his epochal *Spiritual Folk-Songs of Early America,* George Pullen Jackson divides the repertory of the rural books for whites into: (1) religious ballads, with "Poor Wayfaring Stranger" as one of 51 examples; (2) folk hymns, with HOLY MANNA and PISGAH as two examples among 98; (3) revival "spiritual songs," [239] with "Roll Jordan Roll" and "Old-time Religion" as two well-known examples among 101. The third type, "the *spiritual songs,* rather than the *hymns* or the *ballads,*" came into full bloom with the millennial surge of the 1840's, and it was this type "which appealed subsequently most deeply to the Negroes and has reappeared most often among their religious songs," according to Jackson [240] who in *White and Negro Spirituals* (1943) documents his assertion with 114 parallels, extending to even such famed spirituals as "Down by the riverside" (pp. 192–193), "Go down, Moses" (180–181), "Go tell it on the mountain" (214–215), "Roll, Jordan" (180–181), "Sin-Sick Soul" (158–159), and "Were you there" (220–221). Convinced by the wealth of evidence, Jackson summarizes thus: "The Negroes' spirituals were, up to comparatively recent times, adopted from the stock of tunes and texts which originated in the white man's revivals." Since this revival music stemmed from a known folk tradition, "we may conclude then, and with a high degree of certainty, that the Afro-American has been a potent factor in the carrying on of the Celtic-English-American's folk songs." [241]

How the slaves came to learn the white man's repertory has been

[239] For the emergence of this type, see *White and Negro Spirituals,* pp. 118–123. For New England antecedents, see *Down-East Spirituals,* p. 234.

[240] *Spiritual Folk-Songs,* p. 9.

[241] "Early American Religious Folk Songs," in *Proceedings of the Music Teachers National Association, 1934* (Oberlin: The Association, 1935), pp. 78–79.

documented with gratifying fulness in Dena J. Epstein's "Slave Music in the United States before 1860; A Survey of Sources," in *Notes of the Music Library Association,* XX/2–3 (Spring and Summer, 1963), 195–212 and 377–390. The first of eight articles agreed upon by the group of slaves in Boston who early in October of 1693 started assembling themselves for Sunday evening worship reads in part (*Rules For the Society of Negroes. 1693.,* printed at Boston in broadside *ca.* 1706): "between the Two Prayers, a Psalm shall be sung." Cotton Mather's *Diary* records his having preached to the group in that same month on the text: "Princes shall come out of Egypt; Ethiopia shall soon stretch out her hands unto God" (Ps. 68:31). The early date for such a psalm-singing rule among the Boston Negroes takes on added luster when the date of the first New England publication of the Bay Psalm Book with notes is remembered —1698.

Not only did Negro psalm-singing get off to a head start in seventeenth-century Massachusetts, but also an occasional Negro in the north reversed the coin by becoming a singing-school teacher of whites before the end of the eighteenth century. The Congregational preacher and musician Andrew Law is our witness to one such Negro singing-school master in New York City, whom he had himself trained. In a letter to his brother William dated October 1, 1786 (Law Papers, William L. Clements Library), he rather ruefully confesses that his erstwhile Negro protégé is now competing with him.

This evening I opened to see if I could get a school, but very few attended. Frank the Negro who lived with me has about 40 scholars which he engaged to give up when I came, but he does not incline to now. . . . Every one to whom I bestow favours takes the bread out of my mouth.

Just as the Congregationalists began teaching Negroes to sing psalms from the moment that slaves appeared in the colony, so also the Presbyterians farther south insisted on beginning with the same kind of emphasis. Such early white missionaries amongst them as the Presbyterian Samuel Davies wrote from Hanover, Virginia, to a friend in London in the spring of 1755:

The Books I principally want for them are, *Watts's Psalms and Hymns,* and *Bibles.* . . . I am the rather importunate for a good Number of these, as I cannot but observe, that the *Negroes,* above all the Human Species that I ever knew, have an Ear for Musick, and a kind of extatic delight in

Psalmody; and there are no books they learn so soon, or take so much Pleasure in.[242]

Upon receiving the books he wrote on March 2, 1756, a letter of thanks to his London benefactor, "R. C." (reprinted in *The Evangelical and Literary Magazine,* IV/10, October, 1821 [edited by John H. Rice at Richmond, Va.], pp. 544–549). This long letter reads in part:

The books were all very acceptable, but none more so than the *Psalms* and *Hymns* which enable them to gratifie their peculiar taste for psalmody. Sundry of them have lodged all night in my kitchen, and sometimes when I have waked about 2 or 3 o'clock in the morning, a torrent of sacred harmony poured into my chamber, and carried my mind away to heaven. In this seraphick exercise, some of them spend almost the whole night (p. 546).

Davies, who later became president of the college that has now grown into Princeton University, assured "R. C." in this letter that "these sacred concerts" would "surprize and please you more than an Oratorio, or a St. Cecilia's day." For a precedent in teaching the slaves sacred music he had the example of the white missionary in Charleston, South Carolina, who already in 1745 was gathering such large and enthusiastic groups of Negroes to "sing psalms" in his private house that their assemblies were becoming a "nuisance to the neighborhood" (*Evangelical and Literary Magazine,* IV/10, 550). Also, Davies could look to the example of Joseph Ottolenghe, a Piedmont-born Jew who after embracing Christianity emigrated to Georgia in 1751 and within two years had his numerous Negro pupils singing psalms with great gusto (James B. Lawrence, "Religious Education of the Negro in the Colony of Georgia," *Georgia Historical Quarterly,* XIV/1 [March, 1930], pp. 42–49).

In a letter dated November 19, 1753, Ottolenghe had described his daily routine with his Negro charges thus:

I generally sing a Psalm with them, such as are us'd at Church. Several of them have really good Voices, [and] having learn'd ye Words & Tune at Schole, join ye Congregation at Church.

---

[242] Quoted by Epstein, but with wrong date, from Appendix to Benjamin Fawcett, *A Compassionate Address to the Christian Negroes in Virginia* (Salop [England]: F. Eddoes & F. Cotton, 1756), p. 37. The letter was addressed not to "Mr. *Bellamy* of *Bethlem* in *New England*" (Appendix, p. 33) but to "R. C." See George H. Bost, "Samuel Davies: Colonial Revivalist and Champion of Religious Toleration," University of Chicago Ph.D. dissertation, March 1942, p. 291 and especially note on pp. 135–136. "R. C." responded with some five hundred books; John and Charles Wesley contributed books also (*ibid.,* p. 136).

With such recent successes in South Carolina and Georgia to inspire him, Davies obviously had every reason to anticipate good returns on the books requested from "R. C." of London in 1755 "to gratifie their peculiar taste for psalmody," and which were received in 1756.

Somewhat later Davies wrote again to "R. C." (August 26, 1758):

I can hardly express the pleasure it affords me to turn to that part of the gallery where they sit, and see so many of them with their Psalm or Hymn Books, turning to the part then sung, and assisting their fellows, who are beginners, to find the place; and then all breaking out in a torrent of sacred harmony, enough to bear away the whole congregation to heaven.

However, psalm and hymn books were perennially in such short supply that many Southern churches as late as the 1840's still resorted to "lining out" the hymns. "The minister reads a line, and the congregation sing it; then reads the next, and so on. The slaves (to whose accommodation the galleries are frequently devoted,) are so accustomed to this way of singing that they seem to think the tune incomplete without the intervention of *spoken* lines." So wrote a correspondent in *The Musical Gazette*, I/12 (Boston, July 6, 1846), 91, continuing with an anecdote of a lone Negro who alternately spoke and sang. "Many of the slave melodies are well known at the north . . . many of them sing all common psalm tunes with accuracy, and in addition there are verses evidently original."

Dwight's Journal of Music, X/7 (November 15, 1856), 51–52, reprints an article entitled "Songs of the Blacks" from a New York weekly, *The Evangelist*, which had carried it unsigned the previous month. Like much later description of Negro activity, this article loses critical value because the author prefers to indulge in racial theorizing. Nonetheless, the author does record the Negroes' participation in camp meetings.[243] "As hundreds assemble at a camp meeting in the woods, and join the chorus of such a [Watts] hymn as 'When I can read my title clear,/To mansions in the sky,' [244] the unimpassioned hearer is almost lifted from his feet by the volume and majesty

---

[243] For an early description of camp meetings, see Charles William Janson, *The Stranger in America* (London: James Cundee, 1807), pp. 106–107. Epstein invites attention to the abundant literature on the "participation of the Negroes in the camp meeting movement"; see Epstein, p. 202n. The indispensable authority on the music of the movement as such is John Norman Sims's "The Hymnody of the Camp Meeting Tradition," Union Theological Seminary D. S. M. dissertation, 1960.

[244] For the tunes, see indexed entries in Jackson, *Another Sheaf*, p. 232, under "When I can read my title clear." The camp meeting and revival songs often included "Glory, Hallelujah" refrains. For the text of such a refrain song popular in 1831 (printed in 1839) see Epstein, p. 385

of the sound." This open-air singing reflects the fact that "the Negro is a natural musician" who "will learn to play on an instrument more quickly than a white man."

So far as style of singing is concerned, a Russian traveler visiting a Philadelphia Negro Methodist Church [245] published in 1815 a not very sympathetic account of the "loud, shrill" unison wail of the congregation responding to the lined-out psalms, and of the twenty minutes taken up after the sermon by the men and women (seated separately on right and left) singing psalm stanzas alternately.[246] Part-singing was unknown in this church, nor does polyphony seem to have been used farther South. Certainly it was not used in Georgia, on the authority of the antislavery English actress Frances Anne ("Fanny") Kemble, who wrote in her *Journal of a Residence on a Georgian Plantation in 1838–1839* (London: Longmans, Green, 1863, pp. 140 and 159): "the whole congregation uplifted their voices in a hymn, the first high wailing notes of which—sung all in unison . . ."; "they all sing in unison, having never it appears, attempted or heard anything like part-singing." Though agreeing that Negro tunes were "often plaintive and pretty," she claimed that "almost always" they were plagiarized from "white men's" tunes (p. 160). Both she and her son-in-law, who visited the same plantation after the Civil War, agreed that "their voices have a peculiar quality, and their intonations and delicate variations cannot be reproduced on paper."

Although some Negro secular songs were printed before the war and others were transcribed in manuscript collections (Epstein, pp. 209–211 and 390), the first and still one of the most important collections with religious texts appeared in the early Reconstruction period, *Slave Songs of the United States* (New York: A. Simpson & Co., 1867). W. F. Allen, C. P. Ware, and Lucy McKim Garrison co-operated in issuing this *Lyra Africana*—as they dubbed their compilation (p. xxxvii). "The greater part of the music here presented has been taken down by the editors from the lips of the colored people themselves" (p. iii); of the 136 songs, all without harmony because

[245] Janson comments on the great success of the early American Methodists in appealing to "the slaves, whom they receive into their congregation, and place among the most select part of their white brethren" (*op. cit.,* p. 100). Peter Neilson, *Recollections of a Six Years' Residence in the United States of America* (Glasgow: David Robertson, 1830), p. 258, comments on the remarkable success of both Methodists and Baptists in winning Negroes, and gives samples of texts not "reverential or refined" sung by the Negro converts.

[246] Avraham Yarmolinsky, *Picturesque United States of America 1811, 1812, 1813 being A Memoir on Paul Svinin* (New York: William E. Rudge, 1930), p. 20. Original in Pavel Petrovich Svinin, *Opyt zhivopisnago puteshetviĩa po Sĩevernoĩ Amerikĩe* (St. Petersburg, 1815), pp. 48–49.

"the Negroes have no part-singing" (p. xxi), the first 43 were collected "by Mr. Charles P. Ware, chiefly at Coffin's Point, St. Helena Island" (p. iii), but new materials from Virginia and South Carolina enlarged the original corpus threefold. "The songs from Virginia are the most wild and strange" (p. xix), and the editors cite the piece shown in Example 17. The offbeat pattern in this hymn, collected by

Example 17   *O'er the crossing*
Slave Songs of the United States (New York: A. Simpson & Co., 1867), p. 72 (no. 93)

Capt. James S. Rogers, matches similar characteristically Negroid rhythmic patterns in "The Lonesome Valley" (no. 7), "The Graveyard" (no. 21), "I saw the beam in my sister's eye" (no. 23), "Gwine follow" (no. 25), and some dozen other songs in the 115-page anthology. "The preference for off-beats is of African origin," writes Hans Nathan in "Early Banjo Tunes and American Syncopation," in *The Musical Quarterly*, XLII/4 (October, 1956, p. 467), invoking Richard A. Waterman's authority (" 'Hot' Rhythm in Negro Music"). Nathan cites parts of "I saw the beam" and "O'er the crossing." [247]

The year 1867 was made memorable not only by the publication of *Slave Songs* but also by the appearance in the June *Atlantic Monthly* (XIX, cxvi, 685–694) of an epoch-making article entitled "Negro Spirituals." Contributed by Thomas Wentworth Higginson (1823–1911, Harvard Divinity School graduate 1847), the Unitarian minister who left his Worcester pulpit to serve as an infantry colonel with Negro troops in South Carolina 1862–1864, this essay was later to reappear as Chapter IX in his memoirs, *Army Life in a Black Regiment* (Boston: Fields, Osgood & Co., 1870). In this article, Higginson remembers having heard Negro spirituals sung by South Carolina friends visiting Boston as early as the 1830's, and cites

[247] Compare Jackson, *White and Negro Spirituals*, pp. 257–258. For Jackson's discussion of surge singing, see pp. 249–252.

"Blow your trumpet Gabriel" (p. 690, no. 25) as an example. The favorite spiritual among his troops, "Hold your light," was "sung with no accompaniment but the measured clapping of hands and the clatter of many feet" (p. 685). So far as scriptural references were concerned, Revelation and the Pentateuch "constituted their Bible" (p. 688); the rest was dross. "Wrestling Jacob" was the spiritual among the thirty-six collected by Higginson (texts only) that struck him as "wildest and most striking of the whole series" (p. 689). He recognized the musical indebtedness of the Negro spiritual to white camp-meeting forebears ("the three just given are modifications of an old camp-meeting melody," p. 691) but was not sufficiently acquainted with "the Methodist hymn-books" to find the camp-meeting melodies for "Sweet Music," "Good News," and "The Heavenly Road." Of African influences, he saw little trace unless the line "We'll cross de mighty Myo" incorporated the word *Mawa* which "in the Cameroon dialect . . . signifies 'to die' " (p. 686). One spiritual saluted the Blessed Virgin thus: "O hail, Mary, hail! Hail, Mary, hail!" (no. 4); and for this spiritual he postulated Roman Catholic influence, since he "had several men from St. Augustine who held in a dim way to that faith." Tracing the origins of any given spiritual, text or music, was like walking on quicksand, however— because "they often strayed into wholly new versions, which some-times became popular, and entirely banished the others" (p. 693) during only the two years that he spent with his colored regiment. Also, Negroes from one Southern state differed from those of another in the texts which they wedded to any given spiritual melody (p. 686). Higginson was himself not enough of a musician to record the tunes that he kept hearing, nor did he have the scientific interest that moved such an earlier investigator of New World Negro music as Sir Hans Sloane to have someone else write them down.[248] But at least he could recognize the camp-meeting origin of many of the melodies and know that most of the spirituals sung around him were in minor keys (pp. 687, 694).

The Negroes themselves could call a "song that is quite secular in its character" a spiritual, according to Higginson (p. 693). His min-isterial background perhaps accounts for his neglect of the "shout," which he defines as a "rhythmical barbaric dance" accompanied by

---

[248] The earliest New World Negro music to be published was taken on the island of Jamaica in 1688 by a "Mr. Baptiste" and published at pages l–li of Sloane's *A Voyage to the Islands Madera, Barbados, Nieves, S. Christophers and Jamaica* (London: B. M., 1707). Recurrent syncopation and the flatted 7th are already hallmarks of the Negro singing style this early.

their "chanting, often harshly, but always in the most perfect time, [of] some monotonous refrain" (p. 685). The question as to whether the shout should be considered as religious music had already been long agitated. In a letter from Pine Grove Plantation on St. Helena Island, dated April 29, 1862, one of the New England female workers sent South to aid the former slaves wrote as follows of a night praise-meeting:

Then they shook hands all round, when one of the young girls struck up one of their wild songs, and we waited listening to them for twenty minutes more. It was not a regular "shout," but some of them clapped their hands, and they stamped in time. . . . As we walked home we asked Cuffy [Negro ex-slave] if they considered the "shout" as part of their religious worship; he said yes, that "it exercise the frame."

On Saturday nights when new candidates for church membership were being examined, they would begin about ten and continue "the shout till near daylight, when they can see to go home." Even the young children learned the movements: they "move round in a circle, backwards, or sideways, with their feet and arms keeping energetic time, and their whole bodies undergoing most extraordinary contortions, while they sing at the top of their voices the refrain to some song sung by an outsider." [249]

Since the shout—a "rhythmical barbaric dance," as Higginson had labeled it—goes by almost unnoticed in his *Atlantic Monthly* article, a reviewer in *The Nation,* IV, no. 100 (May 30, 1867, p. 432, col. 2), chastised him as follows:

We regret that Mr. Higginson did not also, as he might have done so well, and as is almost necessary to a tolerable appreciation of the "sperichils" describe for us the "shout." This is a ceremony which the white clergymen are inclined to discountenance, and even of the colored elders some of the more discreet try sometimes to put on a face of discouragement.

According to the *Nation* reviewer, the shout brings together as many as half the Negroes on a plantation. A lengthy description follows (p. 433):

The benches are pushed back to the wall when the formal meeting is over, and old and young, men and women, sprucely-dressed young men, grotesquely half-clad field-hands—the women generally with gay handkerchiefs

---

[249] Elizabeth W. Pearson, *Letters from Port Royal written at the time of the Civil War* (Boston: W. B. Clarke Co., 1906), pp. 26–27, 34, 293.

twisted about their heads and with short skirts, boys with tattered shirts and men's trousers, young girls barefooted—all stand up in the middle of the floor, and when the "sperichil" is struck up, begin first walking and by-and-by shuffling round, one after the other, in a ring. The foot is hardly taken from the floor, and the progression is mainly due to a jerking, hitching motion, which agitates the entire shouter, and soon brings out streams of perspiration. Sometimes he dances silently, sometimes as he shuffles he sings the chorus of the spiritual, and sometimes the song itself [i.e., the strophe] is also sung by the dancers. But more frequently a band, composed of some of the best singers and of tired shouters, stand at the side of the room to "base" the others, singing the body of the song and clapping their hands together or on the knees. Song and dance are alike extremely energetic, and often, when the shout lasts into the middle of the night, the monotonous thud, thud of the feet prevents sleep within half a mile of the praise-house.

With these three publications—Higginson's article in *Atlantic Monthly,* the anonymous response in *The Nation* criticizing him for having been too much of a prim clergyman to give the "barbaric shout" its due meed, and best of all, the 136 *Slave Songs of the United States*—1867 ranks among scholars as the most important year of the century, so far as the history of the Negro spiritual is concerned. Authenticity was the goal of the compilers of *Slave Songs,* and authentic interpretation was the aim of Higginson and of his *Nation* critic. The rest of the century saw a procession of "prettied-up" versions and interpretations. Only five years after *Slave Songs,* Biglow & Main [250] in New York issued the first collection of *Jubilee Songs: as sung by the Jubilee Singers of Fisk University.* Theodore F. Seward (1835–1902) [251]—aligned with the Lowell Mason–George F. Root–William B. Bradbury musical axis, sometime supervisor of music at Orange, New Jersey, and prominent editor—claimed in the preface to have "taken down [the melodies] from the singing of the band, during repeated interviews for the purpose" (p. 3). In his "technical analysis" (p. 2) he wrote: "the first peculiarity that strikes the singer is in the rhythm." The following culled from "The Rocks and the Mountains" (p. 24) struck Seward especially:

[250] Organized in 1868, this firm at first specialized in William B. Bradbury's books, later in the "Gospel Hymns" series of Ira D. Sankey (1840–1908), Philip P. Bliss (1838–1876), James McGranahan (1840–1897), and George C. Stebbins (1846–1945). By 1886 the firm claimed having sold 18,000,000 hymn books, and by 1900 50,000,000 of the Sankey variety alone. See *Grove's Dictionary, American Supplement* (1930), pp. 132, 224.

[251] Cf. J. B. I. Marsh, *The Story of the Jubilee Singers* (London: Hodder & Stroughton, 1877 [7th ed.]), pp. 39, 81, 121–122.

Mere authenticity having never been the announced goal of the touring Jubilee Singers, but rather fund-raising for Fisk, Seward therefore hastened to assure the polite public of "the quickness with which they have received impressions and adopted improvements from the cultivated music they have heard" (p. 3). "By the severe discipline to which the Jubilee Singers have been subjected in the school-room, they have been educated out of the peculiarities of the Negro dialect," proudly boasted E. M. Cravath, the Field Secretary of the American Missionary Association (sponsoring agency for the tour), who was to become president of Fisk in 1875.

They have also received considerable musical instruction and have become familiar with much of our best sacred and classical music, and this has modified their manner of execution. They do not attempt to imitate the grotesque bodily motions or the drawling intonations that often characterize the singing of great congregations of the colored people in their excited religious meetings (p. 29).

The enormous success of the group inspired the Reverend Theodore L. Cuyler (1822–1909), pastor of Lafayette Avenue Presbyterian Church in Brooklyn and one of America's most renowned preachers, to write a letter to the *New York Tribune,* duly reprinted in *Jubilee Songs* (p. 32):

I never saw a cultivated Brooklyn assemblage so moved and melted under the magnetism of music before. The wild melodies of these emancipated slaves touched the fount of tears, and grey-haired men wept like little children. In the program last evening were not only the well-known slave songs "Go down, Moses," "Roll, Jordan, roll," and "Turn back Pharaoh's army," but a fresh collection of the most weird and plaintive hymns sung in the plantation cabins in the dark days of bondage. One young negress— exceeding "black yet comely"—sang a wild yet most delicious melody, "I'll hear the trumpet sound in the morning," which was the very embodiment of African heart-music. Listening to their rich, plaintive voices, one might imagine himself in the veritable Uncle Tom's cabin of the "old dispensation."

"I'll hear the trumpet sound in the morning" (included, of course, in the very collection [p. 15] that the Reverend Theo. L. Cuyler's newspaper puff was designed to advertise) joined "Steal away" and "Swing low, sweet chariot" to make a collection of twenty-four *Jubilee Songs,* none of which had ever before reached print—or at least so claimed the American Missionary Association ("neither the words or the music have ever before been published, or even reduced to written form" [p. 29]). The tune for "I'll hear the trumpet" originated "near Atlanta," according to John W. Work (1871–1925), when "a slave was sold from his wife and it seemed that he would really die of a broken heart." James Weldon Johnson corroborates the "Negro" origin of this tune when he calls it "the Negro's piercing lyrical cry." [252]

If so, B. F. White plagiarized it when he published the same tune under the title THE MORNING TRUMPET in *The Sacred Harp, A Collection of Psalm and Hymn Tunes . . . together with nearly one hundred pieces never before published* (Philadelphia: T. K. & P. G. Collins, 1844), crediting himself with its confection. No doubt White was himself a Georgian (residing at Hamilton, Harris County, when he and E. J. King published *The Sacred Harp*). Because so many of the *Jubilee Songs,* of the "Cabin and Plantation Songs as sung by Hampton Students arranged by Thomas P. Fenner in charge of musical department at Hampton" in *Hampton and its Students* (New York: G. P. Putnam's Sons, 1875), and of *Revival Hymns and Plantation Melodies* (Cincinnati: Marshall W. Taylor,[253] 1882) bear affinities with tunes already published in Southern white collections, the Fisk *Jubilee* "unpublished" 1872 version of the "very embodiment

Example 18   *The Morning Trumpet*

The Sacred Harp (Philadelphia: B. F. White (1800–1879)
T. K. & P. G. Collins, 1844), p. 85

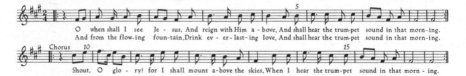

O when shall I see   Je - sus, And reign with Him a - bove, And shall hear the trum-pet sound in that morn-ing.
And from the flow-ing   foun-tain, Drink ev - er-last-ing love, And shall hear the trum-pet sound in that morn-ing.
Shout, O   glo - ry! for I shall mount a-bove the skies, When I hear the trum-pet sound in that morn - ing.

Jubilee Songs (New York: Biglow
& Main, 1872), p. 15

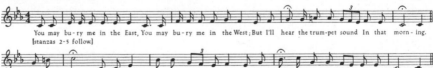

You may bu-ry me in the East, You may bu-ry me in the West; But I'll hear the trum-pet sound In that morn-ing.
[stanzas 2-5 follow.]
In that   morn - ing, my Lord, How I   long   to go, For to hear the trum-pet sound, In that morn-ing.

of African heart-music" is shown in Example 18 for comparison with B. F. White's version of the same tune published at Philadelphia twenty-eight years earlier. "The only essential changes that the Negro

[252] Quoted in *White Spirituals in the Southern Uplands*, p. 254.
[253] Taylor was the only prominent Negro collector of Negro spirituals, but the music is so replete with obvious errors that none of the transcriptions can be trusted.

singers have made in the earlier white camp-meeting melody are their raising the seventh and injecting a sharped sixth," claims Jackson, who adds that even the accidentals may well have been intended in the B. F. White original. "The hymn is a typical campmeeting type, with its 'Shout O Glory!' refrain and trumpet burden added to John Leland's text," says Annabel Morris Buchanan in discussing its origins (*Folk Hymns of America* [New York: J. Fischer & Bro., 1938], p. xviii; music at p. 22).

Wherever the spirituals taken on tour by the Jubilee Singers originated, one fact is sure: these Fisk University singers inspired so many imitators that by 1875 their market was glutted by "rival companies." Hampton Institute engaged Fenner in June, 1872, expressly to build a touring group "for Northern work." By February, 1873, he had them ready to start north on their first tour. As with all these groups, churches served as their base of operations into whatever community they traveled.

Fenner claimed first publication of "Hear de Lambs a-cryin'," "My Lord, what a Mornin'," "Nobody knows the trouble I've seen," "Run, Mary, run," and of several other prime favorites.[254] However, "Nobody knows the trouble" had appeared in *Slave Songs,* 1867 (p. 55), "Swing low, sweet chariot" in *Jubilee Songs* (p. 6), to mention no others. Already in Fenner's preface he confessed that the freed Negroes "have an unfortunate tendency to despise" the spirituals "as a vestige of slavery." He claimed also that the music was so rapidly passing away that it would be lost to future generations if not published.

Apart from the moot questions of white cognates for certain Negro spirituals, and of first publication dates for various favorites, the double meaning of many famous ones such as "Steal away" (= steal away north) has been argued heatedly by the polemicists. The Moses of "Go down, Moses" has been identified as Harriet Tubman (1821?–1913), herself a fugitive slave who became the leader of the Underground Railroad.[255] Some writers argue that even today *double entendre* has not lost its importance, and take for an example such an anthem as "We shall overcome"—the melody of which is much older than the text. Without attempting to trace its ultimate origin, the

[254] See Mary Frances Morgan and Helen W. Ludlow, *Hampton and Its Students* (New York: G. P. Putnam's Sons, 1875), p. 172: "The melodies in this book . . . are published here for the first time."

[255] Harold Courlander, *Negro Folk Music, U. S. A.* (New York: Columbia University Press, 1963), pp. 42–43, 291 (notes 3–4), citing Irwin Silber, *Songs of the Civil War,* p. 270.

date when the melody was first confided to print can be pushed back to at least November, 1792, when *The European Magazine and London Review,* XXII, 385–386, published it under the title of "The Sicilian Mariner's Hymn to the Virgin" (with the text beginning *O sanctissima, O piissima*). But the present text—copyrighted as recently as 1960 by Guy Carawan, Frank Hamilton, Zilphia Horton, and Pete Seeger—carries as large a freight of double meaning as any "Go down, Moses" or "We'll soon be free" of the last century, according to many students of the civil rights movement.[256]

The role of spirituals, regardless of how much veiled meaning is read into the texts, still looms large enough for Harold Courlander to devote a chapter to "Anthems and Spirituals as Oral Literature" in *Negro Folk Music, U. S. A.,* and to transcribe twenty-four songs with "religious" text against only nineteen with "secular" text, when showing the 1963 reader what elements are most vital and alive in the present-day Negro milieu.[257]

Hymnbook editors, who continue to shrink from other types of rural expression, make an exception for spirituals—if "properly" harmonized. *The Pilgrim Hymnal,* 1958, edited musically by Hugh Porter, late head of the Union Theological Seminary School of Sacred Music in New York, includes seven Negro spirituals (against nine tunes by Mason, five by Bradbury, and eleven by John B. Dykes). "Were you there," "Lord, I want to be a Christian," and "Go tell it" are the pentatonic melodies among the seven spirituals in this hymnal for the Congregational Church. As if *entrée* into the genteel company of an official hymnal were insufficient, Negro spirituals have also been saluted by art composers so dignified as Daniel Gregory Mason, who based his String Quartet in G minor, Op. 19 (G. Schirmer for S. P. A. M., 1930) on such spirituals as "Deep River," and Leo Sowerby, who dedicated a prelude on "Were you there" to Vernon de Tar (H. W. Gray, 1956).

Another composer for whom spirituals have served as fertile source-

---

[256] See "Moment of History," *New Yorker,* March 27, 1965, pp. 37–38.

[257] Courlander, pp. 35–79; 223–260. The last musical example, "Russia, Let That Moon Alone" (p. 260), is a street gospel song recorded for Folkways Records from the singing of Sister Dora Alexander in New Orleans. For a history of Negro gospel, based largely on data supplied by the veteran New York radio personality Joe Bostic, see Claude Hall, "Negro Gospel," in *Billboard,* LXXVII/44 (October 23, 1965), p. 71; also Eliot Tiegel, "From Prayer House to Plush Nightclub," same issue, pp. 80–81, 94. The outstanding Negro gospel composers of the 1940's were William Dorsey and Roberta Martin. In the 1950's James Cleveland, Alex Bradford, Raymond Razzberry, Leon Lumpkin, and Jessie Dickson took the lead. Because Negro gospel is "created by Negroes for Negroes . . . the songs lose a lot of their universal appeal" (Hall, "Negro Gospel," p. 71, quoting Bostic).

material must not be overlooked, even though he was not an American: Samuel Coleridge-Taylor (1875–1912). Son of an African physician from Sierra Leone, he first became acquainted with spirituals during the English tours of the Fisk Jubilee Singers; and it was from Seward's already-mentioned "correct" Jubilee transcriptions that Coleridge-Taylor derived "Nobody knows the trouble I see," second version (Overture to his *Song of Hiawatha,* Op. 30, No. 3, premiered Norwich Musical Festival, October 6, 1899) and "I'm troubled in mind" (*Symphonic Variations,* Op. 63, Queen's Hall, Philharmonic Society's Concert, June 14, 1906). "Many thousands gone" prominently enters the original draft of his Violin Concerto, second movement. What is more, he arranged *Twenty-Four Negro Melodies* (Op. 59) for piano, with "Deep River," "My Lord delivered Daniel," "Run, Mary, run," "Sometimes I feel like a motherless child," and "Steal away" forming nos. 10, 18, 21–23—to mention no other Jubilee favorites. Sir Charles Villiers Stanford (1852–1924, professor of music at Cambridge University after 1887 and Coleridge-Taylor's teacher) recognized at once the filiation of many of the Negro Spirituals chosen for this anthology. In a congratulatory letter dated May 16, 1905 (W. C. Berwick Sayers, *Samuel Coleridge-Taylor, Musician* [London: Cassell and Co., 1915], pp. 266–267), he wrote:

MY DEAR COLERIDGE-TAYLOR,—It is very good of you to send me the [Twenty-Four Negro] Melodies. They look most characteristic and interesting. I wish you would send a copy to Percy Grainger, who is greatly interested in folk-songs. By the way, one of the tunes, "The Angels changed my Name," is an Irish tune, and also I think, "The Pilgrim's Song." Like some of the Negro tunes Dvořák got hold of, these have reached the American Negroes through the Irish Americans. A curious instance of the transmigration of folk-songs.—Your very sincerely, C. V. STANFORD.

10

DIVERGING CURRENTS, 1850 – PRESENT

ALREADY by 1850 the American denominations [258] had so drawn their social lines that some ministered to the wealthy and élite in big cities,[259] while others served the common folk on farms and frontiers. Speaking of one "élite" denomination in a course of historical lectures given at Berlin in 1854, Philip Schaff claimed that the Protestant Episcopal Church had addressed itself "heretofore almost exclusively to the higher classes of society, and had rather discouraged the poor man from joining it." [260] With such a constituency, the music published for use in Episcopal churches at mid-century sounded quite a different note from that prevailing in publications for frontier churches, or even for middle-class urban churches.

Typical of the successful city church musician was Henry Wilson (1828–1878). His European studies (1854–1855) resulted from a chance encounter with Alexander Wheelock Thayer—who, having read of an Episcopal church organist in Greenfield (Massachusetts) capable of "taking Jullien's 'Prima Donna Waltz' and in a flash arranging it as a hymn 'A charge to keep I have' for the choir to sing the next Sunday, told a stranger on the train 'that is the sort of man I should like to know.' " [261] As the anecdote runs, the stranger replied,

[258] For music in two denominations neglected in the present study, see Raymond J. Martin, "The Transition from Psalmody to Hymnody in Southern Presbyterianism, 1753–1906," S. M. D. dissertation, Union Theological Seminary, 1963; Carlton Y. Smith, "Early Lutheran Hymnody in America From the Colonial Period to the Year 1850," Ph.D. dissertation, University of Southern California, 1956; Edward C. Wolf, "Lutheran Church Music in America during the Eighteenth and Early Nineteenth Centuries," Ph.D. dissertation, Illinois University, 1960.

[259] Cf. A. P. Allwardt, "Sacred Music in New York City, 1800–1850," S. M. D. dissertation, Union Theological Seminary, 1950. James William Thompson's "Music and Musical Activities in New England, 1800–1838," Ph.D. dissertation, George Peabody College for Teachers, 1963, gathers useful data on city church music in Providence, Boston, and elsewhere.

[260] *America. A Sketch of the Political, Social, and Religious Character* (New York: C. Scribner, 1855), p. 164.

[261] Frances H. Johnson, *Musical Memories of Hartford* (Hartford: Witkower's, 1931), p. 18. This story, though *bien trouvé*, stumbles on one inconsistency: Thayer was not appointed consul at Trieste until 1865.

"I am the man," whereupon Thayer suggested Wilson's accompanying him to Europe. Upon returning home, Wilson accepted in 1855
the position of organist at Christ Church, Hartford, Connecticut,
occupying it for the next twenty-two years.

His *Christ Church Collection of Sacred Music* (New York: S. T.
Gordon, 1861) dons regal attire with forty (of the sixty-five) psalms,
hymns, and canticles borrowed from such purple composers as "Mendelssohn, Mozart, Rossini, Schumann, & others." His "others" include
Handel, Haydn, Weber, Marschner, Thalberg, Herz, and Hérold—but
no Americans except himself. Mendelssohn's *Lieder ohne Worte,* Op.
38, No. 3; Op. 53, No. 2; Op. 19, No. 1; Op. 30, No. 3; and "If
with all your hearts" from *Elijah* (to other words) prove the easily
identifiable originals for Wilson's Psalm 72, Hymns 177, 51, 167, and
18; Mozart's *O Isis und Osiris* is source of his Psalm 87; Handel's
"I know that my Redeemer" becomes his Psalm 18; Weber's "But now
there falls a milder light" (Huon's aria) his Hymn 172. Even when
he condescends to so commonplace a text as Toplady's "Rock of
Ages" (Hymn 139), he elevates it by wedding it to Schumann's
Widmung. Apart from a dozen suavely Mendelssohnian items by
himself, he makes room for a *Benedic anima mea* of his fellow Hartford organist—Henry Greatorex (1811–1858)—whose name is kept
alive in hymnbooks today with a *Gloria Patri,* but who was American
only by adoption.

"Elevated" as were Wilson's musical intentions, a higher level yet
was sought in the 203-page *Cathedral Chants: including the Gregorian
Tones. Adapted to the Canticles, and Occasional Services, of the
Protestant Episcopal Church . . . By S. Parkman Tuckerman, Mus.
Doc.,* published at Boston by Oliver Ditson in 1858. Dr. Tuckerman
(1819–1890),[262] successively organist in New York City of Trinity
Chapel (1855) and in Boston of St. Paul's Church (1863), must
surely be the first American editor who so reveled in his own Lambeth degree (1853) as to have added Mus. Doc. after the names of
every doctor from William Crotch to Edward Hodges (1796–1867)[263]

---

[262] See Janet M. Green's article in "Musical Biographies" (*American History and
Encyclopedia of Music* [Toledo: Irving Squire, 1908], Vol. II), pp. 413–414. In
England Novello, Ewer published Tuckerman's ambitious *A Morning and Evening
Service in Eb* before 1853. He was the first American-born composer to publish settings of the Magnificat and of the uncut Benedictus. (The American Episcopal Church
until 1891 accepted only the evening canticles first allowed in the "black rubric"
prayerbook of 1552.) His *A Morning Service in G* was also published by the same
firm before his Lambeth degree.

[263] Organist and choirmaster at Trinity, New York, 1839–1858, Hodges (born
in Bristol) was a Cambridge Mus. Doc., 1825, who arrived in New York from
Toronto in 1839. For a compendious biography, see A. H. Messiter, *A History of*

who gains admittance to his select book. He proves also to be the morning star of that large group of American church composers whose lights have shown at their brightest in prize contests, by including at pages 191–203 his own Te Deum, "written in competition for a prize of One Hundred dollars offered by the last General Convention of the Protestant Episcopal Church." [264] Further to forestall the future, when nothing is so important as length, he prefaces his Te Deum at page 191 with the astute promise that "the time of performance should not exceed seven minutes."

Wilson and Tuckerman appealed about 1860 to a metropolitan seaboard sector of the American public, and—if Philip Schaff was right [265]—offended the masses by their "exclusiveness and pedantry." What was worse, such snobbery did not always guarantee quality. George W. Morgan's shabby Morning Service (1864) boasted as its best title to fame the fact that it had been "sung at St. Paul's, London" before being introduced at Grace Church, New York, and H. S. Cutler (1824–1902), organist at Trinity Church, tried puffing the two equally vapid canticles in his *Melodia Sacra* (1852) with an "approved-in-England" label. Essentially better music was being heard in New York at the Broadway Tabernacle, where Bradbury [266] spoke the language of the masses not only in his hymns ("Just as I am" [1849], "Sweet hour of prayer" [1860], "He leadeth me" [1864]) but also in such lengthier works as the cantata *Esther, the Beautiful Queen* and the anthem *And it shall come to pass in the last days* ("sung at the closing services of the Broadway Tabernacle Church on April 26, 1857"). At his weakest in such a maudlin effusion as "The Blind Orphan Girl"—a solo to melodeon accompaniment overlaid with many a *rallentando con espressione,* harmonized with barber-

---

the Choir and Music of Trinity Church (New York: Edwin S. Gorham, 1906), pp. 39–72. He composed twenty-five anthems and seven services (p. 69). Apart from his own music, he used nothing but English works spiced with two Italian anthems during his twenty-year reign at Trinity (pp. 71–72).

[264] Te Deum republished with slight alterations in *A Morning Service in F* by J. Alfred Novello (London), pp. 1–10; Benedictus (*Cathedral Chants,* pp. 200–203 ["the proper time of performance is three minutes"]) in Novello, pp. 11–19. The 1789 American prayerbook sanctioned only four verses of the Benedictus (Luke 1:68–71), but the English prayerbook called for eight more (72–79), and therefore Tuckerman had to triple his American Benedictus to suit it for English publication. American nineteenth-century Services were scanty in number, partly because prayerbook variants prevented their finding an English market until remodeled. For a brief history of American Services, see Stevenson, "The English Service," in *American Choral Review,* VI/2 (Jan., 1964), 6.

[265] *America,* p. 163.

[266] Jacob H. Hall, *Biography of Gospel Song and Hymn Writers* (New York: Fleming H. Revell Co., 1914), pp. 23–27; cf. also n. 214 above.

shop chords, and concluding with an operatic flourish on "I'm blind, O! . . . I'm blind," Bradbury was but echoing the Bellini bravura of the *Norma* adaptations being simultaneously sung in nearby silk-stocking Incarnation Church.

Even those able to appreciate Haydn in the concert hall and Bellini in the opera house frequently asked whether such works as the Rossini *Stabat Mater* and Cherubini *Requiem* being sung at Incarnation were properly qualified for the sanctuary. A. J. Rowland, a doctor of divinity, spoke for his own denomination in the *Baptist Quarterly Review,* V/20 (Autumn, 1883), 414, when he decried not only operatic adaptations but also the usual "anthems and voluntaries" as "no adequate part of worship." The Puritan conscience spoke through him when he continued: "God is not to be praised by proxy. . . . The only office that a choir can serve is to lead the congregation in the singing."

Since in the period 1865–1940 each denomination tended to foster its own individual brand of church music, the history of this crucial epoch can now be best understood by separating the strands that belong to Episcopalians, Presbyterians, and the rest. The activist, mission-minded denominations from Mormons [267] to Methodists [268] during this period sponsored official hymnals with a hard core of dignified hymns for polite city congregations surrounded by the juicy fruit of "Blessed assurance" (a long-time favorite in Billy Graham

[267] William L. Wilkes studies intensively the musical complexions of successive Mormon hymnals (1889, 1908, 1927, 1948, 1950) in his "Borrowed Music in Mormon Hymnals," University of Southern California Ph.D. dissertation, 1957. The famous Mormon hymn, "O ye mountains high," is adapted to a mid-century Scottish air, "O Minnie, O Minnie, come o'er the lea," later known as "Lily Dale." *The Songs of Zion* (1908), with 260 tunes, shows more "gospel tune" influence than any other Mormon hymnal. The Latter-Day Saints have gladly used such tunes as that of "In the gloaming," but have so strenuously objected to *In dulci jubilo* that it had to be taken out of the 1948 hymnal when revised (1950); see Wilkes, p. 59. The 1889 Mormon hymnal emphasized music for the choir, and reached a "high-water mark of self-consciousness in Latter-day Saint hymnody" by including many more tunes of Mormon origin than any other edition. The 1948–50 hymnal still retains tunes by John Tullidge (1806–1874), George Careless, Ebenezer Beesley, and other early Mormon worthies; Alexander Schreiner, Leroy Robertson, and Crawford Gates represent the present generation.

[268] See "Methodist Hymn Books," in Jackson, *White Spirituals in the Southern Uplands,* pp. 303–308. Further data on Lemuel C. Everett and R. M. McIntosh ("Gathering home") in J. H. Hall, pp. 97–107. Robert G. McCutchan, *Our Hymnody* (New York: The Methodist Book Concern, 1937), pp. 10–13, surveys "official" Methodist hymnals. His successor, Carlton R. Young, contributes the authoritative résumé, "American Methodist Hymnody: A Historical Sketch" to *The History of American Methodism,* ed. by Emory S. Bucke (New York/Nashville: Abingdon Press, 1964), III, 631–634.

campaigns), "I need Thee every hour" (one of Mrs. Mary Baker Eddy's three favorite hymns, which must never be omitted from Christian Science hymnals [269]), and other like-minded "Songs of Salvation." Side by side with the official denominational hymnal, the same activist denominations allowed a dense orchard of Sunday School and "auxiliary" hymnbooks to grow up, fruited with hymn tunes by such gospel composers as B. D. Ackley, E. O. Excell, W. G. Fischer, Charles H. Gabriel, Phoebe Palmer Knapp, B. B. McKinney,[270] G. C. Stebbins, John R. Sweney, and Will L. Thompson.[271] The composers of the popular tunes in the Sunday School type of books have often been as innocent of any academic training as Dan Emmett. Bricklayer, shoe salesman, or plumber, these composers have found formal musical instruction no more useful than Moody and Sunday found Hebrew and Greek.

Within the last fifty years, their same class of hymn tune has entered even Roman Catholic hymnals designed for American use. One of the more successful of these, *Crown Hymnal,* includes 169 English hymns with tunes that range in quality from T. Haweis's CHESTERFIELD (123) and an adaptation of Mozart's first-movement theme

[269] *Christian Science Hymnal* (1910), preface, p. iii.

[270] McKinney's "Send a great revival in my soul" was the theme song of the 1949 Graham campaign in Los Angeles (rocketing him to national fame). Cf. Marvin L. McKissick, "A Study of the Function of Music in the Major Religious Revivals in America since 1875," University of Southern California Master of Music thesis, 1957, p. 120. McKissick studies the repertory and methods of both Billy Graham's soloist, Beverly Shea, and his group leader, Cliff Barrows. "I'd rather have Jesus," with words by Rhea F. Miller and music by Shea, seems to be his most popular composition (p. 139). The music of the Los Angeles kickoff meetings (1949) is studied at p. 120, and that of the Boston campaign at p. 125. "Blessed assurance," with music by Mrs. Joseph F. Knapp (1873) and text by Fanny Crosby, is probably the all-time favorite in Graham revivals (p. 133), but "What a friend" with music by Charles C. Converse (1870), "Revive us again," and "Near the Cross" (1869) have proved close runners-up (p. 125). The Graham meetings differ from the Moody and Sunday revivals in failing to inspire very much "new" music. Shea's clinching solo, with "He's got the whole, wide world" for a refrain, is adapted to an old tune. When singing "How great Thou art," he adopts the manner of a sentimental light opera star. Further discussion of Graham crusade music below at pp. 126–127.

[271] Hall, pp. 299–302, 131–132, 349–352, 203–206, 149–152, 251–254, summarizes the biographies of Excell, Fischer, Gabriel, Stebbins, Sweney, and Thompson. Stebbins's *Memoirs* were serialized in *The Gospel Choir,* Vol. VIII (1922/3). Published by the Rodeheaver Company and edited by Charles H. Gabriel, this monthly contains in its eight volumes (1915–1923) compendious memorabilia of the gospel song heroes. Cf. Edwin H. Pierce, "Gospel Hymns and Their Tunes," in *The Musical Quarterly,* XXVI/3 (July, 1940), 355–364. A popularity poll conducted by Army chaplains during World War II showed "The Old Rugged Cross," copyrighted in 1913 by George Bennard (1873–1958; Homer A. Rodeheaver owned the copyright when it was renewed in 1941), to be not only the all-time favorite gospel song, but also the most popular of all Protestant hymns, of whatever type. Bennard wrote both the treacly music and the anapest verse, with refrain.

in the "Turkish March" Sonata (34) to a "Softly and tenderly" tune (11) and an equally insipid "In the garden" melody that vie with the popular Protestant "Old Rugged Cross" (music by George Bennard [see note 316]) for sentimental effusiveness. The musical give-and-take in such a hymnal with imprimatur as this [272] is interestingly paralleled by the hymn texts. Charles Wesley, co-founder of Methodism, is in this book at No. 36, for instance—but without credit line.

At the same time that Roman Catholic hymnals in this country were succumbing to the musical idiom of the weaker Protestant Sunday School songs, the vogue of "Brighten the corner where you are," "By and by," "There is glory in my soul," "O that will be glory for me," and the like [273] was sweeping to distant and alien shores. From Cairo to Honolulu, and from São Paulo to Madras, American evangelical missionaries have so thoroughly imbued converts with this kind of song that "gospel" music now dominates nearly every foreign language hymnal. The proof of how quickly this kind of music has won friends in alien fields can be found in such a book as *Standard Buddhist Gathas and Services* (published at Kyoto in 1939), the English-language section of which (items 501–557) is filled with "a body of good, worthy hymns and services" that would do credit to a Homer E. Rodeheaver [274] collection.

Even in Europe, gospel hymnody has not lacked its advocates. After the mammoth Moody-Sankey campaign of 1875, Lord Shaftesbury claimed that had American evangelists done "nothing more than teach the people to sing such hymns as 'Hold the Fort, For I Am Coming' [Philip P. Bliss (1838–1876) [275]] they would have conferred an inestimable blessing on Great Britain." [276] Cliff Barrows [277]

[272] Published in 1912 by Ginn, and edited by the Rev. L. J. Kavanagh and James M. McLaughlin, this book was typical of the many designed to implement the 1903 *Motu proprio* at the parish level.

[273] Charles H. Gabriel (1856–1932) composed all these; they gained enormous popularity during the Billy Sunday revivals. Cf. Daniel I. McNamara, *The ASCAP Biographical Dictionary* (New York: Thomas Y. Crowell, 1952), pp. 171–172.

[274] John T. Howard prints Rodeheaver's apologia for this type of music in *Our American Music* (New York: Thos. Y. Crowell, 1946), pp. 611–612. For further defense, see my *Patterns of Protestant Church Music,* pp. 151–162, and "Evangelistic Song," in *Religion in Life,* XXVI (1957), 436–443.

[275] Despite Bliss's lavish representation in *The Baptist Hymnal* edited by W. H. Doane (1883), *Baptist Hymnal* edited by W. H. Sims (1956), and *Hymns for Christian Service* (Chicago: Tabernacle Publishing Co., 1936), this particular gospel song is not included.

[276] *Patterns of Protestant Church Music,* pp. 152–153.

[277] A member of the "team" since 1945, Barrows graduated from Bob Jones College, played trombone, led choirs in Youth For Christ rallies, and attracted Graham's attention at Asheville during such a rally. See William G. McLoughlin, Jr., *Billy*

and George Beverly Shea did not find that American gospel songs had lost any of their mass appeal when Graham conducted his London campaign in 1954. But Erik Routley, in *The Music of Christian Hymnody: A Study of the Development of the Hymn Tune* (1957), has qualms as to the "inestimable blessing" bestowed by this class of American tune. "At best this music is honestly flamboyant and redolent of the buoyancy of the civilization that created New York and Pittsburgh and Chicago; at its worst it is flabby and futile" in his opinion.[278] Horatio W. Parker (1863–1919)[279] and Winfred Douglas (1867–1944) did something to rescue America from "the slough of sentimental music-hall sloppiness and campfire heartiness" into which it fell after the Civil War. But "American taste has proved itself hard to rescue," he concludes. Even so adept a master of the popular idiom as Stephen Collins Foster could not write anything with religious words that equaled his "Camptown Races," "My Old Kentucky Home," and "Old Folks at Home." Foster's twenty Sunday School songs, divided between Horace Waters's *Golden Harp* and *Athenaeum Collection* (1863), never approach anywhere the vitality of "Old Black Joe" (1860) or "Beautiful Dreamer" (1864). For his hymn "The pure, the bright, the beautiful" he chose two stanzas by so eminent an author as Charles Dickens (*The Athenaeum Collection,* pp. 212–213). However, he failed to rise above routine level whether setting Dickens's poetry or his own.

Since hymn tunes are pre-eminently the food of the common man, their importance in church history exceeds that of all other musical types in a nation so democratic as America. But during the last half of the nineteenth century, city churches began nearly everywhere to depend also on ensembles of paid soloists for their more pretentious Sunday fare. The mixed quartet in a side gallery or above the pulpit became the norm in such churches, even in the newly settled West. As early as 1856, when the *San Francisco Bulletin* published a series of articles on local church music, the reporter thought it odd that "The First Presbyterian Church has a choir of ten instead of the

---

Graham, Revivalist in a Secular Age (New York: Ronald Press, 1960), p. 41, and indexed entries.

[278] Routley, *The Music of Christian Hymnody* (London: Independent Press, 1957), p. 166. He considers "John Brown's Body" our best nineteenth-century hymn tune. For his further remarks on gospel music, see his précis "On the Billy Graham Song Book," in *The Hymn,* VI (1955), 26, 36.

[279] MOUNT ZION by Parker "is probably one of the best hymn tunes of its age" (*The Music of Christian Hymnody,* p. 166).

fashionable quartet so much in vogue in other churches." [280] In Episcopal churches throughout the West—whether at Virginia City in boom days or in Los Angeles at the predecessor of the present cathedral—the taste in the 1870's and 1880's was just as much for the quartet as in the East, where Dudley Buck (1839–1909) reigned as King of church music.

Describing the music in the leading Episcopal church, a reporter for the *Los Angeles Express* wrote in the issue of March 22, 1875, that the "air of the prayer in the opera of *Zampa*" provided "a delicious conclusion to very interesting services." [281] The two female soloists were Miss Florida Nichols, with a soprano voice "which would attract attention in any choir," and Miss Belle Mallard, whose "notes are fresh as a bird's." For such singers as these, Dudley Buck composed scores of highly successful anthems, many of which still "deservedly remain upon our choir programs," according to Peter Lutkin, who praises him above every composer of his generation. Even though "most of his music was intended for the quartette choir, it was a marked advance on anything which had preceded it." [282] Lutkin attributes Buck's weaker moments to his "too frequent cadences giving something of a patchwork effect," and to his "oversentimental" approach to the historic texts of the Bible and the liturgy. Buck—born in the same year as his fellow New Englander John Knowles Paine, educated in Germany as was Paine, honored by Theodore Thomas with exposition commissions at Philadelphia in 1876 and again at Chicago in 1893 (as was Paine, also)—"stood more nearly for a distinctive style of American Church music than any other composer."

---

[280] Quotation taken from July 3, 1856, issue, cited in Cornel Lengyel, ed., *Music of the Gold Rush Era* [History of Music in San Francisco Series, Vol. I (Works Progress Administration, 1939)], p. 59.

[281] Howard Swan, *Music in the Southwest* (San Marino: The Huntington Library, 1952), p. 117. Viewed from a narrowly dogmatic position, much of the "religious" music to be discussed in the rest of the present monograph cannot be counted church music at all. It is merely concert music set to religious texts. However, in defense of mentioning the operatic tidbits that passed for church music in the last century, and of discussing the cantatas, oratorios, and English-language Masses of Horatio Parker, Randall Thompson, and Roger Sessions produced in the present century, is the patent fact that Protestant churches have incorporated them into acts of worship. Even works so outside the Protestant tradition as Haydn's *Lord Nelson* Mass, Beethoven's Mass in C, Mozart's, Verdi's, and Fauré's Requiems are now sung in whole or in part during worship services in churches so influential as the First Presbyterian of Princeton, Christ Church Methodist of New York, and First Congregational of Los Angeles. Just how "worshipful" are these acts of worship is, of course, a question to be endlessly debated. The Wycliffes have the best reason on their side when the music is meretricious, poorly performed, and adapted.

[282] Peter Lutkin, *Music in the Church* (Milwaukee: Young Churchman Company, 1910), pp. 252–253.

In Lutkin's opinion, Buck's approach to an American style sufficiently compensates for his faults.[283]

Buck turned his hand to any text, Latin or English, with the same easy facility and tuneful zest. His *Ave Maria* and *Requiem aeternam* —quartet choruses in *The Legend of Don Munio,* a cantata published by Oliver Ditson in 1874 as Buck's Op. 62—bow just as low to *Vierhebigkeit* and round off the musical cliché just as smoothly as does the choral finale from the same cantata in praise of the Protestant Jehovah, "In thankful hymns ascending."

Besides Buck, several other New England composers wrote cantatas and oratorios that were printed by Oliver Ditson in the 1870's. Eugene Thayer, born at Mendon, Massachusetts, in 1838, and one of the first native-born Americans to win a Mus. Doc. degree at Oxford University, returned to Boston to take up an organist's career; in 1872 Ditson brought out Thayer's *Festival Cantata.*[284] Two years later, the same firm followed with John Knowles Paine's 174-page oratorio *St. Peter* (given its première at Portland, Maine, on June 3, 1873 [285]). This was Paine's first large work performed in this country. A smaller choral work, his sacred ode for four men's voices and orchestra, *Domine salvum fac,* had been sung at the inauguration of Thomas Hill as president of Harvard University on March 4, 1864; it was repeated for the inauguration of Charles Eliot, October 19, 1869. Abroad, he had garnered praise in the German press with a

---

[283] Summarizing Buck's career in the *Hartford Courant* of October 7, 1909, p. 8, col. 5, his best informed fellow townsman (The Rev. Dr. Edwin Pond Parker) wrote: "Mr. Buck's contributions to church music have been voluminous, manifold, and of almost inestimable value. He made an arid wilderness a fruitful field. In his settings of the great canticles and hymns of the church, he seemed to strike precisely the true religious chords." The issue (front page, col. 3) contains an admirably full summary of his career to supplement Rossetter Cole's article in the *Dictionary of American Biography* (New York: Charles Scribner's Sons, 1929), III, 222–223. See also Johnson, *Musical Memories of Hartford,* pp. 2–16. Buck refused the honorary Yale Mus. Doc. for reasons disclosed by Dr. Parker in the *Courant* and by Buck himself in a letter dated June 28, 1884, to President Noah Porter of Yale (Johnson, pp. 13–14).

[284] Mixing German chorales (*Ein' feste Burg,* no. 18), AMERICA with the first incise treated as a fugue subject (no. 21), snatches from Italian opera (Festival March, nos. 1 and 22), and Mendelssohn *Songs Without Words* (no. 11), this Op. 13 cantata unluckily lays itself open to charges of mixing too many styles. "The words chiefly from the psalms" make the same sort of pastiche as Handel's *Occasional Oratorio.*

[285] George T. Edwards, *Music and Musicians of Maine* (Portland: Southworth Press, 1928), pp. 124–126, reprints a review by the celebrated historian John Fiske (program facsimile, p. 125). Kenneth Creighton Roberts, Jr., assembles further data on *St. Peter* in his University of Michigan thesis (1962), "John Knowles Paine," pp. 14–17. At the time it was written, this thesis provided the best available coverage of Paine's life and works.

Mass in D, which he directed at Berlin in 1867.[286] However, it was *St. Peter* that established him as the "first American who has shown the genius and the culture necessary for writing music in the grand style," to repeat John Fiske's encomium. W. S. B. Mathews, discussing "American Oratorio" in *The Nation*, XVI, no. 398 (February 13, 1873), pp. 116–117, added his accolade. Buck is the only composer who comes near Paine, if one may believe *The Nation*, and *St. Peter* "is without doubt the most important musical work yet produced in this country." [287]

Oliver Ditson's other large sacred publications continued with Buck's *46th Psalm* in 1872 and the *Redemption Hymn* and *The Blind King* by James Cutler Dunn Parker (1828–1916; no relation to Horatio W.), issued in 1877 and 1883. J. C. D. Parker, for twenty-seven years organist at Trinity Church, Boston, wrote also a *St. John* cantata (1890). *The Life of Man*, his farewell choral work (introduced to Boston by the Handel and Haydn Society at an Easter concert, 1895), had a powerful Resurrection scene, in the opinion of Louis Elson, and showed "masterly canonic writing in the portrayal of the seven churches of Asia." So evanescent are such triumphs, however, that few students of American music would today recognize a *Doppelmeister* problem.

A Parker so much more eminent rose in the 1890's as to overshadow not only his Harvard-trained namesake but all other American sacred composers of his century. *Hora Novissima*, Horatio Parker's first large choral work (Op. 30), breathed the spirit of the times when he chose Latin for his language. Even Mrs. H. H. A. Beach was in February of 1892 making her Boston début as a composer with a Mass in E♭, Op. 5,[288] performed by the Handel and Haydn Society under Carl Zerrahn. Two months later Parker finished scoring *Hora*

---

[286] Published as Op. 10 by Beer and Schirmer (New York [1866]) with dedication to August Haupt (1810–1891), Paine's teacher in Berlin. Cf. Edwards, p. 124.

[287] For analyses of prior large American sacred works, see Ralph M. Kent, "A Study of Oratorios and Sacred Cantatas Composed in America before 1900," 2 vols., University of Iowa Ph.D. dissertation, 1954. In addition to cantatas expressly for church use, numerous American "secular" cantatas were composed between 1850 and 1930 that contain choruses, ensembles, and solos to religious texts. This large no man's land between the strictly secular and sacred repertories has been sympathetically surveyed in a 1964 University of Michigan Ph.D. dissertation: Jacklin Talmage Bolton's "Religious Influences on American Secular Cantatas 1850–1930." See especially Bolton's chapter 3, "Protestant Worship Music."

[288] *Mrs. H. H. A. Beach* (Boston: Arthur P. Schmidt, 1906 [analytical sketch by Percy Goetschius]), pp. 49–69 (reprints of critical notices and reviews of the Mass, Op. 5). The most authoritative study of her career to date is E. Lindsey Merrill's "Mrs. H. H. A. Beach: Her Life and Music," University of Rochester [Eastman School of Music] Ph.D. dissertation, 1963.

Novissima, which he had started to compose in the spring of the previous year.[289] His daughter alludes to his many personal griefs in the year that he wrote this important oratorio to a text of thirty-five six-line stanzas from *De contemptu mundi.*[290] The poem had been a favorite of his father, Charles Edward Parker, who died in the year Horatio was working at *Hora Novissima,* as did Mary, Horatio's younger sister, and his only son. From these griefs, he turned to the oratorio that more than any work has kept his name alive.[291] First performed by the Church Choral Society of New York under Richard Henry Warren on May 2, 1893, it made an ever more profound impression at the Handel and Haydn Society première in 1894 and the Cincinnati Festival performance under Theodore Thomas in the same year. Before its première at the Three Choirs Festival in Worcester (1899), it had already been acclaimed in the English press as a work worthy of comparison with the best that Europe was producing.[292]

In a clearer sense than any of his later oratorios—*The Legend of St. Christopher,* Op. 43 (New York Oratorio Society, April 15, 1898); *A Wanderer's Psalm,* Op. 50 (Hereford, Three Choirs Festival, September 13, 1900); or *Morven and the Grail,* Op. 79 (Boston, Handel and Haydn Society, April 13, 1915)—*Hora Novissima* qualifies as church music—because it was heard first in a church (Church of the Holy Trinity, New York City). On this account it indeed differs from the familiar oratorios of all such European com-

[289] Autograph score, Library of Congress, ML96.P31, pp. 30 (Jan. 5, 1892), 204 (May 1). Isabel P. Semler, *Horatio Parker* (New York: G. P. Putnam's Sons, 1942), pp. 77–79. The score was engraved in Leipzig by F. M. Geidel and published by Novello (London, 1900). George W. Chadwick, *Horatio Parker* (New Haven: Yale University Press, 1921), p. 11, placed the première a year too early and mistook the conductor of the first performance (corrected in Semler, p. 81). The première was conducted by Richard Henry Warren, organist and choirmaster of St. Bartholomew's Church, New York, 1886–1905. For a résumé of Warren's association with the Church Choral Society and of his other notable services to New York music, see chapter 2 of Jean E. Trautmann's "A History of Music at Saint Bartholomew's Church, New York," Union Theological Seminary thesis, 1951. Leopold Stokowski succeeded Warren at St. Bartholomew's, 1905–1908. (For Stokowski's important but largely unknown services to American church music, see Trautmann, pp. 25–30, 78–81.)

[290] Bernard of Cluny's poem was popularized by John Mason Neale (1818–1866), the darling of the Tractarians. See Leonard Ellinwood, *The Hymnal 1940 Companion* (New York: Church Pension Fund, 1951), pp. 350–351.

[291] Recorded by American Recording Society (ARS 335), William Strickland conducting. The criticisms quoted from Philip Hale and W. J. Henderson (Chase, *America's Music,* p. 377) claiming that parts of the work "might have been written by Hobrecht, Brumel, or even Josquin des Près" shot very wide of the mark for both the Flemings and Parker. Such uninformed criticism inhibits serious study of more than one major American work.

[292] *Musical Times,* XXXIV/608 (Oct. 1, 1893), 586–587.

posers as Handel, Haydn, Mendelssohn, and Elgar. To have had it
performed first in a church redounds all the more to Parker's credit
when we compare its harmonic wealth, the intensity of expression
throughout, the dynamic extremes, the bold modulations, and the
over-all unifying devices with the usages of such contemporaneous
oratorio composers as Parry, Mackenzie, Rubinstein, Saint-Saëns,
Gounod, and even Franck. For an example of his unifying devices:
the head-motif of the instrumental introduction undergoes inversion
to become the vocal fugue subject of *Pars mea* (no. 4); it again
appears, in its original form, as the instrumental counterpoint to a
new choral melody in the finale of Part 1, *Tu sine littore* (no. 6).
Or for another example: the head-motif of the bass aria, *Spe modo
vivitur,* suffers a sea-change into major and emerges as the soprano
melody in *O bona patria.* The instrumental theme first heard at measures 201–203 of the opening chorus, Part 1, returns in the finale of
Part 2 at letters "I" and "N," there to serve as a countermelody to the
principal theme. Another idea carried over from first to last numbers
of the oratorio is the agitated instrumental interlude from measures
42–49 of the plangent introduction to the opening chorus. This particular chromatic interlude—quoted in no. 6 as well as nos. 1 and
11—serves so obviously as keystone in two arches that a reviewer in
1893 almost wished to call it a *Leitmotiv.*[293]

Parker never lets down the high emotional pitch established in the
first chorus. Each of the two principal parts ends splendidly. Nothing
lasts too long. The more voice parts (*Stant Syon* is a double chorus;
Urbs Syon inclyta pits a quartet against the chorus *a 4*), the more
ingenious the conduct of the individual parts. The relief of an *a
cappella* chorus for the antepenultimate number of the oratorio proved
so fine a contrast that Parker reverted to the same scheme when he
wrote his next oratorio (the *a cappella* section *Jam sol recedit*[294] precedes the last scene in *The Legend of St. Christopher*).

Neither of his two Services (E, Op. 18, 1892; B♭, Op. 57, 1904)
continues to be much sung. The rest of his "religious" output has
faded into even dimmer oblivion. Yet parts of the latter oratorios
equal the best in *Hora Novissima.* Like Dudley Buck, whose *The
Legend of Don Munio* is founded on a Washington Irving tale, Parker
describes *The Legend of St. Christopher* on the title page as a "dramatic" oratorio. Against his judgment when he was composing it, he

293 *Ibid.,* p. 586.
294 Semler, p. 100, quotes D. S. Smith's estimate of this chorus as "Parker's finest
and most beautiful composition."

even decided at the time of publication to call the principal divisions "Acts." For the poetry of *St. Christopher* he was indebted to his mother (*née* Isabella Jennings, "Class Poet" at Lasell Seminary when she graduated in 1857 [295]); and for the libretto of *Morven and the Grail* to Brian Hooker, the same Yale English professor who provided him with the librettos of his two operas, *Mona* (G. Schirmer, 1911) and *Fairyland* (1915). The "plots" of both *St. Christopher* and *Morven*—despite the different librettists—show some striking similarities. In both a young low-voiced hero pursues the Ideal, first in the wind, then in the earthquake, then in the fire. Finding the Ideal in none of these, he finally discovers it in the still small voice (or an equivalent). In a general way this is indeed the scheme underlying so secular an oratorio as Schumann's *Paradise and the Peri.*

Parker's gift for composing exciting music did not desert him in either *St. Christopher* or *Morven*. The clamor up to the drawing of the bow in Act I, the raucous meeting with Lucifer in Act II, and the exultant Gloria in Act III, indeed outdo *Hora Novissima*. The repetition of Offerus's vow-motif (score-numbers 17, 34, 55, 91) and of the *Asperges me* music in II, ii and III, ii (= "Tarnhelm" motif) bears witness to Parker's overmastering concern for unity. Throughout *Morven* he constantly reverts to themes first enunciated at measures 5 and 53 of the Introduction (m. 5 = "Compact" motif in *The Ring,* 53 = "Atonement" in *Parsifal*); and to the "Follow the Grail" motif in the opening quartet (= "Gleaming Gold" in *The Ring*).[296] If he adopts Wagnerian unifying principles, and if he works with a harmonic palette as richly hued as Elgar's, Parker still shows such mastery of his craft that he is no more to be deprecated than is Berg for having followed in Schoenberg's wake.

During the years that *St. Christopher* was in gestation (he finished the scoring of the first part in August 1897), his pupils at Yale included Charles Ives. Ives's testimony to Parker's gifts is therefore germane: "I have and had *great* respect and admiration for Parker." [297] Ives continues by praising him for seldom being trivial—even if Parker could toss off a *Valse gracile* that was the first encored number on the only all-American program that Josef Hofmann ever gave.[298]

---

[295] *Ibid.,* p. 29.

[296] These correspondences are cited only to give a quick idea of the character of Parker's ideas, and not because he consciously quoted (any more than Brahms quoted Grieg in his Op. 4 and Op. 79, No. 1).

[297] Henry and Sidney Cowell, *Charles Ives and His Music* (New York: Oxford University Press, 1955), p. 33. (Cowell says that "great" is crossed out.)

[298] Richard Aldrich, *Concert Life in New York, 1902–1923* (New York: G. P. Putnam's Sons, 1941), p. 589.

"His choral works have a dignity and depth" that cannot be ignored, even if Parker was too much swayed by the "German rule." [299] One of Ives's classroom experiments was a fugue in which the entries went around the clock of keys from C to G to D to A. Despite his Germanisms, his training under Rheinberger at Munich, his German wife whom he taught to speak English, and his academic honors, Parker's mind was not so closed as to prevent him from experimenting with just such a scheme of clock-entries in *St. Christopher*, II, ii. The voices enter with a subject successively in B, E, and A, and later in a journey through the relative minors. True, the effect is never close to Ives's. But Parker was destined to make his living out of music, to win more large cash prizes than any American composer in history,[300] and to obtain the honorary D. Mus. from Cambridge University—an unprecedented honor for an American. Ives, by contrast, lived so much above the professional world that recognition might never have reached him had not he earned enough from insurance to publish and distribute his music gratuitously.

Parker's other distinguished Yale pupils included David Stanley Smith, Douglas Moore, and Roger Sessions. As early as 1902, Smith (1877–1949) was writing "large and elegant pieces" in Munich,[301] whither he had followed Parker on sabbatical. When praising Smith to that other paladin of New England musical culture, George W. Chadwick (1854–1931),[302] Parker wrote from Munich: "He is a good boy and will turn out well, unless I am dreadfully mistaken." Smith did turn out well, if succeeding to the deanship of Yale Music

[299] Cowell, p. 33.

[300] For his Op. 31 he received a $300 prize (National Conservatory of Music); for his Op. 45, $250 (Musical Art Society of New York); for his Op. 54, $500 (Paderewski Prize); for his Op. 71, $10,000 (National Federation of Music Clubs). G. Schirmer was the original publisher of his Opp. 3, 6, 14, 15, 17, 20, 22–28, 33–37, 39, 42, 45, 53, 59–62, 64–65, 67–68, 71, 73–75, 77, and of numerous anthems and solo songs without opus number. Already before 1900, G. Schirmer had published 12 important church works without opus number (Magnificat, *Nunc dimittis, Deus misereatur*, Te Deum, *Salve Regina* and seven anthems).

[301] Semler, p. 141.

[302] Chadwick and that other hierarch of Boston music, Arthur W. Foote (1853–1937), were long-time church organists. While not always as successful in their sacred works as in their secular (*Symphonic Sketches*, 1908, and *Suite for Strings in E*, Op. 63, 1909), both Chadwick and Foote left large bodies of respectable church music. Chadwick published some fifty mixed-voice Protestant anthems and an ambitious Christmas cantata ("pastoral"), *Noël*. Douglas G. Campbell's University of Rochester Ph.D. dissertation (1957), "George W. Chadwick: His Life and Works," pp. 47–61, 66–67, discusses these. Foote's numerous Episcopalian canticles and his synagogue music may surprise those who think of him primarily as organist of the Boston First Unitarian Church, 1878–1910. For full information on his church output, see Doric Alviani, "The Choral Church Music of Arthur William Foote," Union Theological Seminary S. M. D. dissertation, 1962.

School for two decades (1920–1941) measures success. But Smith, prolific composer of hymn tunes, anthems, cantatas, and oratorios, lived into an epoch when to be "good" was less a cachet of musical esteem than to be "outrageous." He felt his isolation keenly in later years, and tried self-consciously to paste modernisms on his essentially pre-war pieces. His early church music, such as *The Logos,* Op. 21, a Christmas cantata in four parts (H. W. Gray, 1908), is simple, affecting, and rises to full-throated climaxes at the close of Parts 1 and 4 with quotations of *Veni Immanuel.*[303] Smith reached his high-water mark as a churchly composer with his *Rhapsody of St. Bernard,* Op. 38, the "cantata" of oratorio proportions (G. Schirmer, 1918) that brought his name into the national limelight when it was first given at the Chicago North Shore Festival in the year of publication. The text—translated by Smith himself from Bernard of Clairvaux—begins with *Jesu dulcis memoria,* a stanza that he sets with all the liquid sweetness of the "Victoria" motet. Although he exploits for what they are worth the few dramatic touches in the centonized text, the stanzas stay too close to the pure and the ethereal for much conflict. According to Ives, Parker could become "hard-boiled" on a moment's notice. Smith is never hard-boiled, even in the fugal *Jesu Rex.* Nor does he strive for Parker's over-all unity. In only two numbers does he repeat himself—1 and 12 (the opening melody returns at "F" in the epilogue). Brahms of *How lovely are Thy dwelling places* (letter "A") looked over Smith's shoulder when he wrote *Jesu decus angelicum.* Brahms's influence also accounts for such rhythmic involvements as Smith devises in *Desidero te millies,* for the intercepted phraseology in *Jesu, flos matris,* for the spare orchestration, and even perhaps for the use of the word "Rhapsody" in the title.

Sessions, who in his *Reflections on the Music Life in the United States* (1956) justly calls Parker "the most significant figure in the American music of his time" after MacDowell,[304] and who praises his religious works for "not only a mature technique," but also a "musical nature and profile which were well defined," had the advantage of being twenty years younger than Smith. Such religious music as Sessions's *Mass for Unison Choir and Organ* (1955) speaks to this generation as uncompromisingly as does Stravinsky's *Canticum Sacrum ad honorem Sancti Marci nominis* of the same year. Both works are

---

303 When Smith, or any of his generation, quoted from the past, they always seem to have preferred pseudo-plainsongs such as *Veni Immanuel* to anything of authentic antiquity.

304 *Reflections* (New York: Merlin Press, 1956), p. 142.

so much of their time as to bear all the mid-century stigmata—without which signs no advanced listener will believe that he is hearing music from on High. Denis Stevens, reviewing Sessions's Mass at its première (Cathedral of St. John the Divine, New York, March 11, 1956), saw deeply into its meaning when he wrote for the *Musical Times,* May, 1956 (p. 269), that Sessions's "contribution to English liturgical music is an important one, and it is more than likely that new music of this calibre . . . will do much to revive the adventurous spirit that one so often finds lacking in the purveyors of *ars sacra.*" Irving Lowens found it "austere music," but of high "specific gravity." [305]

Randall Thompson's *Mass of the Holy Spirit* of the year following acknowledges the past with many more learned "devices" than does Sessions's Mass. For instance: Thompson resorts to canons (*Christe,* three-in-one canon at the fourth and seventh below; *Benedictus,* four-in-one at the fifth, ninth, and thirteenth below; *Agnus* at the octave), incorporates a fugue (*Pleni sunt coeli*), and readily repeats or sequences long strains (*Gloria in excelsis* [p. 13] = *Tu solus Dominus* [p. 25]; *Credo in unum Deum* [p. 31] = *Et incarnatus est* [p. 37]; Glory be to Thee [p. 56] = Hosanna [p. 81]). Sessions's Mass, even though he uses key signatures, yields to no conventional harmonic analysis; Thompson's, without such signatures, speaks in an easily assimilable major-minor chordal vocabulary. Throughout, Thompson's Mass is masterfully scored for an *a cappella* group, usually of the conventional SATB kind, but sometimes of as many as seven (*Sanctus*) or eight (*Qui tollis peccata* [p. 21]) parts. Sessions wisely confines himself—as does also Lou Harrison in his *Mass for Mixed Chorus, Trumpet, Harp, and Strings* (introduced in New York, February, 1954)—to unison or octave singing.[306]

The resurgence of the Mass, whether set by Roy Harris (for men's voices with organ, New York, May 13, 1948), Harrison, Sessions, or Thompson,[307] is interestingly paralleled in modern America by

---

[305] *Notes of the Music Library Association,* 2nd ser., XVI/1 (Dec., 1958), 152.

[306] Sessions wrote his Mass for the fiftieth anniversary of Kent School. Thompson's Mass was a commissioned work also. The first version of Harrison's Mass was inspired by a report of WPA research in Indian mission music; he "Europeanized the composition" after moving to New York.

[307] Only the Kyrie of the Sessions and Thompson Masses is in foreign language (both Masses were written for the Episcopal Communion Service). Thompson's Requiem (Boston: E. C. Schirmer, 1958 [131 pp.], 1963 [243 pp.]) is an eighty-minute work for double chorus in five parts (Lamentations, The Triumph of Faith, The Call to Song, The Garment of Praise, The Leave-Taking). "Not a liturgical mass," the Thompson Requiem takes for its libretto a wide assortment of Scriptural passages. "It cannot be proclaimed a composition completely devoid of tedium,"

the use to which such lights as Samuel Barber, Aaron Copland,[308] Ross Lee Finney, Lukas Foss, Howard Hanson, Alan Hovhaness, Norman Dello Joio, Normand Lockwood, Peter Mennin, Vincent Persichetti, and Leo Sowerby have put numerous other classic religious texts. These range from the creation poem in Genesis, psalms in both scriptural prose and rough-hewn Bay Psalm Book meter, selections from such other books of the Bible as Isaiah, Ecclesiastes, and Luke's gospel, to John Chrysostom's Greek liturgy and selected prayers from Kierkegaard. At mid-century our established American composers have almost to a man made some sort of "religious" gesture. In doing so, they differ from MacDowell and Charles T. Griffes. Curiously, the gestures of even the most *avant-garde* have been bows to the traditionally accepted masterpieces of religious prose and poetry.[309]

When, for instance, Copland composes his *a cappella* masterpiece *In the Beginning,* he hews as closely to Scripture as did Handel in *Messiah.* Thompson in his sequence of sacred choruses for unaccompanied mixed voices, *The Peaceable Kingdom,* invokes the painter-preacher Edward Hicks (1780–1849) as his patron,[310] but confines himself to passages from Isaiah so far as text is concerned. When for

---

declared Alan Rich (*The Musical Quarterly,* XLIV/3 [July, 1958], 370) when reviewing the première performance in Berkeley, California. Both Thompson's *Mass of the Holy Spirit* and Requiem have been recorded (Cambridge Records No. 403 includes also the *Alleluia* for mixed voices *a cappella* [premiered Berkshire Festival, G. Wallace Woodworth conducting, July 8, 1940] that ranks already as the most "successful" choral work by a twentieth-century American).

308 For purple prose describing the excellences of Copland's *In the Beginning,* see Hans Redlich, "New Music: A Critical Interim Report," in *The Music Review,* XVI (1955), 264. Copland's best-known instrumental work quoting an American hymn is *Appalachian Spring* (London: Boosey & Hawkes, 1945). Cf. Shaker melody beginning p. 67 (full score) with Edward D. Andrews, "Shaker Songs," in *The Musical Quarterly,* XXIII/4 (Oct., 1937), 495, ex. 1. Chase, p. 229, copies the tune from Andrews's book, *The Gift to Be Simple* (New York: J. J. Augustin, 1940), p. 136, no. 72. The book version differs somewhat from the *Musical Quarterly* version quoted by Copland. Copland's unerring instinct committed him to a tune from the letter-notated legacy that Victor Yellin lauds as unique in the early nineteenth century (*Journal of the American Musicological Society,* XVIII/2 [Summer, 1965], p. 258). No other denominational repertory of the period combined a more "folk-like and spontaneous" burst of song with such receptivity to tunes now called Negro. Shaker manuscripts contain "some of the earliest known records of Negro melody."

309 Virgil Thomson suggests a reason when, in *Harper's,* November, 1960, p. 61, he writes: "The music of today, written by no matter whom, is surprisingly noncommittal." It is easier to remain aloof with an antiquated text. Thomson in his *Stabat Mater* for soprano and string quartet (1932) broke ground with a text that is not liturgical (words by Max Jacob).

310 The anomaly of Hicks's patronage is the more keenly felt when the Quaker antipathy to all art-music is remembered. Hicks, a fanatic, deplored even his multiple-copy paintings, such as the peaceable kingdoms, as pomps of Satan.

a brief interlude he does consent to stray from Scripture in one scene of *The Nativity according to Saint Luke* (composed for the bicentennial of the dedication of Christ Church, Cambridge, 1961), he chooses a poem by Richard Rowlands (1565–1630? [pp. 74–75]) rather than by a contemporary. Leo Sowerby,[311] the most professionally church-oriented of composers, chooses texts from Revelation for *The Throne of God* (1956–1957) or from St. Francis for the Alice Ditson commission, *The Canticle of the Sun* (Carnegie Hall, April 16, 1945). His *Vision of Sir Launfal* (1926) came closer to our time, but no nearer than James Russell Lowell. Both *Christ Reborn* (Philadelphia, November 1, 1953) and *Forsaken of Man* culminate in Scripture. So far as the libretto of the latter is concerned, Sowerby wrote a letter to V. Lee Stallings (reproduced in Stallings's Southern Baptist Theological Seminary thesis, "A Study of *Forsaken of Man,* a Sacred Cantata by Leo Sowerby," 1956, p. 8) identifying Edward Borgers— "arranger" of the text—as a personal friend with whom he "worked it out together." The King James overtones of the text as a whole must therefore be credited as much to Sowerby's taste as that of the announced librettist.

Composers in the West as well as the East obey this same law. When the $25,000-prize-winning Leroy J. Robertson writes a full-scale *Oratorio from The Book of Mormon* (premiered February 18, 1953) he too makes it equally his rule to choose none but classic texts (Part I: Helaman 13:5–7, 29, 22–23, 32; 13:33, 36a, 37; 14: 2–3a, 4b–5a, 6b, 7–8; Isaiah 52:7a; Helaman 14:20, 21a, 23a, 27b, 25a; 16:1–2, 6a; 6b, 7–8a; Part II: 3 Nephi 1:9–12; 13; 15a; Part III: 3 Nephi 8:4–9, 24a; 11:10a, 17a; Matthew 6:9–13). His over-all plan sometimes gives him a choice between versions in English that were first published in either 1611 or in 1830. Here, too, he opts for the version known longer in the English-speaking world (Matthew 6:9–13 instead of 3 Nephi 13:9–13). His setting of Isa. 52:7a ("How beautiful upon the mountains") returns to a text already a favorite with such traditionalists on the East coast as F. Flaxington Harker (1876–1936), whose solo version (Op. 41, No. 3) has been a staple in Protestant sanctuaries since G. Schirmer published it in 1910. Rob-

[311] Ronald M. Huntington gives a painstaking account of Sowerby's church works in "A Study of the Musical Contributions of Leo Sowerby," University of Southern California master's thesis, 1957. See the sections on organ works, pp. 219–227, choral pieces, pp. 227–237, services and settings, pp. 237–239. The style-criticism at pp. 169–170 is illuminating. Since 1957 Sowerby's list has continued to expand rapidly. His unaccompanied *Communion Service in C* (New York: H. W. Gray, 1963) typifies the additions that he has made recently. His Service music makes an instructive comparison with Wilson's and Buck's published exactly a century earlier.

ertson's *Lord's Prayer,* doubtless the best-known excerpt from his three-part 1953 oratorio in the grand manner (recorded on Vanguard VRS–1077), at once calls to mind the setting by the Philadelphia-born Albert Hay Malotte (1895–1964)—published by G. Schirmer in 1935, introduced by John Charles Thomas, interpreted by Mahalia Jackson at Newport, R. I., and now as widely known as "America the Beautiful." The two settings deserve comparison even though Robertson's Prayer eschews operatic climax, requires no independent accompaniment, repeats lines (full score, 1954, pp. 131–133), and sounds best in the original *a cappella* version. They are fittingly compared because both Lord's Prayers form but a minuscule part of their whole output. Yet both composers lived to see their settings of the best-known text cast their other equally inspired music in the shade.

Obviously American composers of our time, whatever their locale, have learned the useful object-lesson taught by *Messiah* (Dublin, April 13, 1742). They know that, of Handel's seventeen English oratorios produced from 1732 to 1752, only *Messiah* and to a much lesser extent *Israel in Egypt*—both with all-scriptural texts—still hold the boards. This is not, of course, to say that the mere choice of a religious classic for text guarantees success in itself—not even the choice of so favorite a text as "God is a Spirit" (John 4:24) or The Lord's Prayer. Other versions of "God is a Spirit" preceded David Hugh Jones's setting (once rated by John Finley Williamson as the best American anthem produced between World Wars I and II). Fulton Oursler, in "The Song You Can't Forget" (*This Week Magazine,* December 27, 1953), claimed that G. Schirmer alone had published 18 Lord's Prayers before Malotte's. But what the rule of the times comes to can be thus summarized: the choice of any new copyrighted text, or for that matter of any text not already agreed upon as a religious classic, gravely handicaps a composer; and no experienced professional ignores the problem.

Even with hymns the same trend prevails. New music requests old texts. Or at least such is the law in hymnals of the larger denominations. The youngest American composer reported out by the Hymnal Committee of the Commission on Worship to the 1964 General Conference of The Methodist Church was Robert J. Powell (b. 1932). But his hymn tune AUTHOR OF LIFE (*Report,* 68) set lyrics by Charles Wesley (1707–1788). Lloyd Pfautsch (b. 1921) composes music for Charles Wesley's "I Want a Principle Within" (156) and for "Christian! Dost Thou See Them" (81) with text by Andrew of

Crete (660–732) translated by John Mason Neale (1818–1866). Austin C. Lovelace (b. 1919), another of the half-dozen composers born since World War I favorably reported (275, 429, 432), sets lyrics translated from Clement of Alexandria (*ca.* 170–220) and verses from Psalms 43, 122, and 134. Reversing the coin, hymn lyrics by such a current Methodist bishop as Gerald Kennedy (b. 1907) seek as their apt composer Joachim Neander (1650–1680).

However ecumenical the times, each denominational publication does still tend to favor its own personnel, even its own editorial personnel. For instance: the just-mentioned 1964 Methodist Hymnal Report pays the current New York-Washington Episcopalian-Presbyterian syndrome little more homage than the inclusion of one C. M. tune by Leo Sowerby (72). But of course the Methodist subcommittee chairman on hymn tunes with his confrères and consultants were under no obligation to return a compliment. In 1958, Sowerby—after surveying the American scene from the organ bench of the Episcopal cathedral in Chicago (where he then served)—awarded merit ribbons to these native-born composers of church music: Seth Bingham, Everett Titcomb, Philip James, Joseph W. Clokey, Randall Thompson, Normand Lockwood, Richard Purvis, Robert Elmore, Searle Wright, and Robert Crandell.[312] Mark Siebert, who published a lengthy White List of anthems by contemporary composers in *Notes of the Music Library Association*, sec. ser., XV/1 (December, 1957), 159, largely anticipated Sowerby's choices (adding a half-dozen names not in Sowerby's list). Obviously these lists threw down no welcome mats before Fort Worth Baptists, Nashville Methodists, or Kansas City Nazarenes. Nor are composers owing allegiance to any of the non-liturgical churches conspicuously mentioned in the usual censcored list. A contemporary work given in 1965 by some such "correct" New York church as Incarnation is therefore much more likely to be "A Child My Choice"—the poetry by Robert Southwell (Jesuit hanged at Tyburn, February 21, 1595), the music by Robert Dirksen of Washington Cathedral (Episcopalian)—than it is to be an anthem by Austin C. Lovelace (Montview Boulevard Presbyterian Church, Denver, and Iliff Seminary) or by Lloyd Pfautsch (Southern Methodist University).

---

[312] *Organ and Choral Aspects and Prospects (10th Music Book, 1958,* compiled and edited by Max Hinrichsen [London: Hinrichsen Edition, 1958]), pp. 42–44. In 1965 Searle Wright was Organist and Director of Music, St. Paul's Chapel, Columbia University; Robert Crandell was Director of Music, Packer Collegiate Institute, Brooklyn, and Organist-Choirmaster of First Presbyterian Church, Brooklyn. Both taught Composition at Union Theological Seminary School of Sacred Music.

To summarize what else is now happening in American church music: famous contemporary American composers continue to pour out a steady stream of first-class services, psalms, anthems, and odes invoking the name of God. Their difficulty often precludes use outside such privileged environments as heavily endowed metropolitan churches or college and university chapels. The hymnals of the larger denominations, except such religious bodies as flourish principally in the South, grow more and more "respectable" musically with each new edition. To ensure propriety in these official hymnals, the few older American compositions have had to undergo extensive cosmetic surgery. Paradoxically, the early American hymn tunes rejected by editors of "respectable" hymnals have become the chief cornerstones of important secular works by composers so "respectable" as Copland, Cowell,[313] Ives,[314] Schuman, and Thomson.[315]

The "hot gospel" denominations continue to depend on numerous late-nineteenth-century salvation songs of the P. P. Bliss and C. H. Gabriel variety. However, even the most successful of modern revival-

---

[313] The *Library of Congress Catalog, Music and Phonorecords,* January–June 1963, p. 31, lists the following tributes by Cowell to the early American repertory: *Hymn and Fuguing Tune No. 1* for symphonic band, *No. 2* for string orchestra, *No. 3* for symphony orchestra, *No. 7* for viola and piano, *No. 14* for organ. These were published in 1945, 1946, 1956, 1953, and 1962, respectively.

[314] Charles Ives rises to a climax in his great solo song *General Booth Enters Into Heaven* (composed 1914, published 1915, on a text by Vachel Lindsay) with a straightforward quotation of the pentatonic CLEANSING FOUNTAIN cited as a "Western Melody" in Asa Hull's *Pilgrim's Harp.* Ives ends his Violin and Piano Sonata No. 4 (*Children's Day at the Camp Meeting*) with the same "Shall we gather at the river" of Robert Lowry that Virgil Thomson varies for the last of his set, *Variations on Sunday-School Tunes* (composed in Paris 1926–1927, published 1954). Ives's whole repertory is indeed so shot through with quotations of old American hymns that a dissertation on his borrowings remains for the writing. Those most likely to discuss his use of WATCHMAN (1830) in his First Sonata for Violin and Piano (composed 1903–1908), of DILIGENCE (1864) in his Fourth Sonata, and of NETTLETON (John Wyeth's *Repository of Sacred Music,* 1813) in his Second Sonata, can praise Ives for having countered the trend of history. Previously, sacred composers had borrowed *Adieu mes amours, Mille regretz, Mein Gmüth ist verwirren,* and *Desilde al caballero* from the secular repertory. Now, Ives permits sacred tunes to interlope in secular environments. See below (p. 129) for further mention of Ives's hymn quotations.

[315] Thomson's masterly *Symphony on a Hymn Tune* (Southern Music Publishing Company, 1954) exploits FOUNDATION, an early American tune traced to Jesse Mercer's *The Cluster of Spiritual Songs,* 1817 (third edition) [McCutchan, *Our Hymnody,* p. 342]. The leading Georgia Baptist preacher of his day, Mercer (1769–1841) published one unbound and two bound editions of *The Cluster* at Augusta before contracting for a Philadelphia edition (1817); 1820, 1826, and 1835 editions followed. See C. D. Mallary, *Memoirs of Elder Jesse Mercer* (New York: John Gray, 1844), p. 85; also, p. 105 (singing), and pp. 450–451 (Mercer's vitriolic comments on "The use of the Violin"). In *The Sacred Harp,* 1844 (compiled by the Georgians, B. F. White and E. J. King), the pentatonic tune now known as FOUNDATION takes the name BELLEVUE (p. 72).

ists (continuing the D. L. Moody and Billy Sunday tradition) fails to surround himself with any composer who can match the appeal of Bliss, Sankey, or Gabriel. As a result, old-time religion in the mouths of the masses means gospel hymns of the type popularized before 1914. To test this generalization, one need but look at "The Old Rugged Cross." The composer died as recently as 1958,[316] but the tune and lyrics were copyrighted in 1913. Apparently newer is "How Great Thou Art," copyrighted in 1955 "by Manna Music, Inc., Hollywood 28, California, not to be reprinted or reproduced without written permission from Manna Music, Inc." But this is an arrangement of a Swedish folk melody, "O Store Gud," according to Stuart K. Hine, translator of the lyrics (credited to Carl Boberg).

With sheet music sales of a million copies claimed during the first decade (*Billboard*, LXXVII/44, p. 92), "How Great Thou Art" in 1965 headed a gospel train pulling enough cars to impress even captains of the secular entertainment industry. As one result, the editors of *Billboard* could announce the shining 96-page issue of October 23, 1965—devoted exclusively to "The World of Religious Music"— as but the first of an intended annual series. The twenty-eight articles in the first issue treated such topics as "Gospel Quartets on Bus," "All Night Sing," "National Quartet Convention," "Gospel Breakthrough," "Fathers of Modern Gospel," "Country and Gospel," and "West Coast Gospel." Emphasizing the biracial strength of the movement, "Negro Gospel," "We Shall Overcome," "Gospel Nightclubs," and "Mahalia Jackson" each rated a separate essay in this adroit anthology of glossy advertisement and folk history. But whether announcing Negro or white gospel attractions, the advertisements always stressed "personality" performers, not composers. When Dwight L. Moody (1837–1899) was still in his thirties, the Rev. E. J. Goodspeed could publish a 743-page *Full History of the Wonderful Career of Moody and Sankey, in Great Britain and America* (Philadelphia: F. Scofield & Co., 1876). Both the Billy Graham Room at the James P. Boyce Centennial Library of the Louisville Southern Baptist Theological Seminary and the advertisements for his music principals in *Billboard* veto the likelihood of a 743-page book at any time soon with the title *A Full History of the Wonderful Career of Graham and Shea*, or of *Graham and Barrows, Tedd Smith*, or *Don Hustad*.

[316] See the Rev. George Bennard's obituary in the *Los Angeles Times*, October 18, 1958, Pt. III, p. 8. Although dead at Reed City, Michigan, October 10, he was buried in Inglewood Park Cemetery after a funeral service at the Church of the Open Door, Los Angeles. According to the Los Angeles obituaries, he started as evangelist in Ohio, became a Salvation Army official, and composed 300 hymns.

So long as America continues diverse enough to be a land in which more than 250 denominations can flourish, church music will probably continue to reflect all the amazing varieties of social background, wealth, education, and aspiration that have called this plethora of religious bodies into being and made their continued support possible. In one sense, this diversity is much to be desired. In a day when uniformity swamps so many other aspects of American life, at least church music can continue to boast of ranging everywhere from the cheaply vulgar to the expensively sublime.

To bridge the gap between what heavily endowed and what smaller and poorer churches can do, some denominations such as Southern Baptists and Methodists began in the 1950's publishing magazines— *The Church Musician* (1950) and *Music Ministry* (1959). By 1965 *The Church Musician* had grown to a 72-page monthly, two-thirds consisting of text, the rest of music. For supplementary distribution with *The Church Musician,* an LP of the monthly music was being recorded by thirteen choristers from Manhattan Baptist Church, New York City, Buryl A. Red, conductor. Noble Cain's setting of Psalm 37: 3–5, "Trust in the Lord," and Carlton R. Young's "Day by Day, Dear Lord" to a text by Richard of Chichester (*ca.* 1197–1253), appearing in the April and December issues, typified the "better music" reaching small churches through *The Church Musician* in 1965. Typically, the texts continued to be proven religious classics, rather than contemporary poetry.

Just as the nineteenth-century southern Baptists William Walker and Benjamin Franklin White gave homegrown American music first place in *Southern Harmony* and *The Sacred Harp,* so also the 1956 *Baptist Hymnal* edited at Nashville by Walter Hines Sims continues the tradition of favoring the native-born. No other major denominational hymnal published between 1940 and 1965 allots these seven native-born Americans so many as ten or more tunes each: P. P. Bliss (12), W. B. Bradbury (11), W. H. Doane (14), C. H. Gabriel (12), L. Mason (15, of which five are arrangements), B. B. McKinney [1886–1952] (16), G. C. Stebbins [1846–1945] (11). J. B. Dykes and Joseph Barnby, the top-ranking foreigners, garner only seven and nine tunes each, respectively.

After a sale of three-and-a-half million copies within eight years of publication, the hymnal inspired a useful handbook by William J. Reynolds, *Hymns of Our Faith* (Nashville: Broadman Press, 1964). This is a vade mecum that Americanists will find especially treasurable because of the detailed and authentic coverage given numerous American composers of tunes in the "Happy Birthday to You" popularity class, but whose biographies enter no standard encyclopedias. The usefulness of this information can be illustrated by referring once more to the hymn-quoting Ives. In his second, third, and fourth symphonies and in his third violin and piano sonata, Ives quoted thirteen hymns. These are tabulated in Kenneth Robert Mays's Indiana University thesis (1961), "The Use of Hymn-Tunes in the Works of Charles Ives," pages 110–111. Whereas only a scattered few enter the usual denominational hymnal, no less than ten of the thirteen tunes quoted by Ives are in the *Baptist Hymnal,* 1956 (nos. 92, 99, 129, 240, 328, 334, 372, 432, 471, 481). For a student of Ives's sources, the data on such tunesmiths as Joseph P. Webster (1819–1875), George A. Minor (1845–1904), and William G. Tomer (1833–1896)—composers of SWEET BY AND BY, HARVEST, and GOD BE WITH YOU (pp. 435, 362, 424)—can therefore prove very gratifying indeed.

In a review published in the *New York Herald Tribune* (Saturday, November 27, 1965, p. 5), Eric Salzman praised Leonard Bernstein's pairing of Ives's Third with Mahler's Ninth Symphony at a New York Philharmonic concert. Salzman also assured his readers that "the Ives suffered not a bit from the juxtaposition." If in this same review Salzman could name as Ives's most "remarkable" achievement his carrying "the simple hymn tunes of a bygone age into an extraordinarily elevated, speaking discourse of scope, character and simple, profound meaning," then surely the research needed to establish the composers of these "simple hymn tunes of a bygone age" has its value. Similar attention given the composers whose works Palestrina quoted in his *Nasce la gioia mia, Dilexi quoniam,* or *In illo tempore* Masses would not be counted labor lost, even were the composers only Primavera, Maffoni, and Moulu.

It must of course be conceded that not all American musicologists are as yet willing to grant the honors to research in American church music, or in American music as a whole, that they bestow on research in European topics. As summed up by the author of "A Profile for American Musicology" (*Journal of the American Musicological Society,* XVIII/1 [Spring, 1965], p. 68):

The student of Marenzio or Louis Couperin is concerned with music that can be brought to life: but Francis Hopkinson or Lowell Mason or Theodore Chanler [1902–1961]—surely they defy all efforts at resuscitation. Man, they are dead.

Among the arguments that can be marshaled to counter the "Man, they are dead" school of thought, the following seem worth repeating: (1) the patent influence of Mason and of much lesser men on the one American symphonist of his generation that university professors do not blush to name; (2) the undeniable fact that Mason's ANTIOCH, Lewis Redner's ST. LOUIS, Richard Storrs Willis's CAROL, John Henry Hopkins's THREE KINGS, and Samuel A. Ward's MATERNA still remain as well known to the bulk of the American public as the best successes of George Gershwin, Irving Berlin, or Jerome Kern; (3) the denominationally restricted, but still sizable, acceptance of another fifty or more tunes by Mason, Hastings, Doane, Bliss, Gabriel, and Bennard. If in a nation so democratically oriented as the United States, the mere fact that fifty million Americans sing the tunes just listed does not sufficiently matter to musicology, at least their currency makes sport of the contention, "Man, they are dead."

Fortunately for the present book, enough younger musicologists have entered the field of American church music since World War II to swell the bibliography at pages 133–151 to significant proportions. From Allwardt and Alviani, Britton and Broucek, Crawford and Crews at the beginning of the alphabet to Wilcox, Wilkes, Willhide, and Yoder at the close, the doctoral dissertations now demand a rewriting of the traditional texts on American music history. Even the master's theses listed in the bibliography often reveal lacunae that need to be filled in currently circulating texts.

Just as scholarship in the American church music field shows signs of radical improvement, so also hopeful signs can be read in much of the new creative output. Several composers already active in the 1950's have become increasingly visible in the 1960's: Crandell, Dirksen, Lovelace, Pfautsch, Purvis, Robertson, Wright, and Young— to list alphabetically a random seven of varied denominational background. The "young" generation includes also such lights as Felciano, Hoiby, McCormick, Mechem, Moe, and Pinkham. The cornucopia of names deserving mention would, however, swell this paragraph to unmanageable dimensions.

Born February 8, 1921, at Freeport, Illinois, and educated at Peabody Conservatory and Johns Hopkins University, Richard Dirksen began his long association with the Washington Cathedral in 1941; in 1965 he was Director of Advanced Programs. On one Sunday the music in this cathedral (directed by Paul Callaway) may well be found to include Dirksen's Communion Service in E minor and his *Chanticleer,* a setting of lyrics by William Austin (1587–1634).

The same representative Sunday will see among the names of other composers performed Byrd, Victoria, Handl, Sweelinck, Vierne, Maleingreau, Reger, Vaughan Williams, and Benjamin Britten (December 26, 1965).

From the Boston area comes the still younger composer Daniel Pinkham, born June 5, 1923, at Lynn. Harvard-educated (A.B. and M.A.) and a faculty member of the New England Conservatory, he published in 1963 a *Requiem* with brass sextet and double bass accompanying the singers, in the same year a *Festival Magnificat* and *Nunc Dimittis* with optional brass accompaniment, and in 1965 *Three Lenten Poems,* the texts by Richard Crashaw (*ca.* 1613–1649). Scored with handbells or celesta or harp as possible accompanying instruments, the Crashaw *Poems* illustrate a current tendency to allow for numerous intriguing options, so far as accompanying instruments are concerned. Pinkham's "I was glad" (1963) for the 275th anniversary of King's Chapel, Boston, and "Thou hast loved righteousness" (1964) for the First Presbyterian Church of Oyster Bay, New York, prove that commissions play no less decisive a role in modern church composition than in secular.

Some of the same trends illuminate the work of Pfautsch. "Reconciliation" (1964), commissioned by the Highland Park Presbyterian Church of Dallas, contravenes convention with a speaking choir and a trumpet in the sanctuary. In his anniversary piece, "I'll praise my Maker," three trumpets, three trombones, and tuba accentuate the festal mood. Still another tendency common to the publications of Pinkham, Pfautsch, Kirke L. Mechem, and Daniel Moe in the 1955–1965 decade was an emphasis on "the power of positive thinking." Even Pinkham's 1963 *Requiem* in memory of a younger brother was reviewed in *The Boston Globe* after its Jordan Hall première with the phrase, "a positive spirit pervades." Commissioned by the Contemporary Music Society of which Leopold Stokowski was president, this fifteen-minute *Requiem* notably lacked any Day of Wrath. Vigorous affirmations of life and of its victory inspire Mechem's "Give thanks unto the Lord," a four-minute setting of Psalm 135:1–5 (1960), of his "Make a joyful noise," a version of Psalm 100 (1961), of Moe's "O praise the Lord" (Psalm 117), his "Hosanna to the Son of David" (Matthew 21:9), and his Easter Te Deum. Anniversaries and festivals breed commissioned works; these match the spirit of the occasion with "the sound of the trumpet" and with the glitter of bells and other percussion instruments.

If the temper of the times was to be gauged by publications, the predominant response of the American sacred composer to the age-old injunction, "Lift up your hearts," was, from 1960 through 1965, "Rejoice, and be glad." Now and then, as in late 1965, a university chapel sought this mood with a so-called "jazz service." Elwyn Wienandt published a thoughtful analysis of "Jazz at the Altar?" in *Christian Century*, LXXVII, March 23, 1960, and returned to the subject in *Choral Music of the Church* (New York: The Free Press, 1965), with allusions to the Dixieland Six in Christ Church Cathedral, St. Louis, February 12, 1961 (p. 432) and to Edgar Summerlin's liturgical jazz (p. 434). The real news of the early 1960's did not consist in these self-conscious gestures, however—nor even in Duke Ellington's highly publicized appearances at Fifth Avenue Presbyterian Church, New York (December 26, 1965), and Coventry Cathedral, England (February 21, 1966). After all, twenty years earlier the New Orleans equivalent of the Dixieland Six was already a commonplace in certain churches of the town and such groups were being heard regularly at the 10:30 A.M. service in Chapel No. 1 of nearby Camp Plauché. The better news of the 1960's was the buoyancy and élan no less real in much new church music. Not limited to the rhythmic tags of "jazz" but exploiting them, not seeking to thwart the mood of worship but to enhance it, the optimistic new church music of the 1960's re-creates in contemporary terms the brisk confidence that has always been a characteristically American trait from its beginnings in Lyon, Billings, Holden, Edson, and Ingalls.

Written not for contemplatives, but rather as an incitement in the upward march to Zion, American Protestant music has at every stage always borne aloft one motto sewn through its insignia—win. By their very nature dependent on consent rather than on coercion, the Protestant denominations have always looked for a music that speaks to their chosen constituencies, and that is sufficiently persuasive to "Bring them in." A sense of urgency and of resolve, the determination to bring in the sheaves before the night falls, a heroic decision to bear the posts of the encompassed city up to the top of the hill, "bar and all," even if night should fall—these have been typical traits of American Protestantism that have found reflection in her historic music. Those sacred composers who remain truest to that legacy will probably for decades yet to come continue writing music to match the optimistic and persuasive mood of the pioneers who believed that even for the Indians there was nothing so good as singing "prettie tuneablie our psalmes."

SELECTIVE
BIBLIOGRAPHY

SELECTIVE BIBLIOGRAPHY

Although intended in the main as a comprehensive list of the works cited in the foregoing text, the bibliography omits materials assigned to either M or MT in the Library of Congress classification system. Dissertations that had to be consulted on microfilm are given the date of publication by University Microfilms, Ann Arbor, Michigan, which does not always match the date when the dissertation was accepted.

A Particular Plain and Brief Memorative Account of the Reverend Mr. Thomas Symmes. Boston: T. Fleet, for S. Gerrish, 1726.

ADAMS, C. FREDERICK. "Notices of the Walter Family," in *New England Historical and Genealogical Register,* VIII/3 (July, 1854).

ALLEN, N. H. "Old Time Music and Musicians," in *The Connecticut Quarterly,* I/3 (July–August–September, 1895) and III/1 (January–February–March, 1897).

ALLWARDT, ANTON PAUL. "Sacred Music in New York City, 1800–1850," Union Theological Seminary D.S.M. dissertation, 1950.

ALVIANI, DORIC. "The Choral Church Music of Arthur William Foote," Union Theological Seminary D.S.M. dissertation, 1962.

ANDERSON, JOHN. *Vindiciae cantus dominici.* Philadelphia: David Hogan, 1800.

ANDREWS, EDWARD D. *The Gift to Be Simple: Songs, Dances and Rituals of the American Shakers.* New York: J. J. Augustin, 1940.

———. "Shaker Songs," in *The Musical Quarterly,* XXIII/4 (October, 1937).

ASBURY, SAMUEL E., AND HENRY E. MEYER. "Old-Time White Camp-Meeting Spirituals," in *Publications of the Texas Folk-Lore Society,* X (1932).

AYARS, CHRISTINE M. *Contributions to the Art of Music in America by the Music Industries of Boston 1640 to 1936.* New York: H. W. Wilson Co., 1937.

BACON, GEORGE B. *Sermon Commemorative of Dr. Lowell Mason.* [Orange, N. J.]: Cushing, Bardua & Co., 1872.

BARBOUR, J. MURRAY. *The Church Music of William Billings.* East Lansing: Michigan State University Press, 1960.

BARTLETT, JOSEPH. *Music as an Auxiliary to Religion.* Boston: Crocker and Brewster, 1841.

BARTON, WILLIAM. *The Book of Psalms In Metre*. London: Thomas Snowden, 1692.

BECK, PAUL E. "David Tanneberger, Organ Builder," in *Papers Read Before the Lancaster County Historical Society,* XXX (January, 1926).

BENSON, NORMAN ARTHUR. "The Itinerant Dancing and Music Masters of Eighteenth Century America," University of Minnesota Ph.D. dissertation, 1963.

BOLTON, JACKLIN TALMAGE. "Religious Influences on American Secular Cantatas, 1850–1930," University of Michigan Ph.D. dissertation, 1964.

BOST, GEORGE H. "Samuel Davies: Colonial Revivalist and Champion of Religious Toleration," University of Chicago Ph.D. dissertation, 1942.

BOWMAN, EMILY JANE. "Music of the Early American Moravians," University of Michigan M.M. thesis, 1963.

BRICKENSTEIN, H. A. "Sketch of the Early History of Lititz. 1742–75," in *Transactions of the Moravian Historical Society,* Vol. II. Nazareth [Pa.]: Whitefield House, 1886.

BRINER, ANDRES. "Wahrheit und Dichtung um J. C. Beissel. Studie um eine Gestalt in Thomas Manns 'Dr. Faustus,' " in *Schweizerische Musikzeitung,* XCVIII/10 (October, 1958).

BRITTON, ALLEN P. "A Bibliography of Early Sacred American Music," in *Musurgia,* Ser. A, Vol. VIII (1951).

———. "Music in Colonial Times," in *Michigan Alumnus Quarterly Review,* LV/16 (March 12, 1949).

———. "The Musical Idiom in Early American Tunebooks," in *Journal of the American Musicological Society,* III/3 (Fall, 1950).

———. "The Original Shape-Note Tune Books," in *Studies in the History of American Education,* ed. by Claude Eggertsen. Ann Arbor: School of Education, 1947.

———. "Theoretical Introductions in American Tune-Books to 1800," University of Michigan Ph.D. dissertation, 1949.

———, AND IRVING LOWENS. "Unlocated Titles in Early Sacred American Music," in *Notes of the Music Library Association,* 2nd ser., XI/1 (December, 1953).

BRODER, NATHAN. "Out of Our Own Heritage . . . Music of the American Moravians," in *High Fidelity,* X/6 (June, 1960).

BROOKS, HENRY MASON. *Olden-Time Music*. Boston: Ticknor and Co., 1888.

BROUCEK, JACK W. "Eighteenth Century Music in Savannah, Georgia," Florida State University Ed.D. dissertation, 1963.

BROWN, ROBERT B., AND FRANK X. BRAUN. "The Tunebook of Conrad Doll," in *Papers of the Bibliographical Society of America,* XLII/3 (1948).

BRUINSMA, HENRY A. "The Organ Controversy in the Netherlands Reformation to 1640," in *Journal of the American Musicological Society,* VII/3 (Fall, 1954).

BUCK, DUDLEY. *Choir Accompaniment.* New York: G. Schirmer, 1888.

BUECHNER, ALAN CLARK. "Yankee Singing Schools and the Golden Age of Choral Music in New England," Harvard University Ph.D. dissertation, 1960.

CAMPBELL, DOUGLAS G. "George W. Chadwick: His Life and Works," University of Rochester Ph.D. dissertation, 1957.

CHADWICK, GEORGE W. *Horatio Parker.* New Haven: Yale University Press, 1921.

CHASTELLUX, FRANÇOIS JEAN, MARQUIS DE. *Travels in North-America, in the years 1780–81–82.* New York: White, Gallaher, & White, 1827.

CHENEY, SIMEON P. "Biographical Department," in *The American Singing Book.* Boston: White, Smith and Company, 1879.

CLOSEN, LUDWIG, BARON VON. *Revolutionary Journal, 1780–1783,* transl. and ed. by Evelyn M. Acomb. Chapel Hill: University of North Carolina Press, 1958.

COOK, HAROLD. "Shaker Music: A Manifestation of American Folk Culture," Western Reserve University Ph.D. dissertation, 1947.

COTTON, JOHN. *Singing of Psalmes a Gospel-Ordinance.* London: M. S. for Hannah Allen, 1647.

COURLANDER, HAROLD. *Negro Folk Music, U. S. A.* New York: Columbia University Press, 1963.

COVEY, CYCLONE. "Did Puritanism or the Frontier Cause the Decline of Colonial Music?," in *Journal of Research in Music Education,* VI/1 (Spring, 1958).

———. "Puritanism and Music in Colonial America," in *William and Mary Quarterly,* 3rd ser., VIII/3 (July, 1951); addendum: IX/1 (January, 1952).

COWELL, HENRY AND SIDNEY. *Charles Ives and His Music.* New York: Oxford University Press, 1955.

CRAWFORD, RICHARD ARTHUR. "Andrew Law (1749–1821): The Career of an American Musician," University of Michigan Ph.D. dissertation, 1965.

———, AND H. WILEY HITCHCOCK. *The Papers of Andrew Law in the William L. Clements Library.* Ann Arbor: [University Library, Bulletin 68], 1961.

CREWS, EMMA K. "A History of Music in Knoxville, Tennessee, 1791 to 1910," Florida State University D.Ed. dissertation, 1961.

DANIEL, RALPH T. "English Models for the First American Anthems," in *Journal of the American Musicological Society,* XII/1 (Spring, 1959).

———. "The Anthem in New England before 1800," Harvard University Ph.D. dissertation, 1955.

DAVID, HANS T. "Background for Bethlehem: Moravian Music in Pennsylvania," in *Magazine of Art,* XXXII (April, 1939).

———. "Ephrata and Bethlehem in Pennsylvania: A Comparison," in

Papers Read by Members of the American Musicological Society, 1941. 1946.

————. "Hymns and Music of the Pennsylvania Seventh-Day Baptists," in *American-German Review,* IX/5 (June, 1943).

————. "Musical Life in the Pennsylvania Settlements of the *Unitas Fratrum,*" in *Transactions of the Moravian Historical Society,* XIII/1–2 (1942).

DEAN, TALMAGE W. "The Organ in Eighteenth Century English Colonial America," University of Southern California Ph.D. dissertation, 1960.

DINNEEN, WILLIAM. "Music in the First Baptist Church, Providence, 1775–1834," in *Rhode Island History,* XVII/2 (April, 1958).

DOOLEY, JAMES EDWARD. "Thomas Hastings: American Church Musician," Florida State University Ph.D. dissertation, 1963.

DOUGLAS, CHARLES WINFRED. *Church Music in History and Practice.* New York: Charles Scribner's Sons, 1937.

DOWNEY, JAMES C. "Frontiers of Baptist Hymnody," in *The Church Musician,* XV/4 (April, 1964).

[DUCHÉ, JACOB.] *Observations on a Variety of Subjects, Literary, Moral and Religious.* Philadelphia: John Dunlap, 1774.

Dudley Buck. A Complete Bibliography of His Works. New York: G. Schirmer, 1910.

DWIGHT, JOHN S. "Address, delivered before the Harvard Musical Association, August 25th, 1841," in *The Musical Magazine; or, Repository,* III/69–70 (Aug. 28, 1841).

EAMES, WILBERFORCE, ED. *The Bay Psalm Book: Being a Facsimile Reprint.* New York: Dodd, Mead & Co., 1903.

EDWARDS, GEORGE T. *Music and Musicians of Maine.* Portland, Me.: Southworth Press, 1928.

ELLINWOOD, LEONARD. "English Influences in American Church Music," in *Proceedings of the Royal Music Association. 80th Session. 1953/54* (November 12, 1953).

————. *The History of American Church Music.* New York: Morehouse-Gorham Company, 1953.

————. "The Praise of God Today," in Charles Winfred Douglas, *Church Music in History and Practice.* New York: Charles Scribner's Sons, 1962.

————, ED. *The Charleston Hymnal of 1792 Compiled by Robert Smith and Henry Purcell.* Charleston: Dalcho Historical Society [*Publications,* No. 10], 1956.

————, AND ANNE WOODWARD DOUGLAS. *To Praise God. The Life and Work of Charles Winfred Douglas.* New York: Hymn Society of America [*Papers,* XXIII], 1958.

ELLIS, HOWARD. "Lowell Mason and the *Manual of the Boston Academy of Music,*" in *Journal of Research in Music Education,* III/1 (Spring, 1955).

ELSON, LOUIS C. *The History of American Music*. New York: Macmillan Co., 1925.

ENGEL, CARL. "Views and Reviews" [Ephrata Music], in *The Musical Quarterly,* XIV/2 (April, 1928).

ENGELKE, HANS. "A Study of Ornaments in American Tune-Books, 1760–1800," University of Southern California Ph.D. dissertation, 1960.

EPSTEIN, DENA J. "Slave Music in the United States before 1860: A Survey of Sources," in *Notes of the Music Library Association,* 2nd ser., XX/2–3 (Spring and Summer, 1963).

ESKEW, HARRY. "Hymnody of Our Forefathers," and "Music of Our Forefathers," in *The Church Musician,* XV/5 and 6 (May and June, 1964).

———. "Joseph Funk's 'Allgemein nützliche Choral-Music' (1816)," in *Fortieth Report. Society for the History of the Germans in Maryland.* Baltimore, 1965.

FELT, JOSEPH B. *Annals of Salem,* Vol. I., 2nd ed., Salem: W. & S. B. Ives, 1845.

FINNEY, THEODORE M. "The Collegium Musicum at Lititz, Pennsylvania, during the Eighteenth Century," in *Papers Read by Members of the American Musicological Society . . . 1937.* N.d.

FISHER, WILLIAM A. *Notes on Music in Old Boston*. Boston: Oliver Ditson, 1918.

———. *Ye Olde New-England Psalm-Tunes, 1620–1820*. Boston: Oliver Ditson, 1930.

FITHIAN, PHILIP. *Journal and Letters 1767–1774*. Princeton: University Library, 1900.

———. *Journal, 1775–1776,* ed. Robt. G. Albion and L. Dodson. Princeton: University Press, 1934.

FLETCHER, FRANCIS. *The World Encompassed by Sir Francis Drake*. London: Nicholas Bourne, 1652.

FOOTE, HENRY WILDER (1839–1889). *Annals of King's Chapel,* Vol. I. Boston: Little, Brown, 1882.

FOOTE, HENRY WILDER (b. 1875). "Musical Life in Boston in the Eighteenth Century," in *Proceedings of the American Antiquarian Society,* XLIX/2 (1939).

———. *Recent American Hymnody*. New York: Hymn Society of America, 1952 [*Papers,* XVII].

———. *Three Centuries of American Hymnody*. Cambridge, Mass.: Harvard University Press, 1940.

FROST, MAURICE. *English & Scottish Psalm & Hymn Tunes c. 1543–1677*. London: Oxford University Press, 1953.

———, ED. *Historical Companion to Hymns Ancient & Modern*. London: W. Clowes, 1962.

GARRETT, ALLEN. "The Works of William Billings," University of North Carolina Ph.D. dissertation, 1952.

GENTRY, LINNELL. *A History and Encyclopedia of Country, Western, and Gospel Music*. Nashville: McQuiddy Press, 1961.

GENUCHI, MARVIN C. "The Life and Music of Jacob French (1754–1817), Colonial American Composer," 2 vols., State University of Iowa Ph.D. dissertation, 1964.

GERSON, ROBERT A. *Music in Philadelphia*. Philadelphia: Theodore Presser Co., 1940.

GOLDMAN, RICHARD F. "Arias, Anthems and Chorales of the American Moravians" [record review], in *The Musical Quarterly*, XLVI/4 (October, 1960).

GOODSPEED, E. J. *A Full History of the Wonderful Career of Moody and Sankey, in Great Britain and America*. Philadelphia: F. Scofield & Co., 1876.

GOULD, NATHANIEL. *Church Music in America*. Boston: A. N. Johnson, 1853.

GRADY, EDYTHE R. "Sacred Music of the Negro in the U. S. A.," Union Theological Seminary M.S.M. thesis, 1950.

GRIDER, RUFUS A. *Historical Notes on Music in Bethlehem, Pennsylvania*. Philadelphia: John L. Pile, 1873; reprinted in *Moravian Music Foundation Publications, No. 4* (1957).

HACH, H. THEODORE. "Review. *The Massachusetts Collection of Psalmody* [etc.]," in *The Musical Magazine; or, Repository*, III, nos. 61 and 62 (May 8 and May 22, 1841).

HALL, CLAUDE. "Negro Gospel. No Other Musical Form is Quite Like It," in *Billboard*, LXXVII/44 (October 23, 1965).

HALL, JACOB H. *Biography of Gospel Song and Hymn Writers*. New York: Fleming H. Revell Co., 1914.

HAMM, CHARLES. "The Chapins and Sacred Music in the South and West," in *Journal of Research in Music Education*, VIII/2 (Fall, 1960).

———. "Patent Notes in Cincinnati," in *Bulletin. Historical and Philosophical Society of Ohio*, XVI/1 (October, 1958).

HARASZTI, ZOLTÁN. *The Enigma of the Bay Psalm Book*. Chicago: University of Chicago Press, 1956.

HARK, J. MAX, TRANSLATOR. *Chronicon Ephratense; A History of the Community of Seventh Day Baptists*. Lancaster: S. H. Zahm & Co., 1889.

HASTINGS, GEORGE E. *The Life and Works of Francis Hopkinson*. Chicago: University of Chicago Press, 1926.

HASTINGS, THOMAS. *Dissertation on Musical Taste*. Albany: Webster and Skinner, 1822.

HAUSSMANN, WILLIAM A. "German-American Hymnology. 1683–1800," in *Americana Germanica*, II/3 (1898).

HEHR, MILTON G. "Musical Activities in Salem, Massachusetts: 1783–1823," Boston University Ph.D. dissertation, 1963.

HESS, ALBERT G. "Observations on *The Lamenting Voice of the Hidden*

Love," in *Journal of the American Musicological Society,* V/3 (Fall, 1952).

HICKMAN, CHARLES LEROY. "Andrew Law: Intellectual Musician," Union Theological Seminary M.S.M. thesis, 1950.

HIGGINSON, J. VINCENT. *Hymnody in the American Indian Missions.* New York: Hymn Society of America, 1954.

HILL, DOUBLE E. "A Study of Tastes in American Church Music as Reflected in the Music of the Methodist Episcopal Church to 1900," University of Illinois Ph.D. dissertation, 1963.

HJORTSVANG, CARL T. "Scandinavian Contributions to American Sacred Music," Union Theological Seminary D.S.M. dissertation, 1951.

HODGES, EDWARD. *An Essay on the Cultivation of Church Music.* New York: J. A. Sparks, 1841.

HODGES, FAUSTINA H. *Edward Hodges, Doctor of Music.* New York: G. P. Putnam's Sons, 1896.

HOHMANN, RUPERT K. "The Church Music of the Old Order Amish of the United States," Northwestern University Ph.D. dissertation, 1959.

HOLMES, CARL T. "A Study of the Music in the 1747 edition of Conrad Beissel's *Das Gesaeng der einsamen und verlassenen Turtel-Taube,* Huntington Library 39957, Evans 5959," University of Southern California Master of Arts thesis, 1959.

HOOD, GEORGE. *A History of Music in New England: with Biographical Sketches of Reformers and Psalmists.* Boston: Wilkins, Carter & Co., 1846.

HOOPER, WILLIAM L. *Church Music in Transition.* Nashville: Broadman Press, 1963.

HOPKINSON, FRANCIS. "A Letter to the Rev. Doctor White, Rector of Christ Church and St. Peter's, on the Conduct of a Church Organ," in *Miscellaneous Essays and Occasional Writings,* Vol. II. Philadelphia: T. Dobson, 1792.

HORN[E], DOROTHY D. "A Study of the Folk-Hymns of Southeastern America," University of Rochester Ph.D. dissertation, 1953.

————. "Dyadic Harmony in the Sacred Harp," in *Southern Folklore Quarterly,* V/4 (December, 1941).

————. "Folk-Hymn Texts in Three 'Old Harp' Books," in *Tennessee Folklore Society Bulletin,* XXII/4 (December, 1956).

————. "Quartal Harmony in the Pentatonic Folk Hymns of the Sacred Harps," in *Journal of American Folklore,* LXXI/282 (October–December, 1958).

————. "Shape-Note Hymnals and the Art-Music of Early America," in *Southern Folklore Quarterly,* V/4 (December, 1941).

————. "Tune Detecting in 19th Century Hymnals," in *Tennessee Folklore Society Bulletin,* XXVI/4 (December, 1960).

HORST, IRVIN B. "Joseph Funk, Early Mennonite Printer and Publisher (with a bibliography)," in *The Mennonite Quarterly Review,* XXXI/4 (October, 1957).

HOUCK, ELIZABETH S. "Johann Conrad Beissel: His Life and Music," Union Theological Seminary M.S.M. thesis, 1956.

HOWARD, JOHN T. "The Hewitt Family in American Music," in *The Musical Quarterly,* XVII/1 (January, 1931).

HOWE, M. A. DeWOLFE. "Venite in Bethlehem," in *The Musical Quarterly,* XXVIII/2 (April, 1942).

HOWELL, LILLIAN POPE. "Lowell Mason, Composer of Hymn-Tunes," Southern Baptist Theological Seminary M.S.M. thesis, 1948.

HUBBARD, JOHN. *An Essay on Music.* Boston: Manning & Loring, 1808.

HUNTINGTON, RONALD M. "A Study of the Musical Contributions of Leo Sowerby," Master of Music thesis, University of Southern California, 1957.

JACKSON, GEORGE PULLEN. "Buckwheat Notes," in *The Musical Quarterly,* XIX/4 (October, 1933).

————. "Early American Religious Folk Songs," in *Proceedings of the Music Teachers National Association. Series 29 [1934].* Oberlin: The Association, 1935.

————. "Pennsylvania Dutch Spirituals," in *The Musical Quarterly,* XXXVIII/1 (January, 1952).

————. "Some Factors in the Diffusion of American Religious Folksongs," in *Journal of American Folklore,* LXV/258 (October–December, 1952).

————. *The Story of the Sacred Harp 1844–1944.* Nashville: Vanderbilt University Press, 1944.

————. "The Strange Music of the Old Order Amish," in *The Musical Quarterly,* XXXI/3 (July, 1945).

————. *White and Negro Spirituals: Their Life Span and Kinship.* New York: J. J. Augustin, 1943.

————. *White Spirituals in the Southern Uplands.* Chapel Hill: University of North Carolina Press, 1933.

JANSON, CHARLES W. *The Stranger in America.* London: James Cundee, 1807.

JEFFREYS, C. P. B. "Music and Singing at St. Peter's, 1761–1783," in *The Pennsylvania Magazine of History and Biography,* XLVIII/2 (April, 1924).

JOHNSON, FRANCES HALL. *Musical Memories of Hartford.* Hartford: Witkower's, 1931.

JOHNSON, H. EARLE. *Hallelujah, Amen! The Story of the Handel and Haydn Society of Boston.* Boston: Bruce Humphries, 1965.

————. *Musical Interludes in Boston, 1795–1830.* New York: Columbia University Press, 1943.

JOHNSON, JAMES WELDON, AND J. ROSAMUND JOHNSON. *The Books of American Negro Spirituals.* New York: Viking Press, 1940.

JONES, MATT B. *Bibliographical Notes on Thomas Walter's "Grounds and Rules of Musick Explained."* Worcester: American Antiquarian Society, 1933.

KENT, RALPH M. "A Study of Oratorios and Sacred Cantatas Composed in America before 1900," Iowa University Ph.D. dissertation, 1954.

KIEFFER, ELIZABETH C. "Three Caspar Schaffners," in *Papers of the Lancaster County Historical Society,* XLII/7 (1938).

KINKELDEY, OTTO. "Beginnings of Beethoven in America," in *The Musical Quarterly,* XIII/2 (April, 1927).

KREHBIEL, H. E. *Notes on the Cultivation of Choral Music and the Oratorio Society of New York.* New York: Edw. Schuberth & Co., 1884.

KRIEBEL, HOWARD W. *The Schwenkfelders in Pennsylvania.* Lancaster: New Era Printing Co., 1904.

KROHN, ERNST C. "The Missouri Harmony: A Study in Early American Psalmody," and "A Check List of Editions of 'The Missouri Harmony,' " in *Bulletin. Missouri Historical Society,* VI/1 and 3 (October, 1949 and April, 1950).

LAFAR, MARGARET FREEMAN. "Lowell Mason's Varied Activities in Savannah," in *The Georgia Historical Society Quarterly,* XXVIII/3 (September, 1944).

LAMECH AND AGRIPPA, BROTHERS. *Chronicon Ephratense Enthaltend den Lebens-Lauf des ehrwürdigen Vaters in Christo Friedsam Gottrecht.* Ephrata: 1786.

LARUE, JAN. "English Music Papers in the Moravian Archives of North Carolina," in *Monthly Musical Record,* 89/995 (September–October, 1959).

LAW, ANDREW. *Essays on Music.* [First-Second Number.] Philadelphia: Printed for the Author, 1814.

LAWRENCE, JAMES B. "Religious Education of the Negro in the Colony of Georgia," in *The Georgia Historical Society Quarterly,* XIV/1 (March, 1930).

LE CHALLEUX, NICHOLAS. *Brief Discovrs et histoire d'vn voyage de quelques François en la Floride,* in Girolamo Benzoni, *Histoire novvelle.* Geneva: Eustace Vignon, 1579.

LEVERING, JOSEPH M. *A History of Bethlehem, Pennsylvania 1741–1892.* Bethlehem: Times Publishing Co., 1903.

LINDSTROM, CARL E. "William Billings and His Times," in *The Musical Quarterly,* XXV/4 (October, 1939).

LIPPENCOTT, MARGARET E. "Dearborn's Musical *Scheme,*" in *New-York Historical Society Quarterly Bulletin,* XXV/4 (October, 1941).

LOESSEL, EARL OLIVER. "The Use of Character Notes and Other Unorthodox Notations in Teaching the Reading of Music in Northern United States," University of Michigan Ed.D. dissertation, 1959.

LOVELACE, AUSTIN C. *The Anatomy of Hymnody.* New York/Nashville: Abingdon Press, 1965.

————. "Early Sacred Folk Music in America," in *The Hymn,* III/1 and 2 (January and April, 1952).

————. "Music in the Special Ministries of the Church," in *The Church Musician,* XVI/1 (January, 1965).

LOWENS, IRVING. "A Plain Introduction to Singing Psalm-Tunes" (Foreword to facsimile of John Tufts's *An Introduction,* 5th edition). Philadelphia: Musical Americana (Harry Dichter), 1954.

————. "A Postscript on Shape-Notes," in *Wyeth's Repository of Sacred Music, Part Second* [facsimile reprint]. New York: Da Capo Press, 1964.

————. "Andrew Law and the Pirates," in *Journal of the American Musicological Society,* XIII/1–3 (1960).

————. "Copyright and Andrew Law," in *Papers of the Bibliographical Society of America,* LIII/2 (1959).

————. "Daniel Read's World: The Letters of an Early American Composer," in *Notes of the Music Library Association,* 2nd ser., IX/2 (March, 1952).

————. "John Tufts' *Introduction to the Singing of Psalm-Tunes* (1721–1744): The First American Music Textbook," in *Journal of Research in Music Education,* II/2 (Fall, 1954).

————. "John Wyeth's *Repository of Sacred Music, Part Second:* A Northern Precursor of Southern Folk Hymnody," in *Journal of the American Musicological Society,* V/2 (Summer, 1952).

————. "Moravian Music—Neglected American Heritage," in *Musical America,* LXXVIII (February, 1958).

————. *Music and Musicians in Early America.* New York: W. W. Norton, 1964.

————. "Our Neglected Musical Heritage," in *The Hymn,* III/2 (April, 1952).

————. "The Bay Psalm Book in 17th-Century New England," in *Journal of the American Musicological Society,* VIII/1 (Spring, 1955).

————. "*The Continental Harmony* by William Billings. Edited by Hans Nathan" (review), in *The Musical Quarterly,* XLVIII/3 (July, 1962).

————. "The Origins of the American Fuging Tune," in *Journal of the American Musicological Society,* VI/1 (Spring, 1953).

————, AND ALLEN P. BRITTON. "Daniel Bayley's 'The American Harmony,' " in *Papers of the Bibliographical Society of America,* XLIX/4 (1955).

————. "*The Easy Instructor* (1798–1831): A History and Bibliography of the First Shape-Note Tune-Book," in *Journal of Research in Music Education,* I/1 (Spring, 1953).

LUCAS, G. W. *Remarks on the Musical Conventions in Boston, &c.* Northampton: Printed for the Author, 1844.

LUTKIN, PETER C. *Music in the Church.* Milwaukee: Young Churchman Co., 1910.

McCorkle, Donald M. "John Antes, 'American Dilettante,'" in *The Musical Quarterly,* XLII/4 (October, 1956).

———. "Moravian Music in Salem," Indiana University Ph.D. dissertation, 1958.

———. "Musical Instruments of the Moravians in North Carolina," in *The American-German Review,* XXI/3 (February–March, 1955).

———. "The Collegium Musicum Salem: Its Music, Musicians, and Importance," in *The North Carolina Historical Review,* XXXIII/4 (October, 1956).

———. "The Moravian Contribution to American Music," in *Notes of the Music Library Association,* 2nd ser., XIII/4 (September, 1956).

McCormick, David W. "Oliver Holden, Composer and Anthologist," Union Theological Seminary D.S.M. dissertation, 1963.

McCutchan, Robert G. *Hymn Tune Names: Their Sources and Significance.* New York: Abingdon Press, 1957.

———. *Our Hymnody.* New York: Abingdon Press, 1942.

Macdougall, Hamilton C. *Early New England Psalmody.* Brattleboro [Vt.]: Stephen Daye Press, 1940.

McElrath, Hugh T., and Edmond D. Keith. *Sing from Your Hearts.* Nashville: Convention Press, 1964.

McKinnon, James. "The Meaning of the Patristic Polemic Against Musical Instruments," in *Current Musicology,* Spring, 1965.

McKissick, Marvin L. "A Study of the Function of Music in the Major Religious Revivals in America since 1875," University of Southern California M.Mus. thesis, 1957.

Mangler, Joyce E. "Music in the First Congregational Church, Providence, 1770–1850," in *Rhode Island History,* XVII/1 (January, 1958).

———. "Oliver Shaw and the Psallonian Society," in *Rhode Island History,* XXIII/2 (April, 1964).

———. *Rhode Island Music and Musicians 1733–1850.* Detroit: Information Service, Inc. [Detroit Studies in Music Bibliography, 7], 1965.

Mann, Thomas. *Doktor Faustus.* Stockholm: Berman-Fischer Verlag, 1947. (English transl. by H. T. Lowe-Porter. New York: Alfred A. Knopf, 1948.)

Marrocco, W. Thomas. "The Notation in American Sacred Collections," in *Acta Musicologica,* XXXVI, II–III (1964).

———. "The Set Piece," in *Journal of the American Musicological Society,* XV/3 (Fall, 1962).

Marsh, J. B. I. *The Story of the Jubilee Singers.* London: Hodder & Stroughton, 1877 [7th ed.].

Martin, Raymond J. "The Transition from Psalmody to Hymnody in Southern Presbyterianism, 1753–1901," Union Theological Seminary S.M.D. dissertation, 1963.

MARTY, MARTIN E. "Composing for the Church: 1960," in *Christian Century,* LXXVII, March 23, 1960.

MASON, DANIEL GREGORY. "A Glimpse of Lowell Mason from an Old Bundle of Letters," in *New Music Review and Church Music Review,* XXVI/302 (January, 1927).

———. "Some Unpublished Journals of Dr. Lowell Mason," in *New Music Review and Church Music Review,* IX/108 (November, 1910); X/110 (January, 1911).

MASON, HENRY L. *Hymn-Tunes of Lowell Mason: A Bibliography.* Cambridge, Mass.: Harvard University Press, 1944.

———. *Lowell Mason: An Appreciation of His Life and Work.* New York: The Hymn Society of America [*Papers,* VIII], 1941.

MASON, JOHN RUSSELL. *American Hymnology: A Bibliography.* New York: Columbia University [School of Library Science], 1933.

MASON, LOWELL. *Address on Church Music.* Boston: Hilliard, Gray and Co., 1826.

———. "Letter to the Editor," in *The Musical Magazine,* III/63 (June 5, 1841).

———. *Musical Letters from Abroad.* New York: Mason Brothers, 1854.

———. *Song in Worship.* Boston: Marvin & Son, 1878.

MATHER, COTTON. *Diary. 1709–1724,* in *Massachusetts Historical Society Collections, 7th Series, Vol. VIII.* Boston [Norwood: The Plimpton Press], 1912.

———. *A Letter; About the Present State of Christianity among the Christianized Indians of New-England.* Boston: T. Green, 1705.

MATHEWS, W. S. B. *A Hundred Years of Music in America.* Chicago: G. L. Howe, 1889.

———. "American Oratorios" [J. K. Paine's *St. Peter* and Dudley Buck's *46th Psalm*], in *The Nation,* XVI/398 (February 13, 1873).

MAURER, JOSEPH A. "Moravian Church Music—1457–1957," in *American Guild of Organists Quarterly,* II/1 (January, 1957).

———. "The Moravian Trombone Choir (Bicentennial of Bethlehem's Historic Music Ensemble)," in *The Historical Review of Berks County,* XX/1 (October–December, 1954).

MAURER, MAURER. "Music in Wachovia," in *William and Mary Quarterly,* 3rd ser., VIII/2 (April, 1951).

MAYS, KENNETH ROBERT. "The Use of Hymn Tunes in the Works of Charles Ives," Indiana University M.M. thesis, 1961.

MERRILL, E. LINDSEY. "Mrs. H. H. A. Beach: Her Life and Music," University of Rochester Ph.D. dissertation, 1963.

MESSITER, A. H. *A History of the Choir and Music of Trinity Church.* New York: Edwin S. Gorham, 1906.

METCALF, FRANK J. *American Psalmody: or, Titles of Books, Containing Tunes Printed in America from 1721 to 1820.* New York: Charles F. Heartman, 1917.

————. *American Writers and Compilers of Sacred Music.* New York: Abingdon Press, 1925.

————. " 'The Easy Instructor': A Bibliographical Study," in *The Musical Quarterly,* XXIII/1 (January, 1937).

MOLNAR, JOHN W. "A Collection of Music in Colonial Virginia: The Ogle Inventory," in *The Musical Quarterly,* XLIX/2 (April, 1963).

MORGAN, MARY F., AND HELEN W. LUDLOW. *Hampton and Its Students.* New York: G. P. Putnam's Sons, 1875.

MORIN, RAYMOND. "William Billings: Pioneer in American Music," in *New England Quarterly,* XIV/1 (March, 1941).

NATHAN, HANS, ED. *The Continental Harmony by William Billings.* Cambridge, Mass.: Harvard University Press, 1961.

NEILSON, PETER. *Recollections of a Six Years' Residence in the United States of America.* Glasgow: David Robertson, 1830.

NICHOLS, ARTHUR H. "Christ Church Bells, Boston, Mass.," in *The New-England Historical and Genealogical Register,* LVIII (1904).

NORTON, M. D. HERTER. "Haydn in America (before 1820)," in *The Musical Quarterly,* XVIII/2 (April, 1932).

OURSLER, FULTON. "The Song You Can't Forget," in *This Week Magazine,* December 27, 1953.

PAGE, PATRICIA ANN. "The Westminster Choir College," Union Theological Seminary M.S.M. thesis, 1953.

PATTERSON, FLOYD H., JR. "The Southern Baptist Sunday School Board's Program of Church Music," George Peabody College for Teachers Ph.D. dissertation, 1957.

PATTERSON, RELFORD. "Three American 'Primitives': A Study of the Musical Style of Hans Gram, Oliver Holden, and Samuel Holyoke," Washington University Ph.D. dissertation, 1963.

PENNSYLVANIA SOCIETY OF THE COLONIAL DAMES OF AMERICA. *Church Music and Musical Life in Pennsylvania in the Eighteenth Century,* 3 vols. (Vol. 3 in 2 parts). Philadelphia: [Lancaster: Wickersham Printing Co.], 1926–1947.

PERKINS, CHARLES C., AND JOHN S. DWIGHT. *History of the Handel and Haydn Society of Boston, Massachusetts.* Boston: Alfred Mudge & Son, 1883–1893.

PFAUTSCH, LLOYD A. "A Curriculum of Church Music for a Theological Seminary: A Historical Justification and a Formulation," Union Theological Seminary M.S.M. thesis, 1948.

PHELPS, AUSTIN, E. A. PARK, AND D. L. FURBER. *Hymns and Choirs.* Andover: W. F. Draper, 1860.

PICHIERRI, LOUIS. *Music in New Hampshire, 1623–1800.* New York: Columbia University Press, 1960.

PIDOUX, PIERRE. *Le Psautier huguenot du XVIe siècle,* 2 vols. Basle: Bärenreiter, 1962.

PIERCE, EDWIN H. " 'Gospel Hymns' and Their Tunes," in *The Musical Quarterly,* XXVI/3 (July, 1940).

————. "The Rise and Fall of the 'Fugue-Tune' in America," in *The Musical Quarterly,* XVI/2 (April, 1930).

PLYMOUTH, MASS., FIRST CHURCH. *Plymouth Church Records 1620–1859: Part I,* in *Publications of The Colonial Society of Massachusetts,* Vol. XXII. Boston: John Wilson and Son, 1920.

POLADIAN, SIRVART. "Rev. John Tufts and Three-part Psalmody in America," in *Journal of the American Musicological Society,* IV/3 (Fall, 1951).

PRATT, WALDO S. *The Music of the French Psalter of 1562.* New York: Columbia University Press, 1939.

————. *The Music of the Pilgrims.* Boston: Oliver Ditson Co., 1921.

PURDY, WILLIAM E. "Music in Mormon Culture, 1830–1876," Northwestern University Ph.D. dissertation, 1960.

QUINN, EUGENE FRANCIS. "A Survey of the Principles and Practices of Contemporary Nonliturgical Church Music," Southern Baptist Theological Seminary D.C.M. dissertation, 1962.

RAU, ALBERT G. "John Frederick Peter," in *The Musical Quarterly,* XXIII/3 (July, 1937).

RAU, ALBERT G., AND HANS T. DAVID. *A Catalogue of Music by American Moravians 1742–1842. From the Archives of the Moravian Church at Bethlehem, Pennsylvania.* Bethlehem: Moravian Seminary, 1938.

REDLICH, HANS. "New Music: A Critical Interim Report," in *The Music Review,* XVI (August, 1955).

REDWAY, VIRGINIA L. "Charles Theodore Pachelbell, Musical Emigrant," in *Journal of the American Musicological Society,* V/1 (Spring, 1952).

————. "James Parker and the 'Dutch Church,' " in *The Musical Quarterly,* XXIV/4 (October, 1938).

REYNOLDS, WILLIAM J. *A Survey of Christian Hymnody.* New York: Holt, Rinehart and Winston, 1963.

————. *Hymns of Our Faith. A Handbook for the Baptist Hymnal.* Nashville: Broadman Press, 1964.

RICE, JOHN H., ED. "Attempts to Evangelize the Negroe-slaves in Virginia and Carolina," in *The Evangelical and Literary Magazine* [Richmond, Va.], IV/10 (October, 1821).

RICH, ARTHUR L. *Lowell Mason.* Chapel Hill: University of North Carolina Press, 1946.

RITTER, FRÉDÉRIC L. *Music in America.* New York: Charles Scribner's Sons, 1890.

ROBERTS, KENNETH CREIGHTON, JR. "John Knowles Paine," University of Michigan M.A. thesis, 1962.

ROOT, GEORGE F. *The Story of a Musical Life.* Cincinnati: John Church, 1891.

ROUTLEY, ERIK. *The Music of Christian Hymnody: A Study of the Development of the Hymn Tune.* London: Independent Press, 1957.

————. "On The Billy Graham Song Book," in *The Hymn,* VI/1 (January, 1955).

SACHSE, JULIUS F. *The German Pietists of Provincial Pennsylvania 1694–1708.* Philadelphia: P. C. Stockhausen, 1895.

————. *The Music of the Ephrata Cloister; also, Conrad Beissel's Treatise on Music.* Lancaster: New Era Printing Co., 1902.

SALTZMAN, HERBERT R. "A Historical Study of the Function of Music among the Brethren in Christ," University of Southern California D.M.A. dissertation, 1964.

SALZMAN, ERIC. "Ives, Mahler and Philharmonic Juxtaposition," in *New York Herald Tribune,* CXXV/43,335 (November 27, 1965).

SASS, HERBERT RAVENEL. "I Can't Help From Cryin'," in *The Saturday Evening Post,* Oct. 3, 1942.

SAYERS, W. C. BERWICK. *Samuel Coleridge-Taylor, Musician.* London: Cassell, 1915.

SCANLON, MARY B. "Thomas Hastings," in *The Musical Quarterly,* XXXII/2 (April, 1946).

SCHALK, CARL FLENTGE. "A Stylistic Analysis of The Christmas Story for Orchestra and Mixed Chorus by Peter Mennin," University of Rochester M.M. thesis, 1957.

SCHOLES, PERCY A. *The Puritans and Music in England and New England.* London: Oxford University Press, 1934.

SCOTT, RUTH. "Music among the Moravians: Bethlehem, Pennsylvania, 1741–1816," Master of Music thesis, University of Rochester, 1938.

SECCOMBE, JOSEPH. *An Essay to Excite a Further Inquiry into the Ancient Matter and Manner of Sacred Singing.* Boston: S. Kneeland and T. Green, 1741.

SEEGER, CHARLES. "Contrapuntal Style in the Three-Voice Shape-Note Hymns," in *The Musical Quarterly,* XXVI/4 (October, 1940).

SEMLER, ISABEL P., AND PIERSON UNDERWOOD. *Horatio Parker.* New York: G. P. Putnam's Sons, 1942.

SESSIONS, ROGER. *Reflections on the Music Life in the United States.* New York: Merlin Press, 1956.

SEWALL, SAMUEL. *Diary 1674–1729,* in *Collections of the Massachusetts Historical Society, Fifth Series, Vols. V–VII.* Boston: [John Wilson and Co.], 1878–1882.

SEYBOLT, ROBERT F. *The Private Schools of Colonial Boston.* Cambridge, Mass.: Harvard University Press, 1935.

SIMS, JOHN N. "The Hymnody of the Camp-Meeting Tradition," Union Theological Seminary D.S.M. dissertation, 1960.

SIMS, WALTER HINES. "Handbook to the Baptist Hymnal," in *The Church Musician,* XV/3 (March, 1964).

SMITH, CARLETON SPRAGUE. *Early Psalmody in America. Series I. The Ainsworth Psalter*. New York: New York Public Library, 1938.

————. "The 1774 Psalm Book of the Reformed Protestant Dutch Church in New York City," in *The Musical Quarterly*, XXXIV/1 (January, 1948).

SMITH, CARLTON Y. "Early Lutheran Hymnody in America From the Colonial Period to the Year 1850," University of Southern California Ph.D. dissertation, 1956.

SONNECK, O. G. "Francis Hopkinson (1737–1791). The First American Composer," in *Sammelbände der Internationalen Musik-Gesellschaft*, V (1903–1904).

————. *Francis Hopkinson, the First American Poet-Composer (1737–1791) and James Lyon, Patriot, Preacher, Psalmodist (1735–1794): Two Studies in Early American Music*. Washington: H. L. McQueen, 1905.

STALLINGS, V. LEE. "A Study of *Forsaken of Man*, a Sacred Cantata by Leo Sowerby," Southern Baptist Theological Seminary M.S.M. thesis, 1956.

STEARNS, CHARLES. *A Sermon: preached at an exhibition of sacred musick*. Boston: Isaiah Thomas and E. T. Andrews, 1792.

STEBBINS, GEORGE COLE. *Reminiscences and Gospel Hymn Stories*. New York: George H. Doran, 1924.

STEVENSON, ROBERT. "Dr. Watts' 'Flights of fancy,' " in *Harvard Theological Review*, XLII/4 (October, 1949).

————. "Evangelistic Song," in *Religion in Life*, XXVI/3 (Summer, 1957).

————. "Ira D. Sankey and Gospel Hymnody," in *Religion in Life*, XX/1 (Winter, 1950–1951).

————. "John Wesley's First Hymnbook," in *Review of Religion*, XIV/2 (January, 1950).

————. "The English Service," in *American Choral Review*, VI/1 and 2 (October, 1963, and January, 1964).

————. "Watts in America," in *Harvard Theological Review*, XLI/3 (July, 1948).

STILES, EZRA. *The Literary Diary*, ed. Franklin B. Dexter, 3 vols. New York: Charles Scribner's Sons, 1901.

STOUTAMIRE, ALBERT L. "A History of Music in Richmond, Virginia, from 1742 to 1865," Florida State University Ed.D. dissertation, 1960.

STROUD, WILLIAM PAUL. "The Ravenscroft Psalter (1621): The Tunes, with a background on Thomas Ravenscroft and Psalm Singing in his Time," University of Southern California D.M.A. dissertation, 1959.

SWAN, HOWARD. *Music in the Southwest*. San Marino: The Huntington Library, 1952.

SWEET, CHARLES F. *A Champion of the Cross being the life of John Henry Hopkins, S. T. D.* New York: James Pott & Co., 1894.

SYDNOR, JAMES R. *The Hymn and Congregational Singing.* Richmond: John Knox Press, 1960.

SYMMES, THOMAS. *The Reasonableness of, Regular Singing, or, Singing by Note.* Boston: B. Green, for Samuel Gerrish, 1720.

————. *Utile Dulci. or, A Joco-Serious Dialogue, Concerning Regular Singing.* Boston: B. Green, for Samuel Gerrish, 1723.

TAYLOR, JEWEL A. "Technical Practices of Negro Composers in Choral Works for A Cappella Choir," University of Rochester M.A. thesis, 1960.

TEAL, MARY EVELYN DURDEN. "Musical Activities in Detroit from 1701 through 1870," University of Michigan Ph.D. dissertation, 1964.

THAYER, ALEXANDER W. "Lowell Mason," in *Dwight's Journal of Music,* XXXIX/1007 and 1008 (November 22 and December 6, 1879).

"The Magazines for June," in *The Nation,* IV/100 (May 30, 1867), 432.

THOMPSON, JAMES W. "Music and Musical Activities in New England, 1800–1838," George Peabody College for Teachers Ph.D. dissertation, 1963.

TROUTMANN, JEAN E. "A History of Music at Saint Bartholomew's Church, New York," Union Theological Seminary M.S.M. thesis, 1951.

TUTHILL, BURNET C. "Leo Sowerby," in *The Musical Quarterly,* XXIV/3 (July, 1938).

UMBLE, JOHN. "The Old Order Amish, Their Hymns and Hymn Tunes," in *Journal of American Folk-Lore,* LII/203 (January–March, 1939).

UNGRODT, JUDITH T. "The Music of Francis Hopkinson," University of Rochester M.A. thesis, 1962.

VARDELL, CHARLES G. *Organs in the Wilderness.* Winston-Salem: Salem Academy and College, 1944.

WALTER, THOMAS. *The Grounds and Rules of Musick.* Boston: J. Franklin, for S. Gerrish, 1721.

————. *The sweet Psalmist of Israel. A Sermon Preach'd at the Lecture held in Boston, by the Society for Promoting Regular & Good Singing.* Boston: J. Franklin, for S. Gerrish, 1722.

WALTERS, RAYMOND. *The Bethlehem Bach Choir.* Boston: Houghton Mifflin Co., 1918.

WARRINGTON, JAMES. *Short Titles of Books relating to or illustrating the History and Practice of Psalmody in the United States 1620–1820.* Philadelphia: Privately Printed, 1898.

WAYLAND, JOHN W. "Joseph Funk: Father of Song in Northern Virginia," in *The Pennsylvania-German,* XII/10 (October, 1911).

WERTENBAKER, THOMAS J. *The Golden Age of Colonial Culture.* New York: New York University Press, 1949.

————. *The Old South: The Founding of American Civilization.* New York: Charles Scribner's Sons, 1942.

WHITEHILL, WALTER M. "Communication" (early Harvard graduates' musical encounters), in *William and Mary Quarterly,* 3rd ser., IX/1 (January, 1952).

WIENANDT, ELWYN A. *Choral Music of the Church.* New York: The Free Press, 1965.

———. "Jazz at the Altar?" in *Christian Century,* LXXVII, March 23, 1960.

WILCOX, GLENN. "Jacob Kimball, Jr. (1761–1826): His Life and Works," University of Southern California Ph.D. dissertation, 1957.

WILKES, WILLIAM. "Borrowed Music in Mormon Hymnals," University of Southern California Ph.D. dissertation, 1957.

WILLHIDE, J. LAWRENCE. "Samuel Holyoke, American Music-Educator," University of Southern California Ph.D. dissertation, 1954.

WILLIAMS, FRANCIS H. "John Kelpius, Pietist," in *New World* (Boston), III/10 (June, 1894).

WILLIAMS, GEORGE W. "Charleston Church Music 1562–1833," in *Journal of the American Musicological Society,* VII/1 (Spring, 1954).

———. "Eighteenth-Century Organists of St. Michael's, Charleston," in *South Carolina Historical Magazine,* LIII/3 and 4 (July and October, 1952).

———. "Jacob Eckhard and His Choirmaster's Book," in *Journal of the American Musicological Society,* VII/1 (Spring, 1954).

———. *St. Michael's, Charleston, 1751–1951.* Columbia: University of South Carolina Press, 1951.

WILLIAMS, THOMAS. *A Discourse on the Life and Death of Oliver Shaw.* Boston: Charles C. P. Moody, 1851.

WINSLOW, EDWARD. *Hypocrisie Vnmasked.* London: Richard Cotes for John Bellamy, 1646.

WOLF, EDWARD C. "Lutheran Church Music in America during the Eighteenth and Early Nineteenth Centuries," University of Illinois Ph.D. dissertation, 1960.

WORK, JOHN, ED. *American Negro Spirituals.* New York: Bonanza Books, 1940.

WRIGHT, LOUIS B., AND MARION TINLING, EDS. *The Secret Diary of William Byrd of Westover 1709–1712.* Richmond: The Dietz Press, 1941.

WUNDERLICH, CHARLES E. "A History and Bibliography of Early American Musical Periodicals, 1782–1852," University of Michigan Ph.D. dissertation, 1962.

YARMOLINSKY, AVRAHAM. *Picturesque United States of America 1811, 1812, 1813 being a Memoir on Paul Svinin.* New York: William E. Rudge, 1930.

YELLIN, VICTOR. "Music in America, An Anthology from the Landing of the Pilgrims to the Close of the Civil War, 1620–1865" (review), in *Journal of the American Musicological Society,* XVIII/2 (Summer, 1965).

YODER, PAUL M. "Nineteenth Century Sacred Music of the Mennonite

Church in the United States," Florida State University Ph.D. dissertation, 1961.

YOUNG, CARLTON R. "American Methodist Hymnody: A Historical Sketch," in *The History of American Methodism,* III, ed. by Emory S. Bucke. New York/Nashville: Abingdon Press, 1964.

———. "John Wesley: Church Musician," in *The Church Musician,* XVI/2 (February, 1965).

ZIMMERMAN, FRANKLIN B. *Henry Purcell 1659–1695, An analytical catalogue of his music.* London: Macmillan, 1963.

INDEX

INDEX

WHILE AN EFFORT has been made to index all names of musical interest, printers' names have usually been omitted. Names of Biblical characters are indexed, but not Biblical citations. To keep the index within bounds, such titles as Reverend, Doctor, Bishop, Captain, and Governor are not used. Place-names that occur scores of times—Boston, New York, and Philadelphia, for instance—go unindexed; on the other hand, places mentioned once or twice are included. Dates not in the text are given only when needed for quick identification. Because of their great number, no attempt has been made to index every hymn tune name, every hymnbook, and every music instructor mentioned in the text. The captions to the plates are not indexed.

Abel: C. F., 43; F. C. (Savannah), 78n
Accomplished Singer, The (Cotton Mather), 22 & n
"A Child My Choice" (Dirksen), 125
Ackley, B. D., 110
Acomb, Evelyn M., 49
Adams, Zabdiel, 22n
Address on Church Music (Mason, 1826), 80
Adgate, Andrew, 30, 50, 88n
Adieu mes amours, 126n
African Methodist Episcopal Church, 70
Agrippa, King, 40
Ainsworth, Henry, 6, 7n, 12–13
Albany: Dutch missionary at, 10; Hastings publication at, 78n
Aldersgate, Wesley's conversion at, 40
Alembert, Jean le Rond d', *see* D'Alembert
Alexander, Dora, 104n
Alleluia (Randall Thompson), 122n
Allen, Richard (1760–1831), founder African Methodist Episcopal Church, 70
Allen, W. F., 96
Allison, Richard, 15
Allwardt, Anton Paul, 106n, 130
ALSEN (F. C. Abel), 78n

Alsted, Johann Heinrich, 24–25
Altdorf, University of, 32
Alviani, Doric, 119n, 130
AMANDA (Justin Morgan), 72
AMERICA: Billings, 62; British national anthem, 114n
American Harmony, The (Daniel Bayley), 60 & n, 86n; (Holden, 1792), 72
American Missionary Association, 101
American Singing Book, The (Read, 1785), 65n, 66n, 79n; 4th ed. (1793), 75
AMHERST (Billings), 62–63
Amish, singing among, 22n
Amsterdam, 6, 12n, 13
Anastasia, Sister (= Anna Thomen), Ephrata disciple, 33, 35–36 & n
Andrew of Crete, 124–125
Andrews, Ebenezer T., 66, 74n, 75n, 90n
Anleitung zum Gesang-Unterrichte (Kübler, 1826), 78 & n
Annotations Upon the second book of Moses (Ainsworth), 6n
Antes, John, 38 & n, 41–42
anthem: definition of, 76n; New England composers, before 1800, 70–73; 1810–1820, 76; representative

153

composers not included in the New
England group before 1820:
Bradbury, 108; Buck, 113; Chadwick,
119n; Hopkinson, 47; Jones, 124;
Lyon, 50–51; Mason, 84–85;
Moravian, 41–44 (& n); Parker,
119n; Pfautsch, 125, 131; Tuckey, 49
Antigua (Leeward Islands), 52
Appalachian Spring (Copland), 122n
Army Life in a Black Regiment
(Higginson), 97
Arne, Thomas, 46
Arnold, John, 60n, 61n
Arnold, Samuel, 75
Asaph, Levite leader of Temple music,
29
Asbury, Francis, 70
Athenaeum Collection, The (1863),
112
AUGHTON ("He leadeth me"), 83n,
108
Augustine of Hippo, 49
Avlcvns pseaulmes et cantiques mys
en chant (1539), 4n
Austin, William, 130

Babcock, Samuel, 30
Bach: J. C. F. ("Bückeburg"), 43;
J. S., 19, 43, 55, 82; K. P. E., 75
Bacon's Rebellion, 53
Baltimore, Christmas Conference at,
69
banjo tunes, 97
Baptist Hymnals, 111n, 128
Baptists: music among, 48, 65n, 68n,
83n, 96n, 109, 111n, 126n; Southern
Baptists, 128–129; *see also* Southern
Baptist Theological Seminary
Barber, Samuel, 122
Barbour, J. Murray, 63, 66n, 91n
Barnby, Joseph, 128
Barrows, Cliff, 110n, 111 & n, 127
Barry, John, 30 & n
Barton, William, 13n
Bayley, Daniel, 28n, 50, 59n, 60 & n,
86n
Bay Psalm Book: 8n, 12, 14–16; 9th
ed., 18n, 93; 26th ed., 27n
Beach, Mrs. H. H. A., 115 & n
"Beautiful Dreamer" (Foster), 112
Bechler, Johann Christian, 41
Becker, Peter, 33
Bedford, Arthur, 84
Beesley, Ebenezer, 109n
Beethoven, Ludwig van, 72–73, 77
& n, 79, 80n, 83n
Beissel, Johann Conrad, 32–37
Belcher, Supply, 30, 79
Belknap, Daniel, 30

bells, church, 55
Benedictus: prayerbook variants of,
108; Tuckerman's setting of, 107n,
108n; *see also* service music
Bennard, George, 110n, 127n, 130
Benzoni, Girolamo, 3
Berkeley, California, première at, 122n
Berkeley, George, 55
Berlin, Irving, 91n, 130
Bernard of Cluny, 116n
Bernstein, Leonard, 129
BETHANY ("Nearer my God to Thee"),
82
Bethlehem, Pennsylvania, music at,
38–39 & n, 41, 43, 45n
Bienheureux est quiconques (Ps. 128),
3–6, 8
Billings, William, 19n, 30n, 42, 46,
59n, 60, 62–66, 71 (anthems), 75n,
76n, 79, 132
Bingham, Seth, 82, 125
Birchensha, John, 25n
"Blessed assurance" (Knapp), 109
Bliss, Philip P., 100n, 111, 127–128,
130
"Blow your trumpet Gabriel" (spirit-
ual), 98
Blum, Ludwig, 35 & n
Bob Jones College, 111
Boehler, Peter, 40
Book of Common Prayer, 57 & n,
107n, 108n
Book of Psalmody, A (John Chetham,
1752), 84
Borgers, Edward, 123
BOSTON (Billings), 62, 64–65
Boston Academy's Collection of
Church Music, The (Mason, 1835),
79
Boston Anthem Book, The (Mason,
1839), 76n, 84–85
Boston Handel and Haydn Society
Collection of Church Music (1822),
77, 83; 1829 ed., 82; 1832 ed.,
90n
Boudinot, Elias (Cherokee, d. 1839),
9n
Bourgeois, Louis, 4
Bovicelli, Giovanni Battista, 27
"Bow thine ear" (Byrd's *Ciuitas*
sancti tui), 76 & n
Boyce, William, 57, 59, 75
Boyd, Charles N. (1875–1937), 89
BOYLSTON ("Blest be the tie that
binds"), 82
boy's voices, Mason's objections to, 80n
Bradbury, William B., 80, 83 & n,
100n, 104, 108, 128
Bradford, Alex, 104n

Bradford, Massachusetts, Symmes's
sermon preached at (1720), 24–25
Brahms, Johannes, 118n, 120
Brattle, Thomas (1658–1713), 24n, 48
BRATTLE STREET (Pleyel), 90n
Braut des Lamms, Die (Beissel), 35
Brewster, William, 15
Bridgewater Collection (Bartholomew
Brown, 1802), 90n
*Brief Introduction to the Skill of
Musick* (Playford), 16 & n, 19
"Brighten the corner where you are"
(Gabriel), 111
Britten, Benjamin, 131
Britton, Allen P., 15n, 16n, 18n,
19n, 22n, 59n, 60nn, 62, 86n, 87n, 130
Broadway Tabernacle, New York
City, 108
Broder, Nathan, 42
Broucek, Jack W., 52, 130
Brown, Bartholomew, 90n
Browne, Simon, 25
Brumel, Antoine, 116n
BRUNSWICK, 26 & n
Buchanan, Annabel Morris, 88, 103
Buck, Dudley, 113–114, 117, 123n
Bucke, Emory S., 109n
Buckman, Jacob, 30
Bull, Amos, 71
Burdick, Jane, 75n
Burney, Charles, 13n
"By and By" (Gabriel), 111
Byrd, William: (1543–1623), 76, 131;
(1674–1744, Virginia gentleman), 30,
53

California, Indians of (1579), 8
Callaway, Paul, 130
Calvin, John, unison congregational
singing endorsed by, 20
CAMBRIDGE, 16n
Cambridge, Massachusetts: first
minister at, 8; first New World
Bible printed at, 10; 200th anni-
versary music at, 123; *see also*
Harvard University
Cambridge University, 105, 107n, 119
Camp Plauché (New Orleans), 132
"Camptown Races" (Foster), 112
cantata, *see* oratorio and cantata
CANTERBURY, 18
Cantica Laudis (Mason, 1850), 82
Canticle of the Sun (Sowerby, 1945),
123
*Canticum Sacrum in honorem Sancti
Marci nominis* (Stravinsky, 1955),
120
Carawan, Guy, 104
Careless, George, 109n

Carissimi, Giacomo, 85
*Carmina Sacra: or Boston Collection
of Church Music* (Mason, 1841),
79n, 83 & n
Carrell, James P., 90 & n
Carter, Robert, 54
*Cathedral Chants: including the
Gregorian Tones* (Tuckerman,
1858), 107
Cathedral of St. John the Divine, New
York City, 121
Chadwick, George, 116n, 119 & n
Chanler, Theodore, 129
Chanticleer (Dirksen), 130
Chapin: Amzi, 88n; Lucius, 87–90;
Nathan, 51, 73
Charles II, 32, 61
Charleston, S. C., 54–57; Negro
singing at, 94
Charlestown Collection (Wesley,
1737), 40
Chase, Gilbert, 20n, 42, 90 & n, 91n,
116n, 122n
Chastellux, François Jean Marquis
de (1734–1788), 48
Chauncey, Nathaniel, 22n
Chauncy, Charles, 30n
Cherokee Singing Book, The (1846),
9n
Cherubini, Luigi, 79, 109
CHESTER (Billings), 65 & n
Chetham, John, 84
*Choir; or Union Collection of Church
Music, The* (Mason, 1832), 82–83
chorale preludes (Bach), 19
Christ Church: Boston (bells at),
55; Cambridge, 123; Hartford,
107; Philadelphia, 34, 47
*Christ Church Collection of Sacred
Music* (Wilson, 1861), 107
Christian Harmonist, The (Holyoke),
65n, 74n
Christian Harmony, The (Ingalls,
1805), 89n
Christian Science, hymnals of, 110
Christ Reborn (Sowerby, 1953), 123
Christus am Ölberge (Beethoven, Op.
85), 77
Church Melodies (Hastings, 1858),
66n, 67
Church Musician, The, 128
Church of the Holy Trinity, New
York City, 116
Church of the Open Door, Los
Angeles, 127n
Cincinnati: festival at, 116; orchestra,
41
clarinets, early Moravian use of,
45n

Clarke, Jonas, 22n
clavichord (Charleston, S. C.), 55
Clayton, David L., 90 & n
Clement of Alexandria, 125
clerk, functions of, 16n, 31
Cleveland, James, 104n
Clokey, Joseph W., 125
Closen, Ludwig von, 49
Cluster of Spiritual Songs, The
    (Mercer), 126n
Coke, Thomas, 70
Cole, Rossetter, 114n
Coleridge-Taylor, Samuel, 105
Collection of Psalm Tunes, A
    (Hopkinson, 1763), 47
Collegium Musicum, 39–40
Columbian Harmonist (Read), 72, 76
Columbian Harmony (William Moore,
    1825), 91n
Comenius, Johann Amos, 24n
Commuck, Thomas (Indian), 9
Communion Service: in C (Sowerby,
    1963), 123; in E minor (Dirksen),
    130; see also service music
Compleat Melody: or, The Harmony
    of Sion (Tans'ur [4th. ed., 1738]),
    86n
Compleat Psalmodist, The (Arnold,
    1740), 60n, 61n
Concerto in C minor (Beethoven,
    Op. 37), 73
Congregationalists, Chapters 1–3
    passim, 48–49, 93, 104, 113n
CONSECRATION ("Sweet hour of
    prayer"), 83n, 108
Continental Harmony, The (Billings),
    19n, 65, 66n, 71, 76n
Converse, Charles C., 110n
Copland, Aaron, 122 & n, 126
copyright laws, influence of, 83, 124
cori spezzati, 43
CORONATION (Holden, 1793), 57–58,
    68n
Cotton, John: (1584–1652), 14, 15n;
    (1640–1699), 14
Couperin, Louis, 129
Courlander, Harold, 103n, 104 & n
Courteville, Raphael, 26n
Courtship of Miles Standish, The
    (Longfellow, 1858), 6n
Covey, Cyclone, 8n
Cowell, Henry, 118n, 126 & n
Crandell, Robert, 125, 130
Crashaw, Richard, 131
Cravath, Erastus Milo (1833–1900),
    101
Crawford, Richard Arthur, 74n, 85n,
    87n, 88n, 130
Creation, The (Haydn), 43, 80

Crespin, Jean, 4
Crews, Emma K., 89n, 130
Croft, William, 21n, 75–76
Crosby, Frances Jane ("Fanny"
    [1820–1915]; married name, Van
    Alstyne), 91n
Crotch, William, 78n, 107
Crown Hymnal (Kavanagh and
    McLaughlin, 1912), 110
Cutler, H. S., 108
Cuzzoni, Francesca, 53

D'Alembert, Jean le Rond, 80
Daman, William, 13n, 19n
Daniel, Ralph T., 60n, 70–72, 76n
Dare, Elkanah K., 87 & n
Dartmouth College, 76
David, King, 25, 29
David, Hans T., 34 & n, 38n, 39n,
    41–42, 43 & n, 45n, 55n
Davies, Samuel, 51, 93–95
Davisson, Ananias, 66nn, 88–90
Da werdet Ihr singen (Peter anthem),
    45
Day, Stephen, 8n, 12n
Dearborn, Benjamin, 87
Death Song of an Indian Chief, The
    (Gram), 75n
"Deep River," 104–105
Delights of Harmony, The (Jenks,
    1805), 84
Dellius, Godfried, 11
Dello Joio, Norman, 122
Dencke, Jeremias, 32, 38n, 45n
Der Herr ist in Seinem heiligen
    Tempel (Peter, 1786), 43–44
Deshon, Moses, 30
Desilde al caballero, 126
Des Prez, Josquin, 116n
de Tar, Vernon, 104
Detroit, 81
Dickens, Charles, 112
Dickerson, Joseph L., 51, 73
Dickson, Jessie, 104n
Die mit Thränen (Peter anthem), 44n
DILIGENCE (Mason), see WORK SONG
Dinneen, William, 48n
Di render mi la calma (Palma), 46
Dirksen, Robert, 125, 130
Dissertation on Musical Taste
    (Hastings, 1822), 78n
Ditson: Alice, 123; Oliver, 107,
    114–115
Dixieland Six, 132
Doane, W. Howard, 68n, 91n, 111n,
    128, 130
Doktor Faustus (Thomas Mann),
    33 & n

Domine salvum fac (Paine), 114
DORCHESTER (Billings), 62–63
Dorsey, William, 104n
Douen, Orentin, 7n
Douglas, Charles Winfred, 112
"Down by the riverside," 92
Downes, Olin, 41
Drake, Sir Francis, 8
Duché, Jacob, 34
Dudley, Paul, 18n, 30
Du fons de ma pensée (Ps. 130),
    3, 6–8
Dulcimer, The (Woodbury), 68–69
DUNDIE, 19n
Dunkers (Church of the Brethren), 34
Dunster, Henry, 15
Dutch: influence of, 12; *see also*
    Dellius, Reformed Protestant Dutch
    Church
Dvořák, Antonin, 105
Dwight: John S., 80n; Josiah, 22n
Dwight's Journal of Music, 59n, 78nn,
    83n, 95
DYING PENITENT, THE *(Virginia
    Harmony),* 90n
Dykes, John Bacchus, 81, 104, 128

Eames, Wilberforce, 8n, 14n, 15n
Eastcheap, Friday lecture in, 21
Easy Instructor, The (Little and
    Smith), 15, 86–87
Eckhard, Jacob, 56 & n
Eddy, Mary Baker, 110
Edson, Lewis, 66 (& n)–67, 75, 132
Ein' feste Burg, 34 & n, 114n
Elgar, Edward, 117–118
Elijah (Mendelssohn), 107
Eliot: Benjamin, 16 (& n)–17, 20;
    Charles, 114; Jacob, 16–17; John
    (1604–1690), 10 11, 15n, 16 (& n)–
    17
Ellington, Duke, 132
Ellinwood, Leonard, 57n, 77n, 116n
Elmore, Robert, 125
Elson, Louis C., 16n, 115
Emmett, Dan, 110
Endecott, John, 8n, 10, 15
Engel, Carl, 35n, 36n, 77n
Enstone, Edward, 48
Ephrata, Pennsylvania, music at, 34–38
Episcopalians, 23 (Church of England),
    48–49, 53–57, 106–109, 113, 119n,
    121n, 125
Epstein, Dena J., 93, 94n, 95nn, 96
Espinosa, Aurelio, 61n
Esther, the Beautiful Queen
    (Bradbury), 108
Estro poetico-harmonico (Marcello),
    85

*European Magazine and London
    Review, The,* 18, 104
Evans, Charles, 5n, 30n, 37
Everett, Lemuel C., 109n
Excell, E. O., 110
Exodus 15, metrical version of, 6n, 15n

faburden, Ravenscroft's "definition"
    of, 7n
Fairyland (Parker), 118
Farmington, Connecticut, 26n
"fasola" folk, 90–91
Fauré, Gabriel, 113n
Federal Harmony (Asahel Benham,
    1795), 73
Felciano, Richard, 130
Fenner, Thomas P., 102–103
Festival Cantata (Eugene Thayer), 114
Festival Magnificat (Pinkham), 131
Feyring, Philip, 47
Figueroa, Bernardino de, 41n
figured bass, 47, 57, 78n
Finney: Ross Lee, 122; Theodore M.,
    39n, 40n
First Baptist Church, Providence, 48
First Congregational Church, Los
    Angeles, 113n
First Congregational (now Unitarian)
    Church, Providence, 48
First Presbyterian Church, Brooklyn,
    125n
First Presbyterian Church, Oyster
    Bay, N. Y., 131
First Presbyterian Church, Princeton,
    N. J., 113n
First Unitarian Church, Boston, 119n
Fischer, W. G., 110
Fisk University, 100–103, 105
Fiske, John, 114n, 115
Fithian, Philip, 31nn, 51, 54
Fletcher, Francis, 8
Florida, Indians of, 3–4, 8
Folk Hymns of America (Annabel
    Morris Buchanan), 88, 103
Foote: Arthur W., 119n; Henry W.
    (b. 1875), 10n, 16n, 17nn, 20n,
    24n
Forsaken of Man (Sowerby), 123
Foss, Lukas, 122
Foster, Stephen Collins, 112
FOUNDATION (= BELLEVUE), 126n
Foxcroft, Thomas, 17n
Francis of Assisi, 123
Franck, César, 43n, 117
Franklin: Benjamin, 5, 18, 20n,
    35n, 38, 45n; Josiah, 18
French, Jacob, 30, 66 & n, 72, 75
Freylinghausen, J. A., 33
"Friendship" (Lyon), 50

Frost, Maurice, 6n, 12n, 13nn, 16n,
    18nn, 19nn, 68n
fuge-tunes, 59n, 65n, 66 (& n)–70, 90,
    126n

Gabriel, Charles H., 91n, 110 & n,
    127–128, 130
gamut, rules of, 21
Gardiner, William, 77, 78n
Garrison, Lucy McKim, 96
Gasparini, Francesco, 53
Gates, Crawford, 109n
"Gathering home" (McIntosh), 109n
"General Booth Enters Into Heaven"
    (Ives, 1914), 126n
Gentleman and Lady's Musical
    Companion, The (1774), 47n, 50
Genuchi, Marvin C., 66n, 72
George I, favorite tune of, 26n
Germantown, Pennsylvania, 4, 33
Gershwin, George, 130
Gibbons, Orlando, 19
GILEAD (Billings), 66n
"Give thanks unto the Lord"
    (Mechem), 131
Go, Congregation, Go! (Antes), 42
"God is a Spirit" (Jones), 124
"Go down, Moses," 92, 101, 103–104
Goetschius, Percy, 115n
Goldman, Richard Franko, 42
Goodspeed, E. J., 127
Gospel Choir, The, 110n
gospel hymns: definition of, 90n;
    literature concerning, 110n, 127;
    sale of, 100n
"Go tell it on the mountain," 92
Goudimel, Claude, 4n
Gould, Nathaniel, 76n
Gounod, Charles, 117
Grace Episcopal Church, New York
    City, 45n, 108
Graham, Billy, 109, 110n, 111n,
    112 & n
Grainger, Percy, 105
Gram, Hans, 74 (& n)–75 (& n)
Granada, 41n
Graun, Karl Heinrich, 79n
Greatorex, Henry, 107
Greene, Maurice (1695–1755), 75
Greenfield, Massachusetts, 106
Gregor, Christian, 39n, 41n
Grieg, Edvard, 118n
Griffes, Charles T., 122
Grimm, Johann Daniel, 39n, 44n
Grove's Dictionary, 18, 25n, 89
    (American Supplement)
Grubé, Bernhard Adam, 40n
Guerrero, Francisco, 41n

Guidonian syllables, 25; see also
    solmization
"Gwine follow," 97

HACKNEY, 16n, 56n
Hagen, Francis F., 41
Hale, Philip, 116n
Hallelujah, The (Mason, 1854), 82
"Hallelujah to the Father" (= Welten
    singen Dank und Ehre, Beethoven),
    77
Hallowed Songs (Philip Phillips), 91n
HAMBURG ("When I survey the
    wondrous cross"), 58, 82
Hamilton, Frank, 104
Hamm, Charles, 88nn
Hammett, John, 22n
Hampton and its Students, 102, 103n
Hampton Institute, 102–103
Handel, George Frideric, 46n, 53,
    72, 75–76, 80n, 85, 107, 114n
Handel and Haydn Society, Boston,
    77, 115–116
HANOVER (Croft), 21n
Hanover: Germany, 85; Virginia, 93
Hanson, Howard, 122
Haraszti, Zoltán, 15n, 16nn
"Hark! the herald angels sing," 84
Harker, F. Flaxington, 123
Harmonia Americana (Samuel
    Holyoke, 1791), 74n
Harmonia Sacra (Hewitt, 1812), 75
harpsichord: Pachelbell's playing of,
    55; Gram's, 75n
Harris, Roy, 121
Harrison, Lou, 121 & n
Hart, Andro, 20
Hartford, Connecticut, 107, 114n
Harvard College (later University):
    Divinity chair at, 22; Dunster
    resigns presidency of, 15; graduates
    of, see Benjamin Eliot, Samuel
    Holyoke, Jacob Kimball, Daniel
    Pinkham, Thomas Symmes, John
    Tufts, Thomas Walter; musical
    theses accepted at (17th century),
    24; music at presidential inaugura-
    tions, 114; tercentenary of, 20n;
    university choir of, 76
Harvard Musical Association, 80n
Hasse: Faustina, 53; Johann Adolph,
    53
Hastings: Eurotas P., 81; Thomas, 9,
    66 (& n)–67, 68n, 78n, 81–82, 84n,
    130
Haupt, August, 115n
Hauser, William, 90–91
Hawkins, Sir John, 85n

Hawley, Joseph, 26n
Haydn: F. J., 43 & n, 44n, 79, 80n, 107, 113n; Michael, 38
Hayes, Philip (1738–1797), 75
"Hear de Lambs a-cryin'," 103
Hearken! Stay close to Jesus Christ (Michael), 42
"Heavenly Road," 98
Heavenly Vision, The (Jacob French anthem), 72
Hedge, Lemuel, 22n
Heidelberg, 33
"He leadeth me," *see* AUGHTON
Heman, Levite leader of Temple musicians, 29
Henderson, W. J., 116n
Herbst, Johannes, 38, 41 (& n)–42, 43 & n
Hérold, Louis-Joseph-Ferdinand, 107
Herrnhut, Moravian European head-quarters, 39–40
Herz, Henri, 107
Hess, Albert G., 38n
Hesselius, Gustavus, pioneer organ builder, 38n
Hewitt, James, 42, 75 & n
Hickman, Charles Leroy, 74n
Hicks, Edward, 122
Higginson: J. Vincent, 9n; Thomas Wentworth, 97–100
HIGH DUTCH, 18 (& n)–19
Highland Park Presbyterian Church, Dallas, 131
Hildebrand Song, 22n
Hildeburn, Charles, 5n
Hill, Thomas, 114
Hillman, Joseph, 90n
Hine, Stuart K., 127
Hitchcock, H. Wiley, 74n, 87n
Hodges, Edward, 107
Hofmann, Josef, 118
Hoiby, Lee, 130
Holbrook: Abdiah, 35n; Joseph P., 81
Holden, Oliver, 30, 57, 66n, 68 & n, 71–72 (anthems), 75, 79, 132
Holdroyd, Israel, 61n
"Hold the Fort" (Bliss), 111 & n
"Hold your light" (spiritual), 98
Hollis, Thomas, 22
Holmes, Carl T., 37–38
HOLY MANNA (William Moore), 91n, 92
Holyoke, Samuel, 30, 65n, 66, 74 & n
Hommann, Charles, 41
Hood, George, 14n, 15n, 22n
Hooker, Brian, 118
Hopkins, John Henry, 130
Hopkinson, Francis, 5, 7, 42, 46–47, 57n, 129

Hora Novissima (Parker, Op. 30), 115–118
Horton, Zilphia, 104
"Hosanna to the Son of David" (Moe), 131
Houck, Elizabeth S., 35
Howard, Samuel (1710–1782), 75
Howe, Solomon, 30
"How Great Thou Art," 110n, 127
"How lovely are Thy dwelling places" (Brahms), 120
Hubbard, John, 76
Huguenots, music of, 3–4, 54n
Hull, Asa, 126n
Huntington Library, San Marino, 37–38, 113n
Hustad, Don, 127
Hymnal, The (Presbyterian, U. S. A., 1935), 80
Hymnal 1940, The (Episcopalian), 19, 80
Hymns Ancient & Modern, 19, 26n, 68n
Hymns of Our Faith (Reynolds), 128–129
Hypocrisie Vnmasked (Winslow, 1646), 13n

Iam Christus astra ascenderat, 13n
Ich werde aufs Neue (Beissel), 37
"I'd rather have Jesus" (Shea), 110n
"If with all your hearts" (*Elijah*), 107
"I know that my Redeemer" (*Messiah*), 107
Iliff Seminary, 125
"I'll hear the trumpet sound in the morning," 101–102
"I'll praise my Maker" (Pfautsch), 131
"I'm troubled in mind," 105
Incarnation Church, New York City, 109, 125
Independents, London congregation of, 21
Indian mission music, research in, 9n, 121n
In dulci jubilo, 109n
"I need Thee every hour," 110
Ingalls, Jeremiah, 66n, 75, 89n, 132
instrumental accompaniment (apart from organ), 39 & n, 48, 131; *see also* oratorio
In the Beginning (Copland), 122 & n
"In the garden" (C. Austin Miles), 111
"In the gloaming," 109n
INVITATION (Kimball), 74n
Iphigenia, Sister, Ephrata disciple, 36
Irish, folk song influence from, 105
"I saw the beam in my sister's eye," 97

Isidore of Seville, 24
Isle of Wight, 25
Israel in Egypt (Handel), 124
Italian augmented sixth chord, use of, 29, 72
Ivers, James, 30
Ives: Charles, 118–119, 126 & n, 129; Samuel A., 6n
"I will sing you a song of a beautiful land" (Phillips), 91n

Jackson: George K., 75 & n, 77–78; George Pullen, 22n, 79n, 88nn, 89 & n, 90, 91n, 92, 103; John B., 89n; Mahalia, 124, 127
Jacksonville, Florida, 3
Jamaica, Negro music recorded on (1688), 98n
James, Philip, 125
James P. Boyce Centennial Library (Louisville), 127
Janson, Charles William, 95n, 96n
jazz, 132
Jeduthun, Levite chief musician, 29
Jefferson, Thomas, 53
"Jehovah reigns" (= Liverpool = *An Anthem taken out of the 97th Psalm,* Tuckey), 49 (& n)–50
Jenks, Stephen, 66, 79, 84
Jennings [Parker], Isabella, 118
Jesu dulcis memoria, 120
Jesus, unser Hirt (Peter anthem), 44n
John Chrysostom, 122
Johnson: James Weldon, 102; Thor, 39n, 41
Jonah, prayer of (sung version), 15n, 17
Jones, David Hugh, 124
Jubilate Deo (Tans'ur), 60n
Jubilee Singers, Fisk University, 100–101, 103, 105
Jubilee Songs, 100–102
Jullien, Louis Antoine (1812–1860), 106
"Just as I am," *see* Woodworth

Karpeles, Maud, 91
Keeble, John (1711–1786), 57
Kelpius, Johannes, 32 (& n)–33 (& n)
Kemble, Frances Anne ("Fanny"), 96
Kennedy, Gerald, 125
Kent School, 121n
Kentucky Harmony, The (Davisson), 66nn, 88 (& n)–89 (& n)
Kern, Jerome, 130
Kierkegaard, Sören, 122
Kimball, Jacob, 30

King, E. J., 102, 126n
King, Robert, 88n
King's Chapel, Boston, 48, 75, 131
Kingsley, George, 80–81
Kinkeldey, Otto, 8, 77nn
Kircher, Athanasius, 29n
Klemm, Johann Gottlieb, 38 & n
Knapp, Phoebe Palmer (= Mrs. Joseph F.), 110 & n
Knobloch, Johann, 4n
Knolton, Peter, 39n
Knoxville (Monday), 89n
Knoxville Harmony, The (John B. Jackson, 1838), 89n
Kocher, Conrad (1786–1872), 82
Köpfel, Wolfgang, 19
Kollmann, A. F. C. (1756–1829), 80
Koželuch, Leopold Anton (1752–1818), 79n
Kübler, G. F., 78–79

Lafayette Avenue Presbyterian Church, Brooklyn, 101
Lambeth degree, 107 & n
Lamech and Agrippa, Brothers, Ephrata disciples, 33n, 34n
Lamentation over Boston (Billings), 63
Lamentations, metrical version of, 15n
Lancaster, Pennsylvania, 38
Landon, H. C. Robbins, 43n
LaRue, Jan, 43n
Lassus, Orlandus, 7n
"Last Rose of Summer, The," 90n
Latrobe, Christian I., 39nn, 44 & n
Laudonnière, René de, 3, 8
Laus Deo, or the Worcester Collection (1786), 72
Law: Andrew, 42, 49n, 51, 66n, 67–68, 74 & n, 79, 85n, 86 & n (innovations of), 87, 88n (correcting hand), 93 (Negro assistant); William, 93
Lawrence, James B., 94
Lebanon (Billings), 62–63, 79
Lebanon, Tennessee, 89
Le Challeux, Nicolas, 3
Legend of Don Munio, The (Buck, Op. 62), 114, 117
Legend of St. Christopher, The (Parker, Op. 43), 116–119
Leinbach, E. W., 42
Leite mich in Deiner Wahreit (Peter, 1770), 43, 45n
Leland, John (1754–1841), 103
Lenox (Edson), 66–67, 75, 85n
"Let the shrill trumpets" (Lyon), 50
Leverett, John (1662–1724), 24n
Library of Congress, holdings of,

27, 35n, 38, 46n, 78n, 83n, 89n, 90 & n, 116n, 126n
Lieder ohne Worte (Mendelssohn), 107, 114n
Life of Man, The (J. C. D. Parker), 115
"Lily Dale," 109n
Lindsay, Vachel, 126n
"lining out," custom of, 95; *see also* clerk, functions of
LITCHFIELD, 16n, 17, 18 & n, 19
Lititz, Moravian music at, 38, 39n, 40
Little, William, 15, 86–87, 90
Lobet den Herrn (Peter), 44
Lobwasser, Ambrosius, 5n
Lockwood, Normand, 122, 125
Logos, The (D. S. Smith, Op. 21), 120
Longfellow, Henry W., 6n
"Lord, I want to be a Christian," 104
Lord Nelson Mass (Haydn), 113n
Lord's Prayer: Malotte, 124; Robertson, 124
Los Angeles, 113 & n, 127n
LOVE DIVINE (*Virginia Harmony*), 90n
Lovelace, Austin C., 125
LOW DUTCH, 18 & n
Lowell, James Russell, 123
Lowens, Irving, 8n, 15 & n, 16n, 19n, 25n, 28n, 40n, 42n, 59nn, 60n, 66nn, 68n, 72, 78n, 80n, 86nn, 87nn, 88n, 89n, 120
Lowry: J. C., 91n; Robert, 91n, 126n
Lucas, G. W., 83n
Lumpkin, Leon, 104n
Luther, Martin, 75, 79n
Lutherans, music among, 106n
Lutkin, Peter, 113–114
Lyon: James, 28n, 30, 46–51, 132; Richard, 15
LYONS (Michael Haydn), 38

McCorkle, Donald M., 38nn, 40n, 41 (& n)–42 (& n), 44n
McCormick, David W., 68n, 74n
McCurry, John Gordon, 91
MacDowell, E. A., 120, 122
McGranahan, James, 100n
McIntosh, R. H., 109n
Mackenzie, Sir Alexander Campbell, 117
McKinney, B. B., 110, 128
McKinnon, James, 49
Madan, Martin (1726–1790), 75
Maffoni, 129
Magnalia Christi Americana (1702), 15n
Magnificat, metrical version of, 15n; prayerbook: Parker's setting, 119n.

Pinkham's, 131, Tuckerman's, 107n; *see also* service music
Magnificat â 8 voci (Pachelbell), 55
Mahler, Gustav, 129
MAJESTY (Billings), 85n
major-minor, relative frequency of (early American repertory), 75–76 (& n); *see also* minor
"Make a Joyful Noise": Mechem, 131; Peter, 44n
Maleingreau, Paul de, 131
Mallard, Belle, 113
Malotte, Albert Hay, 124
Mangler, Joyce E., 48n
Manhattan Baptist Church, New York City, 128
Manigault family (Pierre, d. 1729; Gabriel, 1704–1781; Peter, 1731–1773), 54n
Mann: Elias, 51, 68, 75; Thomas, 33
Manna Music, Inc., 127
Mannheim, 33
Manual of the Boston Academy of Music (Mason, 1834), 78
"Many thousands gone" (spiritual), 105
maqam (= "melody type"), 22
Marburg, 5n
Marcello, Benedetto, 85 & n
Marenzio, Luca, 129
Marot, Clément, 3
Marpurg, Friedrich Wilhelm, 78
Marrocco, W. Thomas, 84n
Marschner, Heinrich, 107
Martin, Roberta, 104n
MARTYRS, 16n, 18, 19n
Mason: Daniel Gregory, 77n, 104; Lowell, 57–58, 68 & n, 76n, 77–85, 90n, 104, 128–130
Massachusetts Collection of Sacred Harmony (1807), 51, 75
Masses: Beach, Op. 5, 115; Beethoven, Op. 86, 113n; Op. 123 (*Missa Solemnis*), 82; Harrison ("for Mixed Chorus, Trumpet, Harp and Strings"), 121; Haydn, see *Lord Nelson* Mass; Mozart, *K. Anh. 233,* 77; Palestrina, *Dilexi quoniam, In illo tempore, Nasce la gioia mia,* 129; Sessions ("for Unison Choir and Organ"), 120–121; Thompson ("of the Holy Spirit"), 121
MATERNA ("America the Beautiful"), 130
Mather: Cotton, 11, 15n, 18n, 22 (& n)–23 (& n), 93; Richard, 15n
Mathews, W. S. B., 115
Mattheson, Johann, 78
Mayhew, Matthew, 11

Mays, Kenneth Robert, 129
Mechem, Kirke L., 130–131
Mein Gmüth ist verwirren, 126n
Mendelssohn, Felix, 79, 107, 114n
Mennin, Peter, 122
Mercer, Jesse, 126n
Merrill, E. Lindsey, 115n
Messiah (Handel), 43, 50, 72, 80, 124
Metcalf, Frank, 5n
Methodist hymnals, 80–81, 98, 109 & n,
    124–125; see also *Charlestown Col-
    lection*
Methodists: magazine published by,
    128; musical rules sanctioned by, 68–
    70; Negro congregations of, 96 & n;
    see also Dare, Pfautsch, Young
mi, importance of (in four-syllable
    solmization), 21 & n, 27, 28n
Michael, David Moritz, 41–42
Military Glory of Great Britain, The
    (Lyon, 1762), 47
Mille regretz (Josquin), 126n
Miller: Edward (1731–1807), 75;
    Peter, 35n, 38; Rhea F., 110n
Mills, Samuel John, 22n
Minor, George A., 129
minor, prevalence of (in early reper-
    tory), 19n
Missionary Hymn ("From Green-
    land's icy mountains"), 58, 82
Mocquereau, Dom André, 37
Modern Psalmist (Mason, 1839), 83
Moe, Daniel, 130–131
Mohawk, singing in, 39n
Mona (Parker), 118
Monday (= Munday), R., 89
Montview Boulevard Presbyterian
    Church, Denver, 125
"moods," meaning of, 86 & n
Moody, Dwight L., 110–111, 127
Moore: Douglas, 119; William, 91n
Morales, Cristóbal de, 41n
Moravians, music of, 32, 38–45
Morgan: George W., 45n, 108; Justin,
    72–73
Morison, Samuel E., 25n, 57
Mormons, music among, 109 & n, 123
Morven and the Grail (Parker, Op.
    79), 116, 118
motetts, Mason's collection of, 84
Motolinía, Toribio de, 10
Moulu, Pierre, 129
Mount Zion (Parker), 112n
Mozart, Wolfgang Amadeus, 44n, 77,
    80n, 107, 110, 113n
Müller, Georg Gottfried, 38, 41
Munich, 119
Murray, James A. H., 84

"Musica Ecclesia" (Read), 80
Musical Instructor, The (Chapin and
    Dickerson, 1808), 51, 73
Musical Letters from Abroad (Lowell
    Mason), 78n, 82nn
Musical Magazine; or, Repository
    (H. T. Hach), 79n, 80n, 83n
Music in Miniature (Billings), 65n
Music Ministry, 128
Musurgia universalis (Kircher, 1650),
    29n
"My Lord delivered Daniel," 105
"My old Kentucky home," 112

Nägeli, Johann Georg, 79
Nares, James, 57, 59
Narragansett Indians, 9
Nashville, musical publications at, 128
Nathan, Hans, 66n, 97
Nativity according to St. Luke
    (Thompson), 123
Nazarenes, 125
Neale, John Mason, 116n, 125
Neander, Joachim, 125
Negro Folk Music, U.S.A. (Cour-
    lander), 103n, 104
"Negro Gospel," 104n, 127
Neilson, Peter, 96n
Neuer Helicon (Nuremberg, 1684), 32
*Neu-vermehrt und vollsta'ndiges
    Gesang-Buch* (1753), 4
New American Melody (French,
    1789), 72
Newark, 46
New England Harmony (Swan, 1801),
    84, 86n
New-England Psalm-Singer, The
    (Billings, 1770), 60 & n, 62, 64, 65n,
    66n, 71
New England Triptych (Schuman,
    1956), 65
New London, 30
New Orleans: gospel singing at, 104n;
    "jazz services" at, 132
Newport, R. I., 124; *see also* Trinity
    Church, Newport
New York Public Library, 37, 41
Nichols, Florida, 113
Noble, Oliver, 22n
"Nobody knows the trouble I've seen,"
    103
Nóbrega, Manuel da, 10
Noël (Chadwick), 119n
Nomini Hall, Virginia, 54
Non nobis Domine (round ascribed to
    Byrd), 76n
Northfield (Ingalls), 66n, 75
Norton, M. D. Herter, 43n

Nunc Dimittis: metrical version of, 15n; Parker setting, 119n; Pinkham, 131
Nuremberg, 32, 55

O Anblick, der mirs Herze bricht (Simon Peter anthem), 44n
Octante trois pseavmes de David (1554), 4–5
Odi che lodi (Marcello's Psalm 8), 85
"O give thanks" (Purcell anthem), 76n
O HOW I LOVE JESUS, 90n
O Isis und Osiris (*Die Zauberflöte*), 77, 107
"Old Black Joe," 112
Old Colony Collection of Anthems (1818), 76nn, 77
"Old Folks at Home," 112
"Old Rugged Cross," 110n, 111, 127
OLD SHIP ZION, 90n
Old South Church, Boston, 16, 17n, 18, 30n
"Old-time Religion," 92
Olive Leaf, The (Hauser, 1878), 90–91
OLIVET ("My faith looks up to Thee"), 82
"O Minnie, O Minnie, come o'er the lea," 109n
"On the Divine Use of Music," 26n
oratorio and cantata, American, 115n; see also *Canticle of the Sun; Christ Reborn; Esther, the Beautiful Queen; Festival Cantata; Hora Novissima; The Legend of Don Munio; The Legend of St. Christopher; The Life of Man; The Logos; Morven and the Grail; Noël; The Peaceable Kingdom; Rhapsody of St. Bernard; St. John; St. Peter; The Throne of God; A Wanderer's Psalm*
Oratorio from The Book of Mormon (Robertson), 123
Oré, Gerónimo de, 10
organs: conscientious objections against, 48–49; Mason's attitude toward, 80; see also Hesselius, Klemm, Snetzler, Tanneberger
O sanctissima, O piissima (SICILIAN MARINERS), 104
"O that will be glory for me" (Gabriel), 111
"O Thou to whom all creatures bow" (Billings anthem), 71
Ottolenghe, Joseph, 94
Oursler, Fulton, 124
OXFORD, 16n, 19 & n
"O ye mountains high" (Mormon hymn), 109n

Pachelbel, Johann (1653–1706), 55
Pachebell, Charles Theodore, 54–55, 78n
Packer Collegiate Institute, Brooklyn, 125n
Paderewski Prize, 119n
Paine, John Knowles, 113–115
Palma, Giovanni, 46–47
parallel fifths and octaves, prevalence of, 28n, 60 (& n)–61 (& n), 78n, 90
Parker: Edwin Pond, 114; Horatio W., 112 & n, 113n, 115–120; James, 5; James Cutler Dunn, 115
Parry, Sir Charles H. H., 117
Parsifal (Wagner), 118
Parthien for winds (Michael), 41
part-singing: Negro abstinence from, 96–98; Walter's advocacy of, 29
passing notes, addition of (psalmody), 9
"Pass me not, O gentle Saviour," 91n
PEACE ("God is the king," Billings anthem), 71
Peaceable Kingdom, The (Thompson), 122
Pelham, Philip, 54 & n
Penn, William, 32
Pergolesi, Giovanni Battista, 79
Persichetti, Vincent, 122
Pestalozzi, Johann Heinrich, 78
Peter: Johann Friedrich, 32, 38, 41–45; Simon, 41, 44n
Pfautsch, Lloyd, 124, 130–131
Philadelphia Harmony (Adgate and Spicer, 1788), 88n
Pidoux, Pierre, 4n, 18n
pietist hymnody, German, 33–34, 40
Phillips, Philip, 91n
Pichierri, Louis, 87n
Pilgrim Hymnal, The (1958), 104
Pilgrim's Harp (Asa Hull), 126n
Pinkham, Daniel, 130–131
PISGAH (J. C. Lowry), 91n, 92
plainsong, see *Iam Christus astra ascenderat, Veni Immanuel*
Playford, John, 16 & n, 18 (& n)–19, 76n
"playnsong," Ravenscroft's use of, 7n
Pleyel, Ignaz J., 90n
Plymouth, psalm singing at, 7n, 12–14
Poladian, Sirvart, 27n
polyglot singing, 39
Porter: Hugh, 104; Noah, 114n
Portland, Maine, 114
Port Royal, South Carolina, 99n
Powell, Robert J., 124
Pratt, Waldo S., 6n, 89
precentor, functions of, 16n, 17–18

Presbyterians: music among, 31, 48–49, 89, 93; U. S., 106n, 112, 131
Primavera, Giovanni Leonardo, 129
Prince, Thomas, 17 & n; library of, 16n
Princeton Theological Seminary, 52
Princeton University ("Nassau Hall"), 47–48, 51–52, 94
Providence, Rhode Island, 48, 106n
Psalm: VIII (Marcello), 85; XXIII, John Cotton translation of, 14, 18n; Tate-Brady version (Francis Hopkinson setting of), 47; XXIV (= BELLA), 26 & n; XLII (Marcello), 85; XLVI (Buck), 115; LXXII, 19 & n; LXXXV, 18; C (Mechem), 131, (Peter), 44n; CIV, 13n; CXV, 16n; CXVII (Moe), 130; CXIX, 19 & n; CXXVIII, see *Bienheureux;* CXXX, see *Du fons*
Pseavmes de David mis en rime (1553), 19
PUMPILY (Billings), 62–63
Purcell, Henry: (1659–1695), 53, 76 & n; (1742–1802), 55–56
Purvis, Richard (b. 1915), 125, 130
Pyrlaeus, John Christopher, 40n

Quakers, musical attitude of, 49
quartet choir, 112–113

Rameau, Jean-Philippe, 53
Rau, Albert G., 39n, 41n, 43nn, 44n, 45nn
Ravenscroft, Thomas, 7, 12, 15, 18n, 19–20, 75
Razzberry, Raymond, 104n
Read, Daniel, 59n, 65n, 66n, 67–69, 72 (anthems), 75–76, 78n, 79 & n
Reasonableness of, Regular Singing, The (Symmes), 24 (& n)–25 (& n)
Red, Buryl A., 128
Redlich, Hans, 122n
Redner, Lewis, 130
Redway, Virginia, 5n, 55nn
Reformed Protestant Dutch Church, 4n, 5, 48
Reger, Max, 131
"Regular Singing," 17n, Chapter 3 *passim*
Reinagle, Alexander, 42
Relly, James, 64
Repository, The (Amos Bull, 1795), 71
Repository of Sacred Music (Wyeth), 66n, 126n; *Part Second,* 74n, 86n, 87 (& n)–89 (& n)
Requiem: Brahms, 120; Cherubini, 109; Fauré, 113n; Pinkham, 131; Thompson, 121n; Verdi, 113n

Revere, Paul, 55n
Revivalist, The (Hillman, 1868), 90n
"Revive us again," 110n
Reynolds, William J., 128
Rhapsody of St. Bernard (D. S. Smith, Op. 38), 120
Rhea, Archibald, 89
Rheinberger, Josef, 119
Rice, John H., 94
Rich, Alan, 122n
Richard of Chichester, 128
Richter, Franz Xaver, 53
Righini, Vincenzo (1756–1812), 79
Roberts, Kenneth Creighton, Jr., 114n
Robertson, Leroy J., 109n, 123, 130
ROCKBRIDGE (Chapin), 88 & n
ROCKINGHAM (Chapin), 88 & n
"Rock of Ages," 66, 107
Rodeheaver, Homer A., 110n, 111 & n
Rogers: James S., 97; William, 9, 26n, 27
"Roll, Jordan, roll," 92, 101
Roman Catholics, 98, 110–111
Romance for Violin (Beethoven, Op. 40), 77
Romberg, Andreas (1767–1821), 79
Root, George F. (1820–1895), 100
Rosenroth, Christian Knorr von, 32
Rossini, Gioacchino, 45n, 109
Routley, Erik, 112 & n
Rowland, A. J., 109
Rowlands, Richard, 123
Royal Harmony or the Beauties of Church Music (Aaron Williams, 1765), 76n
Royal Melody Compleat, The (Tans'ur), 60–61
Rubinstein, Anton, 117
Rudhall, Gloucester (England), 55
Rudiments of Music, The (Law), 51, 66n
Rules For the Society of Negroes, 1693 (Boston, *ca.* 1706), 93
"Run, Mary, run," 103, 105
Rural Harmony, The (Kimball, 1793), 74
Russell, Skiner, 30
RUSSIA (Read), 68–69, 72, 75

SABBATH ("Safely through another week"), 90n
Sabbath Hymn and Tune Book, The (Mason, 1859), 82
Sacred Harp, The (B. F. White and E. J. King), 102, 126n, 128
Sacred Melodies (William Gardiner), 77, 78n
Sahagún, Bernardino de, 10
ST. ANNE (Croft), 21n

St. Augustine, Florida, 98
St. Bartholomew's Church, New York City, 116n
St. Cecilia's Day, 94
ST. DAVID'S, 16n, 18 & n, 19, 25
St. Helena Island, S. C.: spirituals collected on, 97; "shout" heard on, 99
ST. JAMES, 26
St. John (J. C. D. Parker cantata), 115
ST. LOUIS (Redner), 130
ST. MARY'S (= HACKNEY), 16n
St. Michael's Church, Charleston, 54–55
St. Paul's Chapel, Columbia University, New York City, 125n
St. Paul's Church, Boston, 107
St. Peter (Paine), 114–115
St. Peter's Church, Philadelphia, 47
St. Philip's Church, Charleston, 54
Saint-Saëns, Camille, 117
St. Thomas's, Leipzig, congregational singing at, 82n
St. Thomas' Church, New York City, 45n
Salem: Massachusetts, psalm singing at, 7n, 13; North Carolina, Moravian music at, 40
Salvation Army, 127n
Salzman, Eric, 129
San Francisco, 112–113
Sankey, Ira D., 100n, 127
Saur, Christopher, 4–5
Savannah, Georgia: music at, 52, 58 (Mason's sojourn), 77; Wesleys at, 40
Sayers, W. C. Berwick, 105
Schaff, Philip, 106, 108
Scheme for Reducing the Science of Music to a More Simple State, A (Dearborn, 1785), 87
Scholes, Percy, 8 & n, 16nn
Schreiner, Alexander, 109n
Schuman, William, 65
Schumann, Robert, 107
"scientific" composition, 78 (& n)–79
Scots tunes, 19nn, 20 & n, 109n
Seeger: Charles, 91; Pete, 104
Sessions, Roger, 113n, 119–121
Selby, William, 75–76
Senesino, Francesco, 53
service music, 60n, 107n, 108 & n, 117, 119n, 123n
"set pieces," 84–85 (& n)
Sewall, Samuel, 16 (& n)–19 (& n)
Seward, Theodore F., 100–101, 105
Seyboldt, Robert F., 22n, 23n, 30n
Shaftesbury, Lord (= Anthony Ashley Cooper, 7th earl, 1801–1885), 111
"Shaker Songs," 122n

"Shall we gather at the river," 91n, 126n
shape notes (= character notes), 73, 86–87
Sharp, Cecil, 61n, 91
Shea, George Beverly, 110n, 112, 127
Shepard, Thomas, 9n
SHEPHERD ("Saviour, like a shepherd lead us"), 83n
SHERBURNE (Read), 66n, 75, 85n
SHILOH (Billings), 63, 65
"shout" (Negro), 98–100
Shurtleff, N. B., 15n
"Sicilian Mariner's Hymn to the Virgin," 104
Siebert, Mark, 125
Sierra Leone, 105
Silcher, Friedrich (1789–1860), 79n
simplified music notation, 86–87
Simpson, Christopher, 61n
Sims: John Norman, 95n; Walter Hines, 111n, 128
Singet Ihr Himmel (Peter anthem), 45 & n
Singing Master's Assistant, The (Billings, 1778), 62–64, 65n
"singing lecture," 30
Singing of Psalmes A Gospel-Ordinance (1647), 14
singing schools, 22 (& n)–23, 30–31, 53 (Virginia), 57
"Sin-sick Soul," 92
Siroe (Handel, 1728), 46n
Slave Songs of the United States (1867), 96–97, 103
Sloane, Sir Hans, 98 & n
Smith: Carleton Sprague, 4n, 44n; David Stanley, 117n, 119–120; Robert (1732–1801), 56n; Tedd, 127; William, 15, 86–87, 90
Snetzler, Johann, organ builder, 55
Social Harp, The (McCurry, 1868 ed.), 91
"Softly and tenderly," 111
solmization: four-syllable, 21; seven-syllable, 28n; see also shape notes
sonatas, organ: 49
sonatas, piano: Beethoven, Op. 2, No. 1, 77; Mozart, K. 331 in A, 111
sonatas, violin and piano: Beethoven, Op. 23, 77; Ives, Nos. 1, 2, 4, 126n
Song-Garden, The (Mason, 1864), 82
Song of Hiawatha (Coleridge-Taylor), 105
Song of Songs (Song of Solomon), metrical version of, 6n, 15n, 34 (German)
Sonneck, O. G., 45n, 46 & n, 47n, 49n, 51 & n

Sophronia, 88n
Southern Baptist Theological Seminary, 123, 127
Southern Harmony, The (William Walker, 1835), 88n, 90, 91n, 128
Southern Methodist University, 125
SOUTHWELL, 27
Sowerby, Leo, 104, 123, 125
Spangenberg, Augustus, 40
Spell, Lota M., 48n
Spiess, Lincoln B., 48n
Stabat Mater: Rossini, 109; Thomson (1932), 122
Stallings, V. Lee, 123
Stamitz, Johann (1717–1757), 43, 53
Standard Buddhist Gathas and Services (1939), 111
STANDISH, 26 & n
Stanford, Sir Charles Villiers, 105
Staunton, Virginia, 31
"Steal away," 101, 103, 105
Stebbins, George C., 100n, 110 & n, 128
Steffani, Agostino, 85
Stephenson, Joseph, 59 & n, 60n
Sternhold and Hopkins, version of, 6, 7n, 8, 10, 12n, 50
Stevens: Denis, 121; Jervis Henry, 56
Stickney, John, 47n, 50
STILT, THE, 20
Stokowski, Leopold, 116n, 131
Stone, Joseph, 66n
Strassburg, 4n, 19
Stravinsky, Igor, 120
Strickland, William, 116n
String Quartet in G minor (D. G. Mason, Op. 19), 104
Strong, Joseph, 22n
Stroud, William Paul, 7n
Suffolk Harmony, The (Billings, 1786), 65
Suite for Strings in E (Foote, Op. 63), 119n
Summerlin, Edgar, 132
Sunday, Billy, 110, 111n, 127
Sunday School songs, 110–112, 126n
Svinin, Pavel Petrovich, 96n
Swan: Howard, 113n; Timothy, 79, 84, 86n
Sweelinck, J. P., 131
"Sweet hour of prayer," *see* CONSECRATION
Sweney, John R., 110
"Swing low, sweet chariot," 101
Symmes, Thomas, 6n, 16nn, 17n, 22 & n, 24 (& n)–26 (& n), 27, 28n
Symphonic Sketches (Chadwick, 1908), 119n

Symphonic Variations (Coleridge-Taylor, Op. 63), 105
Symphony: Ives, No. 3, 129; Mahler, No. 9, 129; Mozart, in E flat, 44n; Thomson, "on a Hymn Tune," 126n

Tanneberger (= Tannenberg), David, 38
Tans'ur, William, 60 (& n)–61 (& n), 86n
Tate, Nahum, 46
Tate and Brady, version of (1696), 5, 23, 47, 50, 56n
Taylor, Marshall W. (1846–1887), 102
Teal, Mary Evelyn Durden, 81
Te Deum, 108, 119n, 131
Telfair Family Papers, 52
Templum musicum (Alsted), 24–25
Thacher, Peter, 22n
Thalberg, Sigismond, 107
Thayer: Alexander W., 59n, 78nn, 83 (& n)–84, 106 (& n)–107; Eugene, 114
"The Angels changed my Name," 105
"The Lonesome Valley," 97
THE MORNING TRUMPET, 102
"The Pilgrim's Song," 105
"There is glory in my soul" (Gabriel), 111
"The Rocks and the Mountains," 100
Thomas: Isaiah, 65, 72, 74nn, 75n, 90n; John Charles, 124; Theodore, 113, 116
Thompson: Randall, 113n, 121 (& n)–123, 125; Will L., 110
Thomson, Virgil, 122n, 126 & n
thorough bass, Mason's knowledge of, 78n
Thorp, Giles, 6, 12n, 13
three-part singing, Walter's advocacy of, 29
Throne of God, The (Sowerby), 123
"Thy mercy, O Lord, is in the heav'ns" (Hubbard anthem), 76n
Timothy, Lewis, 40
Titcomb, Everett, 125
Tomer, William G., 129
TOPLADY (Hastings), 66, 107
Toplady, Augustus, 107
Trimble, John, 31
Trinity Church: Boston, 75, 115; Newport, R. I. (organ at), 48, 55; New York City, 38n (1741 organ at), 49–50 (& n), 55 (1764 organ), 107n (Hodges at), 108 (Cutler)
Trio for clarinet, 'cello, and piano (Beethoven, Op. 11), 77
Tubman, Harriet, 103

Tuckerman, S. Parkman, 107 (& n)–108 (& n)
Tuckey, William, 49–50
Tufts. John, 16n, 18n, 19 & n, 22, 25 & n, 26, 27 (& n)–28 (& n), 29, 86n, 87
Tullidge, John, 109n
"Turn back Pharaoh's army," 101
Turtel-Taube (Beissel), 35 (& n)–37
Twenty-Four Negro Melodies (Coleridge-Taylor, Op. 59), 105
Tyburn, 125

Underground Railroad, 103
Union Harmony, The (Holden, 1793), 71
Union Theological Seminary, School of Sacred Music, 35, 74n, 95n, 104, 106nn, 116n, 119n, 125n
Unitarian churches: Boston, 119n (see also King's Chapel); Providence, 48
UNITIA (Chapin), 89
University of Michigan, 74n, 81, 114n, 115n
University (formerly College) of Pennsylvania, 46
University of Southern California, 7n, 37, 38n, 74n, 106n, 110n
Uns ist ein Kind geboren (Peter anthem), 43n
Unto us a Child is born (Peter), 43–44
Urania, 28n, 30nn, 49–50
Uranian Academy (Philadelphia), 30
Utile dulci (Symmes), 6n, 16n, 17n, 22nn, 25, 26n, 28n

Valse gracile (Parker), 118
Valton, Peter, 56–57
Van Vleck, Jacob, 38, 41n
Variations on Sunday-School Tunes (Thomson), 126n
Vater unser im Himmelreich, 19
Vaughan Williams, Ralph, 131
Veni Immanuel, plainsong, 120 & n
Verdi, Giuseppe, 113n
VERNON (Chapin), 88 & n
Vetancurt, Agustín de, 48n
Victoria, Tomás Luis de, 41n, 131
Vierhebigkeit, 114
Vierne, Louis, 131
Vignon, Eustace, 3n
Village Harmony, The, 88n
violin: Beissel's proficiency on, 33; Josiah Franklin's playing of, 18; Mercer's denunciation of, 126n; Negro slaves' adeptness with, 53
Virginia, spirituals collected in, 97
Virginia Harmony, The, 90 & n, 91n

Vision of Sir Launfal (Sowerby), 123
Vivaldi, Antonio, 53

Waghorne, John, 30
Wainwright, Robert (1748–1782), 75
Walker: Nehemiah, 17; William, 90, 128
Walter, Thomas, 16n, 17n, 18nn, 19, 22, 26nn, 27, 28 (& n)–29 (& n)
Wame Ketoohomae uketoohomaongash David, 10–11, 16n
Wanderer's Psalm, A (Parker, Op. 50), 116
Ward, Samuel A., 130
Ware, Charles P., 96–97
Warren, Richard Henry, 116 & n
Washington, George, 46n
Washington Cathedral (Protestant Episcopal), 125, 130
WATCHMAN ("Watchman, tell us of the night"), 82, 90n, 126n
Waterman, Richard A., 97
Watts, Isaac, 16n, 21n, 64, 66n, 84, 93, 95
Webb, George J. (1803–1887), 83n
Weber, Carl Maria von, 79, 107
Webster, Joseph P. 129
Welde, Thomas, 15n
"We'll cross the mighty Myo," 98
"Were you there," 92, 104
"We shall overcome," 103–104, 127
WESLEY ("Hail to the Brightness"), 82
Wesley: Charles, 40, 84, 94n, 111, 124; John, 40, 55, 94n
West, Elisha, 66n
WESTMINSTER, 19
Westminster Choir College, 52
"We Three Kings of Orient are," 130
"What a Friend we have in Jesus," 110n
"When I can read my title clear," 95
"When I survey the wondrous cross," 84; see also HAMBURG
White, Benjamin Franklin, 102–103, 126n, 128
WIDMUNG (Schumann), 107
Wienandt, Elwyn, 132
Wightman, Valentine, 22n
Wilcox, Glenn, 74n, 130
Wilkes, William, 109n, 130
Willhide, J. Lawrence, 74n, 130
William L. Clements Library, Ann Arbor, 87n, 93
Williams: Aaron, 59 & n, 76n; George W., 40n, 54nn, 55n, 56n; Roger, 48
Williamsburg, Virginia, 53
Williamson, John Finley, 124
William Tell Overture (Rossini), 45n
Willis, Richard Storrs, 130

Wilson, Henry, 106, 108, 123n
WINDHAM (Read), 79 & n
WINDSOR, 16n, 18 (& n)–19 (& n)
Winslow, Edward, 13n
Winston-Salem, 41, 43n
Winter, Peter (1754–1825), 79
Wither, George, 19
Witt, Christopher, 33
WOBURN (Kimball), 74n
Wo geh ich hin (Beissel), 36
Wolle, Peter, 41 & n
WONDROUS LOVE, 91
Woodbridge, Timothy, 22n, 30
Woodbury, Isaac B., 68 (& n)–69
Woodruff, Merit, 30
Woodward, G. R., 13 & n
WOODWORTH ("Just as I am"), 83n, 108
Woodworth, G. Wallace, 122n
Worcester, Samuel A., 9n

Work, John W., 102
WORK SONG (= DILIGENCE, "Work for the night is coming"), 82, 126n
Wright: Andrew, 84, 88n; Searle, 125 & n, 130
Wyeth, John, 66n, 74n, 87, 126n

Yale University, 74, 78n, 114n, 118–119
Yellin, Victor, 122n
Y Glomen (Welsh air), 89n
Yoder, Paul H., 130
YORK, 16n, 18 & n, 19–20
Young, Carlton R., 109n, 128, 130

Zampa (Hérold), 113
Zarlino, Gioseffo, 76n
Zerrahn, Carl, 115
Zinzendorf, Nikolaus Ludwig von, 40